RAND NATIONAL SECURITY RESEARCH DIVISION

T0306705

Chinese Engagement in Africa

Drivers, Reactions, and Implications for U.S. Policy

Larry Hanauer, Lyle J. Morris

This research was conducted within the International Security and Defense Policy Center of the RAND National Defense Research Institute, a federally funded research and development center sponsored by the Office of the Secretary of Defense, the Joint Staff, the Unified Combatant Commands, the Navy, the Marine Corps, the defense agencies, and the defense Intelligence Community.

Library of Congress Cataloging-in-Publication Data is available for this publication.

ISBN: 9780-0-8330-8411-8

The RAND Corporation is a nonprofit institution that helps improve policy and decisionmaking through research and analysis. RAND's publications do not necessarily reflect the opinions of its research clients and sponsors.

Support RAND—make a tax-deductible charitable contribution at www.rand.org/giving/contribute.html

Cover image: China's President Xi Jinping (left) walks with his Tanzanian counterpart Jakaya Kikwete upon his arrival in Dar es Salaam, Tanzania, March 2013 (Reuters/Thomas Mukoya).

RAND OFFICES

SANTA MONICA, CA • WASHINGTON, DC

PITTSBURGH, PA • NEW ORLEANS, LA • JACKSON, MS • BOSTON, MA

DOHA, QA • CAMBRIDGE, UK • BRUSSELS, BE

www.rand.org

Preface

Most analyses of Chinese engagement with African nations focus on what China gets out of these partnerships—primarily natural resources and export markets to fuel its burgeoning economy, and agricultural products to feed its increasingly urbanized population. Some studies have described the impacts—both positive and negative—that China's aid and investment policies have had on African countries. However, few analyses have approached Sino-African relations as a vibrant, two-way dynamic in which both sides adjust to policy initiatives and popular perceptions emanating from each other.

In an effort to characterize the dynamic nature of Chinese-African relations, RAND comprehensively examined Chinese and African objectives in the political and economic spheres and the means by which they work to achieve their goals. RAND then examined the reactions of both African governments and populations to Chinese engagement and assessed the ways in which China adjusted its policies to accommodate these often-hostile responses. RAND also considered whether the United States and China are competing for influence, access, and resources in Africa and whether opportunities might exist for the two powers to cooperate in ways that advance their mutual interests, as well as those of their African partners.

This report should be of interest to analysts and policymakers concerned with U.S. policy in Africa, as well as those interested in understanding the ways in which China formulates its foreign policy. This research was conducted within the International Security and Defense Policy Center of the RAND National Defense Research Institute, a federally funded research and development center sponsored by the Office of the Secretary of Defense, the Joint Staff, the Unified Combatant Commands, the Navy, the Marine Corps, the defense agencies, and the defense Intelligence Community.

For more information on the International Security and Defense Policy Center, see http://www.rand.org/nsrd/ndri/centers/isdp.html or contact the director (contact information is provided on web page).

Contents

Figures and Table

Figures

Table

Summary

China's role in Africa defies conventional stereotypes and punchy news headlines. China is both a long-established diplomatic partner and a new investor in Africa. Chinese interests on the continent encompass not only natural resources but also issues of trade, security, diplomacy, and soft power. China is a major donor of aid to Africa, but the scope, scale, and mode of Chinese aid practices are poorly understood and often misquoted in the press.

China portrays its principle of non-interference and friendly relations as an altogether new and positive model for external engagement with Africa. Drawing clear distinctions with the European colonial past and Western policies that China believes are based on a paternalistic interference in political affairs, China promotes its presence in Africa as based on equality, mutual respect, and mutual benefit.[1] China chafes at criticisms that its role in Africa supports authoritarian despots and erodes efforts at improving human rights. The fundamental needs of food, security, and economic development, according to Chinese officials, are themselves forms of human rights, which China helps to promote through robust economic development and trade with Africa.[2]

Few non-Chinese experts accept the notion that Chinese-African relations represent interactions among equals, pointing out the inherent imbalance between a large, wealthy, powerful state and a grouping of 54 nations that rarely, if ever, coordinate on economic or foreign policy issues.[3] Instead, Western observers tend to depict China as a "spoiler" in Africa, whose "insatiable" and "voracious" appetite for mineral resources is nothing more than a neo-colonial grab for raw materials that perpetuates African countries' underdevelopment.[4] China's willingness to engage autocratic regimes in Sudan

1 "Chinese Envoy Briefs UN on China-Africa Relations," Xinhua, September 11, 2007. See also Fumbuka Ng'wanakilala and George Obulutsa, "China's Xi Tells Africa He Seeks Relationship of Equals," Reuters, March 25, 2013.

2 Ian Taylor, "Sino-African Relations and the Problem of Human Rights," *African Affairs*, Vol. 107, No. 426, 2008, p. 67.

3 Ross Anthony, "Should China Keep Its 'Africa Dreams' to Itself?" *The Diplomat*, April 3, 2013.

4 Peter Marton and Tamas Matura, "The 'Voracious Dragon', the 'Scramble' and the 'Honey Pot': Conceptions of Conflict over Africa's Natural Resources," *Journal of Contemporary African Studies*, Vol. 29, No. 2, April 2011, p. 155.

and Zimbabwe are highlighted as examples of China's willingness to circumvent, or even completely ignore, international efforts to curtail violence, human rights abuses, and corruption.[5] China's policy of tying economic development aid to government loans is often portrayed as a challenge to the prevailing aid regime among international financial institutions and an effort to foster long-term African dependence on China.

African perceptions of China include a mix of approval, apathy, and contempt. Overall, African citizens and governments hold positive views of Chinese engagement in Africa. African officials overwhelmingly view China's role in Africa as a positive development, welcoming China's heavy emphasis on government-to-government contracts with few, if any, strings attached. Many Africans praise China's contributions to their nations' infrastructure, highlighting visible improvements that contribute to expanded economic activity, job creation for local workers, and tangible improvements to roads, rails, bridges, and other transportation networks—all things that benefit ordinary citizens, albeit indirectly. Most accept Chinese engagement on the continent as a positive development for African economic growth and are seeking ways to leverage the opportunity to their advantage.

Some in Africa, however, are critical of Chinese engagement. Labor unions, civil society groups, and other segments of African society criticize Chinese enterprises for their poor labor conditions, unsustainable environmental practices, and job displacement. Good governance watchdogs warn that China negotiates unfair deals that take advantage of African governments' relative weaknesses, fosters corruption and wasteful decisionmaking, and perpetuates a neo-colonial relationship in which Africa exports raw materials in exchange for manufactured goods. In some countries, resentment at Chinese business practices has led to popular protests and violence against Chinese businessmen and migrants.

China has not maintained a static policy in the face of such obstacles; rather, Beijing has responded to both foreign and local pressures by modifying its approach to the continent. In an effort to make Chinese trade and investment appear less one-sided, Beijing has promoted "sustainable" economic development through "win-win" commercial deals that generate tangible, long-term economic benefits for African nations in the form of jobs, training, and technology. It has also increasingly worked to shape broader Sino-African relations through people-to-people ties, cultural and educational exchanges, Mandarin language training, and a robust public diplomacy campaign. Beijing's policy adjustment has the potential to benefit both China and its African partners. Closer cultural ties and aggressive outreach will likely foster broader public support for China; the resulting favorable climate will enable Chinese investments

---

[5] Philippe D. Rogers, "Dragon with a Heart of Darkness? Countering Chinese Influence in Africa," *Joint Forces Quarterly*, No. 47, 4th Quarter 2007, pp. 22–27. Last Moyo, "From Sudan to Zimbabwe, China Is Part of the Problem," newzimbabwe.com, November 12, 2009.

to continue securing natural resources and generating profits while also contributing increasingly to local job creation and economic development.

China's activities in Africa present both challenges and opportunities for the United States. Chinese engagement in the region is primarily concerned with natural resource extraction, infrastructure development, and manufacturing. U.S. engagement, in contrast, concentrates on higher-technology trade and services as well as aid policies aimed at promoting democracy, good governance, and human development. While China's "no strings attached" approach to investment enables, and perhaps even fosters, inefficient decisionmaking and official corruption, Chinese engagement does not fundamentally undermine U.S. economic and political goals on the continent. On the contrary, Chinese-built infrastructure helps to reduce businesses' operating costs and to expand the size of regional markets, increasing opportunities for profitable ventures by African and U.S. investors. U.S. and Chinese approaches and interests do not inherently contradict each other, and U.S. officials—including Presidents George W. Bush and Barack Obama—have denied that Washington and Beijing are engaged in a "zero-sum" competition for influence and access in Africa. In short, China is not necessarily a strategic "threat" to U.S. interests in Africa.

While the U.S. and Chinese governments may not be strategic rivals in Africa, the two countries could increasingly compete commercially if American businesses become more engaged in African markets—something that President Obama clearly hopes to foster through the multiple trade- and infrastructure-related initiatives he announced during his summer 2013 trip to Senegal, South Africa, and Tanzania. Such business competition would both benefit African countries and advance U.S. interests. African governments might be able to negotiate more favorable commercial terms if they are not beholden to Chinese financing. African communities would benefit, as American companies are more likely than their Chinese counterparts to hire local laborers for both skilled and unskilled positions, transfer industrial technologies in order to work with local partners, require humane working conditions, and contribute to initiatives that promote the health and welfare of their workforce. Such business practices would likely encourage Chinese enterprises to do the same so as to secure deals, compete in local labor and consumer markets, and enhance China's image in Africa.

To effectively engage both China and Africa, however, the U.S. government needs to devote more time and effort to understand the benefits that African countries seek from Chinese engagement, the motivations behind China's policies, the ways in which Africans have reacted, and the ways in which China is positioned to adjust. An examination of Chinese experiences in Africa could prove useful to the U.S. government and to American companies if they, too, should find themselves criticized for fostering one-way relationships despite the optimism that economic cooperation will generate mutually beneficial rewards.

Acknowledgments

We wish to express our appreciation for the valuable insights offered by Ambassador David Shinn of George Washington University and Andrew Scobell of the RAND Corporation in their comprehensive peer reviews. Their thoughtful suggestions immeasurably improved the arguments and analyses made in this report. We would also like to thank the Chinese academics and government officials interviewed for this report. Their willingness to share their views and time greatly enhanced our understanding of Chinese perspectives on Africa and of Beijing's objectives on the continent.

We are also extremely grateful to the RAND International Security and Defense Policy Center, whose leadership provided helpful contributions and critical support for this research.

Abbreviations

AfDB	African Development Bank
AFRICOM	U.S. Africa Command
AIDS	acquired immunodeficiency syndrome
AU	African Union
bpd	barrels per day
CITIC	China International Trust and Investment Corporation
DAC	Development Assistance Committee
DOTS	Direction of Trade Statistics
EAC	East African Community
FDI	foreign direct investment
FMF	Foreign Military Financing
FOCAC	Forum on China-Africa Cooperation
GAO	U.S. Government Accountability Office
GDP	gross domestic product
HIV	human immunodeficiency virus
IMF	International Monetary Fund
MFA	Ministry of Foreign Affairs
MOF	Ministry of Finance
MOFCOM	Ministry of Commerce
NDRC	National Development and Reform Commission
NGO	nongovernmental organization
ODA	Official Development Assistance
OECD	Organisation for Economic Co-operation and Development
OOF	other official flows
OPIC	overseas private investment corporation
PLA	People's Liberation Army

PRC	People's Republic of China
SASAC	State-owned Assets Supervision and Administration Commission
SEZ	special economic zone
SIPRI	Stockholm International Peace Research Institute
SOE	state-owned enterprise
TDA	Trade and Development Agency
UAV	unmanned aerial vehicle
UN	United Nations
USAID	U.S. Agency for International Development

CHAPTER ONE

Introduction

Most analyses of Chinese engagement with African nations focus on what China gets out of these partnerships—primarily natural resources and export markets to fuel its burgeoning economy, and agricultural products to feed its increasingly urbanized population. Some studies have described the impacts—both positive and negative—that China's aid and investment policies have had on African countries. However, few analyses have approached Sino-African relations as a vibrant, two-way dynamic in which both sides adjust to policy initiatives and popular perceptions emanating from the other.

Moreover, China's global intentions have increasingly become the focus of debate among scholars and practitioners. Some analysts hold the view that as China's power grows, it will become increasingly ambitious in its efforts to expand its global influence and domination.[1] Others contend that China's ambitions remain limited, with continued domestic economic and social challenges curtailing Beijing's ability to exert global influence.[2] In this context, Africa presents a unique case study upon which to assess China's goals and ambitions on the world stage.

Scope of This Research

In an effort to characterize the dynamic nature of Chinese-African relations, RAND comprehensively examined Chinese and African objectives in the political and economic spheres and the means by which they work to achieve their goals. RAND then examined the reactions of both African governments and populations to Chinese engagement and assessed the ways in which China adjusted its policies to accommodate

1 See, for example, Martin Jacques, *When China Rules the World: The End of the Western World and the Birth of a New Global Order*, second edition, New York: Penguin Books, 2012; Aaron Friedberg, *A Contest for Supremacy: China, America, and the Struggle for Mastery in Asia*, first edition, New York: W. W. Norton & Company, 2012.

2 See, for example, Andrew J. Nathan and Andrew Scobell, *China's Search for Security*, New York: Columbia University Press, second edition, 2012; David Shambaugh, *China Goes Global: The Partial Power*, New York: Oxford University Press, 2013.

these often-hostile responses. RAND also considered whether the United States and China are competing for influence, access, and resources in Africa and whether opportunities might exist for the two powers to cooperate in Africa in ways that advance their mutual interests, as well as those of their African partners.

This report characterizes China's interests in Africa; highlights the subtle intersection between Chinese financial, political, and security activities in Africa; assesses the influence of these policies on Africa and among Africans themselves; and weighs the impact of China's Africa engagement on U.S. political, economic, and security interests in the region, drawing associated recommendations for U.S. policy.

Given that the countries of the Maghreb are often treated as separate from the countries south of the Sahara, it is important to clarify the geographic area being considered. For the most part, this report examines China's engagement with all 54 countries on the African continent (three of which recognize Taiwan and thus have no political relations with Beijing). One reason for this is that all of these countries participate in pan-African institutions such as the African Union, even if some of them also participate in regional organizations oriented toward the Arab world. A second reason is that China engages the countries of the Maghreb through Africa-focused diplomatic initiatives such as the Forum on China-Africa Cooperation (FOCAC),[3] even though the Chinese Ministry of Foreign Affairs groups the countries of the Maghreb (Morocco, Tunisia, Libya, and Algeria), as well as Egypt, Sudan and Mauritania, with the department that handles the Middle East.[4] (The U.S. government also takes a mixed bureaucratic approach; in the Defense Department, the Maghreb falls under the jurisdiction of U.S. Africa Command [AFRICOM] and the Secretary of Defense's African policy office, while at the State Department the Maghreb falls under the purview of the Bureau of Near Eastern Affairs.) Finally, many of the available statistics regarding Chinese engagement in Africa include data from North Africa, making it easier and more consistent to include these countries in the report as a whole.

Organization of This Report

The second chapter of the report examines the intertwined interests of China and its African partners, exploring what each wants from the other; both sides derive significant political and economic benefits from their interactions.

The third chapter describes the ways in which Chinese-African relations have developed, focusing in particular on political relations, economic and commercial

[3] Forum on China-Africa Cooperation, "FOCAC ABC," website, April 9, 2013.

[4] Ministry of Foreign Affairs of the People's Republic of China, "Department of African Affairs," website, no date. Also, Ministry of Foreign Affairs of the People's Republic of China, "Department of West Asian and North African Affairs," website, no date.

engagement, and security interests. China's commitment to non-interference in the domestic affairs of other countries—a principle driven in part by its own efforts to fend off criticism of its policies toward Tibet and Xinjiang—underpins much of its engagement on the continent; this policy explains Beijing's willingness to do business with African governments regardless of the economic value of a particular deal or the legitimacy of a particular regime. The chapter also provides extensive details on the rapid growth in Chinese-African trade and in Chinese aid and investment on the continent.

Chapter Four describes the impact that Chinese engagement has had on the continent. African leaders have often claimed credit for delivering services funded by China, thereby bolstering their legitimacy. Some particularly abusive regimes have used Chinese assistance to maintain their grip on power. Economically, while Chinese trade and investment have created thousands of jobs in construction, mining, and other sectors, they have also contributed to Africa's continued dependence on raw material exports and undermined Africa's own manufacturing sector. Finally, the limited transparency associated with Chinese aid and investment has contributed to corruption and the inefficient use of state resources, both of which undermine African countries' economic health.

Chapter Five examines African reactions to Chinese activities on the continent. While African governments generally welcome Chinese engagement, African publics display a diverse range of views. In many countries, hostile interactions with Chinese managers and migrants, negative perceptions of Chinese goods, and anger that Chinese ventures often fail to generate concrete economic benefits have combined to create social unrest, violence, and resentment of both the Chinese and local governments alike.

Chapter Six considers China's response to this hostile environment. Over the past four years, China—through a combination of senior-level visits, contributions to peace and security, economic and commercial concessions, aggressive media outreach and public diplomacy efforts, and new initiatives designed to promote Chinese culture and "soft power"—is attempting to preserve its access and influence by demonstrating that it is, in fact, a constructive partner in Africa's development.

Chapter Seven considers the implications of China's influence for U.S. political, economic, and security interests in Africa, particularly by examining whether and to what extent the two countries are engaged in a strategic competition for access, influence, and resources on the continent and whether Washington and Beijing might be able to collaborate to advance shared objectives. The chapter offers recommendations for encouraging China to behave more constructively in Africa—not by pressuring Beijing directly, but rather by empowering African governments and civil society to demand changes in Chinese policy. The chapter concludes with some thoughts on issues that should be examined in greater detail in order to understand China's Africa strategy and China-Africa relations writ large.

CHAPTER TWO

Intertwined Interests of China and Africa

China and its African partners interact in a wide range of political, economic, and military-related arenas in ways that advance mutual interests, but economic pursuits lie at the heart of Sino-African relations. China seeks to acquire oil, gas, minerals, and other natural resources to fuel its economic growth, and many African countries have plentiful resource reserves whose extraction represents their primary economic output. Beijing also seeks markets for Chinese companies to sell their goods and services; consumers in many less-developed countries on the continent welcome inexpensive Chinese manufactured goods, while African governments purchase inexpensive Chinese military materiel and hire Chinese construction and engineering companies to develop much-needed physical infrastructure.

In the political arena, China seeks allies at the United Nations and in other international fora, and African governments are eager to be courted by a global power that treats them as sovereign equals instead of lecturing them about democracy, good governance, and free markets. China provides extensive development assistance to demonstrate its good intentions and create an environment conducive to commerce and friendly political relations, while African countries generally welcome China's willingness to provide aid without preconditions that they respect human rights or ensure government transparency, as typically required by the United States and many other international donors.

What China Wants from Africa

China has four overarching strategic interests in Africa:

1. access to natural resources, particularly oil and gas
2. markets for Chinese exports
3. political legitimacy in international fora, particularly in regards to China's principle of non-interference, "South-South solidarity," and adherence to the "One China" policy

4. prosperity, security, and stability on the continent, both for Africans' well-being and to ensure safety of China's investments and the continuation of its commercial activities.

Natural Resources and Chinese Exports

Despite public relations efforts to portray the relationship as comprehensive and multifaceted, China's number one interest in Africa remains securing access to oil, minerals, and other raw materials to fuel its ambitious industrialization efforts. Such keen interest in Africa can be seen as part of the broader "going out" strategy that China initiated in the late 1990s, which encourages state-owned and private companies to invest abroad, particularly in countries rich in natural resources. By 2020, China is predicted to overtake the United States in terms of oil imports worldwide and will become the largest global consumer by 2035.[1] To guarantee future supply, China is heavily investing in the upstream and downstream oil sectors in countries such as Sudan, Angola, and Nigeria.

Africa also presents a huge untapped market for Chinese goods. Africa's collective gross domestic product (GDP) is estimated to grow to $2.6 trillion by 2020.[2] Investment in Africa can potentially facilitate China's efforts to restructure its own economy away from labor-intensive industries, especially as labor costs in China increase. These two factors—feeding Chinese energy needs and absorbing Chinese exports—remain the central drivers of China's engagement with Africa.

Additional details on Chinese economic initiatives in Africa are provided in Chapter Three.

International Legitimacy

In Beijing's eyes, Africa represents a key diplomatic, strategic, and geopolitical platform upon which China can operationalize its core principles of equality, non-interference, and "South-South solidarity" among developing nations. The Chinese government believes that strengthening Sino-African relations helps raise China's own international influence and helps Beijing's cause of building a more "just international order" that advances peace, prosperity, and equality worldwide.[3] Furthermore, China considers itself the largest developing country in the world, while Africa is home to the greatest number of developing countries. China's "success in Africa," write journalists Serge

---

1 International Energy Agency, *World Energy Outlook 2011*, November 9, 2011.

2 Charles Roxburgh, Norbert Dörr, Acha Leke, Amine Tazi-Riffi, Arend van Wamelen, Susan Lund, Mutsa Chironga, Tarik Alatovik, Charles Atkins, Nadia Terfous, and Till Zeino-Mahmalat, *Lions on the Move: The Progress and Potential of African Economies*, McKinsey Global Institute, June 2010.

3 "FOCAC Beijing Declaration Calls for More Just and Reasonable International Order," *China Daily*, July 20, 2012.

Michel and Michel Beuret in their 2009 book, *China Safari*, "has reinforced its status as a global superpower."[4]

Maintaining and increasing its influence in the United Nations also drives China's engagement with Africa. African countries account for more than one-quarter of United Nations (UN) member states and occupy three non-permanent member seats from the Africa Group regional block in the UN Security Council. As such, Africa represents an important voting bloc for Chinese-led initiatives or against Western-led initiatives with which China disagrees. Africa has played a major role in the diplomatic jostling between the People's Republic of China (PRC) and the Republic of China in the United Nations. African countries constituted 26 of the 76 total votes supporting the PRC taking over the China seat from Taiwan in 1971,[5] which led Mao Zedong to claim that "it is our African brothers who have carried us into the UN."[6]

African votes in the UN also function to shield Beijing from criticism of its human rights policies. Motions by Western nations to censure China over its human rights record at the UN Commission on Human Rights Council have failed on numerous occasions due to support from African countries.[7]

While China and Taiwan have settled into a truce of sorts over diplomatic competition on the continent, Beijing still works actively behind the scenes to bring about cessation of ties between Taipei and its three remaining diplomatic partners on the continent—Burkina Faso, São Tomé and Príncipe, and Swaziland. Gambia's severing of diplomatic ties with Taiwan in November 2013 illustrates Taiwan's ever-dwindling diplomatic clout on the continent.[8] Indeed, Beijing provides no economic assistance to the countries that recognize Taiwan, and it has rewarded African countries that have switched their allegiance from Taipei to Beijing by rapidly expanding its economic engagement. Soon after recognizing Beijing in January 2008, for example, Malawi received an infusion of Chinese aid and investment, including a new parliament building, national conference center, schools, roads, wells, medical assistance, and scholar-

[4] Serge Michel and Michel Beuret, *China Safari: On the Trail of Beijing's Expansion in Africa*, New York: Nation Books, 2009, p. 4.

[5] Marius Fransman, South African Deputy Minister of International Relations and Cooperation, "Keynote Address to the Ambassadorial Forum on China–South Africa Diplomatic Relations at 15 Years," Pretoria, South Africa, September 19, 2013.

[6] Qi Li, "The 'Secrets' Behind the Success of China-Africa Relations," *China Daily*, July 20, 2012.

[7] Joshua Eisenman, "China's Post–Cold War Strategy in Africa: Examining Beijing's Methods and Objectives," in Joshua Eisenman, Eric Heginbotham, and Derek Mitchell, eds., *China and the Developing World*, New York: M. E. Sharpe, 2008, pp. 35–36.

[8] Pap Saine and Michael Gold, "Gambia to Cut Ties with Taiwan, China Says Unaware," Reuters, November 15, 2013.

ships.[9] As Deborah Brautigam, a scholar of Chinese engagement in Africa, has written, "Chinese aid agreements follow diplomatic ties."[10]

Security

China regards prosperity, security, and stability of the African continent as inextricably linked to the overall health of the China-Africa relationship. An Africa that is economically vibrant and whose government institutions and security apparatus are capable of sustaining continued trade and investment not only benefits the people of Africa, it benefits Chinese commerce on the continent. Thus, key terms such as "common prosperity," "peace," "security," and "human development" are featured prominently in China's various white papers on Africa.

Beijing has realized that insecurity and instability in Africa can impact its economic interests. Piracy off the coast of Somalia threatens the shipping lanes that are critical to China's increased trade with Africa and other parts of the world. Internal strife and civil unrest have threatened the safety of Chinese employees working for Chinese entities in Africa.

On the one hand, China has also derived commercial benefits from internal strife in Africa. It is a major provider of arms to African governments, constituting roughly 25 percent of conventional arms sales to Africa.[11] It has continued to sell weapons to pariah regimes such as those in Sudan and Zimbabwe, arguing that sovereign states have the right to purchase military equipment, despite considerable global criticism. Critics argue, however, according to British academic Ian Taylor, that China's insistence on the rights of sovereign states "simply camouflages its bottom line of profit and resource procurement, which arms sales to Africa possibly facilitate."[12]

In part because of such criticism, and in part to mitigate security-related threats to China's economic interests, China has sought a more constructive role as contributor to stability in the region. China is the largest contributor to UN peacekeeping operations in Africa among the five permanent UN Security Council members.[13] These deployments enable China to contribute to regional security, to be seen using its security forces to promote stability, and to gain experience with overseas deployments. The

---

9 David Smith, "China's Booming Trade with Africa Helps Tone Its Diplomatic Muscle," *The Guardian*, March 22, 2012. See also Lok-Sin Loa and Jenny W. Hsu, "China Plans to Take Over Projects in Malawi: Report," *Taipei Times*, January 24, 2008.

10 Deborah Brautigam, "Chinese Development Aid in Africa: What, Where, Why, and How Much?" in Jane Golley and Ligang Song, eds., *Rising China: Global Challenges and Opportunities*, Canberra: Australian National University Press, 2011b, pp. 208–210.

11 Colum Lynch, "China's Arms Exports Flooding Sub-Saharan Africa," *Washington Post*, August 25, 2012.

12 Ian Taylor, *China's New Role in Africa*, Boulder, Colo.: Lynne Rienner Publishers, 2009, p. 32.

13 Kossi Ayenagbo, Tommie Njobvu, James V. Sossou, and Biossey K. Tozoun, "China's Peacekeeping Operations in Africa: From Unwilling Participation to Responsible Contribution," *African Journal of Political Science and International Relations*, Vol. 6, No. 2, February 2012, pp. 22–32.

People's Liberation Army (PLA) has also deployed naval assets in support of international anti-piracy efforts off the coast of Somalia. Security issues in Africa will only increase in importance and will present both challenges and opportunities for China's leaders in the future.

What Africa Wants from China

African governments look to China to provide political recognition and legitimacy and to contribute to their economic development through aid, investment, infrastructure development, and trade. To some degree, many African leaders hope that China will interact with them in ways that the United States and other Western countries do not—by engaging economically without condescendingly preaching about good governance, for example, or by investing in high-risk projects or in remote regions that are not appealing to Western governments or companies.

Some African officials aspire to replicate China's rapid economic development and believe that their nations can benefit from China's recent experience in lifting itself out of poverty. The vice chairman of Tanzania's ruling party, for example, said in 2012 that "China's development model sets a very good example for African nations, in Tanzania in particular. . . . It is a model which shows how a country can develop from a low level of production to very high level of production and it is the correct model for all developing nations, especially for African nations."[14]

Many African leaders simply believe that as a fellow developing country, China has more altruistic motives than exploitative Western corporations. The Tanzanian party official, for example, asserted, "Companies in the west are business-oriented, they are to make profits whatever projects they participate in, they look for what they can get out of it, not what African countries would get out of it. China does not have that approach. China is to help the African nations build their own capacity to develop and that's the difference we very much appreciate."[15] As will be discussed in Chapters Five and Six, however, China has been widely criticized by both political leaders and ordinary citizens in Africa for failing, in reality, to live up to its promises to contribute to African countries' indigenous economic capacity—a dynamic that has led China to make a more concerted effort to generate economic benefits for its African partners.

---

14 "China's Development Model Good Example for African Nations: CCM Vice-Chairman of Tanzania," Xinhua, June 21, 2012.

15 "China's Development Model Good Example for African Nations: CCM Vice-Chairman of Tanzania," 2012.

Political Stature

In part because Africans remain conscious of the inequities of the colonial era, African leaders are eager to be treated with respect on the international stage, both in bilateral interactions and in multilateral fora such as the United Nations and the World Bank.[16] China goes out of its way to emphasize that its African partners are equal, sovereign states, and it frequently contrasts its position with Europe's history of exploiting the continent.[17] China's special envoy to Africa, Zhong Jianhua, made this point most recently in the run-up to President Xi Jinping's March 2013 trip to Africa, stating, "Africa wants to be treated as an equal, and this is what many Western countries do not understand, or are at least are not willing to do. China at least knows that we have to treat people in Africa as equals."[18]

Many African political leaders have welcomed China's approach, portraying Beijing's respect for their sovereignty almost as proof that they have moved beyond dependency on the West. At the 2012 FOCAC meeting, South African President Jacob Zuma remarked, "We are particularly pleased that in our relationship with China we are equals and that agreements entered into are for mutual gain. . . . We certainly are convinced that China's intention is different to that of Europe, which to date continues to intend to influence African countries for their sole benefit."[19]

Chinese support for African nations' sovereignty is not just a philosophical matter. African elites cite Chinese backing as justification for their continued leadership. At an August 2011 ribbon-cutting ceremony for 3,200 Chinese-built apartments, for example, Angolan President Eduardo dos Santos praised the project as an example of Angola's successful emergence from decades of civil war and demonstrated that his administration was following through on his pledge to alleviate the widespread shortage of housing.[20]

Investment

African countries are without question eager to attract Chinese investment. Western private investment has been held back by a wide range of obstacles, and most Western aid has been focused in areas that advance human development more than economic

---

[16] Stephanie Rupp, "Africa and China: Engaging Postcolonial Interdependencies," in Robert I. Rotberg, ed., *China into Africa: Trade, Aid, and Influence*, Washington, D.C.: Brookings Institution Press, 2008, p. 68.

[17] Dennis Tull, "The Political Consequences of China's Return to Africa," in Chris Cyn, Daniel Large, and Ricardo Soares de Oliveira, eds., *China Returns to Africa: A Rising Power and a Continent Embrace*, New York: Columbia University Press, 2008, p. 118.

[18] George Obulutsa and Fumbuka Ng'wanakilala, "Africa's Trade Ties with China in Spotlight as Xi Visits," *Business Day Live*, March 24, 2013.

[19] "Checkbook Diplomacy? China Pledges $20 Billion in Credit to Africa," nbcnews.com, July 19, 2012.

[20] Wang Bingfei, "Interview: China Plays Active, Responsible Role in Angola's Post-War Reconstruction," *People's Daily Online*, August 20, 2011.

development. African countries need foreign investment in minerals, manufacturing, and construction to create much-needed jobs, and their economic growth is hindered by critical shortcomings in infrastructure.

Natural Resource Extraction

A number of African countries are dependent on natural resources to generate the revenues needed to keep their governments running. The World Bank reported that revenues from natural resources generated an average of 60 percent of government funding in oil-rich African countries and 45 percent of government budgets in African countries rich in other natural resources. Furthermore, a combination of extensive reserves, continued exploration, and high commodity prices is likely to cause these countries to remain dependent on their raw materials throughout the near and medium term.[21]

Almost all of these natural resources are sold abroad. A December 2011 study by Oxford Policy Management, a British consultancy, assessed that the majority of African countries (34) were "mineral dependent," which it defined (consistent with the International Monetary Fund's definition of export dependence) as relying on both fuel and non-fuel minerals for more than 25 percent of their tangible exports. Of the 34 countries, a majority (19) relied on minerals for more than half of their exports, and three-quarters (27) became increasingly dependent on mineral exports over the previous 15 years (1995–2010).[22]

Not surprisingly, then, a great deal of Western investment in Africa is focused on natural resources, particularly oil, gas, and minerals. As of 2011, 84 percent of total U.S. imports from Africa were in natural resources. Moreover, U.S. foreign direct investment (FDI) in Africa is largely concentrated in mining and extractive industries, which together make up $33 billion of the $57 billion total stock of U.S. FDI in Africa.[23]

China invests heavily in natural resources as well. According to the U.S. International Trade Commission, as of 2011, approximately 80 percent of Chinese imports from Africa consisted of natural resources. Furthermore, from 2003 to 2010, more than half of China's FDI in Africa was directed to the petroleum industry.[24] For a variety of reasons that will be explained in Chapter Three, Chinese entities have pursued

---

21 World Bank, *Africa's Pulse*, Vol. 6, October 2012, pp. 15–17.

22 Dan Haglund, "Blessing or Curse: The Rise of Mineral Dependence Among Low- and Middle-Income Countries," Oxford, UK: Oxford Policy Management, December 2011. See also United Nations Economic Commission for Africa, *Making the Most of Africa's Commodities: Industrializing for Growth, Jobs, and Economic Transformation*, United Nations: Addis Ababa, Ethiopia, 2013, pp. 120–121 (Annex Table 3.1).

23 Vivian C. Jones and Brock R. Williams, *U.S. Trade and Investment Relations with Sub-Saharan Africa and the African Growth and Opportunity Act*, Congressional Research Service report, RL31772, November 14, 2012, pp. 10–13.

24 Lauren Gamache, Alexander Hammer, and Lin Jones, *China's Trade and Investment Relationship with Africa*, United States International Trade Commission Executive Briefings on Trade, April 2013.

resources in areas where Western firms have proven unwilling to invest; China is more willing to seek natural resources in countries that have especially strained political relations with the West (such as Sudan) or that exhibit particularly high levels of political risk (such as the Democratic Republic of Congo).

Oil and gas production in Africa is expected to grow faster than in other parts of the world. Oil reserves in Africa grew by over 25 percent over the past two decades while natural gas grew by over 100 percent, and oil production is expected to continue to rise at an average rate of 6 percent per year for the foreseeable future.[25] Foreign investment in Africa's energy sector by both Chinese and Western companies is thus likely to continue to increase.

Diversified Investment

Many African countries—particularly those with few valuable natural resources—are eager to attract investment in a wider range of sectors. African leaders have expressed frustration at the continent's continued absence of manufacturing and other forms of value-added production. At a 2011 meeting of African finance ministers hosted by the International Monetary Fund (IMF) and the World Bank, Chadian Finance Minister Gata Ngoulou lamented Africa's dependence on commodity exports, which are particularly vulnerable to price fluctuations. Lesotho's finance minister, Timothy Thahane, stated at the same meeting that "Africa's economic strategy going forward should be to diversify—that is the challenge for all of us."[26] A UN Economic Commission for Africa report in 2013 echoed these comments, recommending that African countries move away from commodity exports in favor of value-added manufacturing and commodity-based industrialization;[27] "Africa's economic future," the Economic Commission for Africa's executive secretary wrote, "will be determined by how the continent will design and implement effective industrial policies needed to promote industrialization and economic transformation."[28]

African countries desperately need to create stable jobs. The McKinsey Global Institute, a consulting firm, found that only 28 percent of the African labor force has stable salaried jobs—far less than other developing regions, such as Latin America (63 percent) and East Asia (48 percent). McKinsey estimates that while African countries (including Egypt and the Maghreb) will create roughly 54 million stable jobs over the

---

25 African Development Bank and African Union, *Oil and Gas in Africa: Joint Study by the African Development Bank and the African Union*, Oxford, UK: Oxford University Press, 2009, p. xxvvi.

26 "Africa Should Cut Reliance on Commodity Exports—Ministers," *IMF Survey Magazine*, April 16, 2011.

27 United Nations Economic Commission for Africa, 2013, pp. 7, 79.

28 Carlos Lopes, "Large Scale Commodity-Based Industrialization in Africa Is Imperative, Possible and Beneficial," United Nations Economic Commission for Africa, *Africa Cheetah Run* blog, March 1, 2013.

next decade, as many as 122 million additional people will enter the workforce during that period.[29]

African countries would presumably welcome investments that create jobs, particularly through value-added production, no matter where it comes from. However, foreign investment in African manufacturing, particularly from the West, is minimal. Deborah Brautigam of Johns Hopkins University writes that a Nigerian official told her, "the West comes to Nigeria, and it's oil, oil, nothing but oil. But the Chinese come and they are interested in every sector of our economy."[30] The dearth of Western investment or aid for large-scale private sector manufacturing, Brautigam states, "leaves the Chinese alone in their growing involvement in this sector."[31]

Infrastructure

Many African countries are particularly eager for foreign investment in infrastructure. "Poor infrastructure," according to a 2012 study by Ernst & Young, "is currently a major contributor to Africa's underdevelopment."[32] Compared with other developing regions, Africa has one-fifth the density of paved roads, two-thirds the density of total roads, and one-ninth the power generation capacity. To develop infrastructure that is on a par with other such regions, the World Bank assesses, Africa needs $93 billion in infrastructure improvements each year.[33]

Unreliable or inadequate water and electricity impede efficient production, and poor roads and limited rail networks raise the cost of transportation and the amount of time needed to ship both manufacturing inputs and products—all of which makes African goods more expensive and more vulnerable to competition from less costly imported goods (many of which come from China). Indeed, the poor state of infrastructure in many African countries increases manufacturing input costs by as much as 200 percent,[34] lowers private sector productivity by as much as 40 percent,[35] and

---

[29] These data include North African countries; since Tunisia, Egypt, and Algeria are in the top four—with 78, 60, and 59 percent holding stable, wage-earning jobs—the average for Sub-Saharan African countries is lower than 28 percent. David Fine et al., *Africa at Work: Job Creation and Inclusive Growth*, McKinsey Global Institute, August 2012, pp. 14–20, 27–31.

[30] Deborah Brautigam, "China in Africa: Think Again," *European Financial Review*, August 16, 2010.

[31] Deborah Brautigam, *The Dragon's Gift: The Real Story of China in Africa*, Oxford, UK: Oxford University Press, 2009, p. 230.

[32] Ernst & Young, *Building Bridges: Ernst & Young's 2012 Attractiveness Survey—Africa, 2012*, EYGM Limited, 2012, p. 9.

[33] Vivien Foster and Cecilia Briceño-Garmendia, *Africa's Infrastructure: A Time for Transformation*, Washington, D.C.: World Bank Africa Infrastructure Country Diagnostic, 2010, p. 6.

[34] World Economic Forum, *Enabling Trade: Valuing Growth Opportunities*, 2013, p. 6.

[35] United Nations Conference on Trade and Development, *Economic Development in Africa Report 2013—Intra-African Trade: Unlocking Private Sector Dynamism*, July 11, 2013, p. 84. Also, Foster and Briceño-Garmendia,

makes African manufacturers less competitive in world markets.[36] "For most countries" in Africa, the World Bank reported in 2010, "the negative effect of deficient infrastructure is at least as large as that of crime, red tape, corruption, and financial market constraints."[37] Meeting the requirements identified by the World Bank's Africa Infrastructure Country Diagnostic program in the power sector alone could increase African GDP by as much as 2 percent.[38]

In addition to making manufacturing more efficient, improved infrastructure will also foster greater regional integration, which will create bigger markets for African goods and promote intra-African trade, which has huge opportunities for growth. (A mere 10 percent of African countries' trade is with other countries in their region, as compared with 40 percent in North America and 63 percent in Western Europe.)[39] Infrastructure spending in Africa has grown rapidly over the past decade and a half, quadrupling from $3 billion in 1998 to $12 billion in 2008.[40] "Bridging the infrastructure gap," writes Ernst & Young, "will be a key enabler of regional integration, growth and development" in the future.[41]

The West has largely stopped financing large infrastructure projects, wrote World Bank economist David Dollar in 2008, primarily because

> they thought the private sector could fill this void. Private investment has in fact met much of the demand in telecom, a sector that is very amenable to private delivery. However, in power, expressways, and rail, it has proved harder to attract private finance. The returns are very long term, and political and economic uncertainties in poor countries mean that private investors demand a very high return to compensate risks. The result is the current hard infrastructure deficit in Africa.[42]

Rapid development of multiple modes of infrastructure poses a particular challenge, particularly in countries with weak legal systems and minimal government

---

2010, p. 2; Martyn Davies, "How China Is Influencing Africa's Development," background paper for *Perspectives on Global Development 2010: Shifting Wealth*, OECD Development Center, April 2010, p. 19.

36 World Economic Forum, 2013, p. 38.

37 Foster and Briceño-Garmendia, 2010, p. 2.

38 Richard Schiere, Léonce Ndikumana, and Peter Walkenhorst, eds., *China and Africa: An Emerging Partnership for Development?* Tunis: African Development Bank Group, September 30, 2011, p. 96.

39 Otto Bakano, "Multiple Barriers Hamper Trade Within Africa," Agence France Presse, January 26, 2012.

40 Rod Cloete, Felix Faulhaber, and Markus Zils, "Infrastructure: A Long Road Ahead," in *McKinsey Quarterly—Africa's Path to Growth: Sector by Sector*, McKinsey & Company, 2010, p. 8.

41 Ernst & Young, 2012, p. 6.

42 David Dollar, "Supply Meets Demand: Chinese Infrastructure Financing in Africa," World Bank blog, July 10, 2008. Approximately 87 percent of private-sector infrastructure investments have been in the telecommunications sector. See United Nations Office of the Special Advisor on Africa and the NEPAD-OECD Africa Investment Initiative, *Infrastructure in Africa*, Policy Brief No. 2, October 2010.

transparency. The high value of such efforts, combined with the often central role of government entities in financing, building, and/or operating such infrastructure, creates enormous opportunities for official corruption.[43] Such corruption, where it exists, likely increases the costs of infrastructure projects to African countries (thereby deterring foreign private investment) and contributes to less-reliable workmanship.

Trade

African governments seeking export markets are hopeful that they can expand bilateral trade with China, though for the most part trade patterns have mirrored those of the European colonial era, in which African countries export raw materials and import manufactured goods.[44] For reasons described above, other than natural resources and agricultural products, Africa produces few things that China needs that can be manufactured and transported to Asia in a cost-effective manner. Thus, natural resources (primarily oil, gas, and minerals) make up about four-fifths of African exports to China.[45] China's imports from Africa are highly geographically concentrated; about 90 percent of African exports to China (by dollar value) come from ten resource-rich countries.[46]

At the same time, Chinese consumer goods can be manufactured and transported to Africa very cost-effectively, resulting in an abundance of cheap Chinese imports throughout the continent. While African consumers have undoubtedly welcomed more affordable goods,[47] low-priced Chinese goods have displaced locally made products that could not compete on price and thus contributed to the loss of local jobs related to manufacturing.[48] A "flood of cheap goods" from China, according to Harvard scholar Robert I. Rotberg, has put "hundreds of thousands of Africans out of work."[49] Ultimately, African countries seek more balanced trade flows so as to mitigate these negative effects.

---

[43] Robert I. Rotberg, "China's Quest for Resources, Opportunities, and Influence in Africa," in Robert I. Rotberg, ed., *China into Africa: Trade, Aid, and Influence*, Washington, D.C.: Brookings Institution Press, 2008, p. 7.

[44] He Wenping, "China's Perspective on Contemporary China-Africa Relations," in Chris Alden, Daniel Large, and Ricardo Soares de Oliveira, eds., *China Returns to Africa: A Rising Power and a Continent Embrace*, New York: Columbia University Press, 2008, p. 157.

[45] David H. Shinn, "The Impact of China's Growing Influence in Africa," *The European Financial Review*, April–May 2011, p. 17.

[46] Lo Wing, *China-Africa Trade—Setting the Scene for the Future*, Standard Chartered Global Research Special Report, April 1, 2011.

[47] Barry Sautman and Yan Hairong, "Friends and Interests: China's Distinctive Links with Africa," in Firoze Manji and Dorothy-Grace Guerrero, eds., *China's New Role in Africa and the South: A Search for a New Perspective*, Oxford, UK: Fahamu, 2008, p. 89, and also in *African Studies Review*, 2007, p. 91.

[48] Aleksandra Gadzala and Marek Hanusch, *African Perspectives on China-Africa: Gauging Popular Perceptions and Their Economic and Political Determinants*, Afrobarometer Working Paper No. 117, January 2010, p. 6.

[49] Rotberg, 2008, p. 11.

Human Development

As will be explained in Chapter Three, although China defines "foreign aid" differently from the West, Chinese development assistance programs do many of the same things—train African students, support rural development, provide or improve health care in poorly served communities, etc. Chinese assistance helps African governments demonstrate that their deals with China have resulted in concrete improvements for local citizens.

Chinese aid also allows African leaders to highlight their willingness to stand up to Western donors. The perception that Western aid money largely supports expatriates living visibly extravagant (by local standards) lifestyles has generated some anti-Western resentment; foreign aid workers often live in large houses, drive imported four-wheel drive vehicles, have household staff, and stay in five-star hotels when they visit. In contrast, most Chinese working in Africa—whether on aid projects or profit-making enterprises—live more frugally.[50] Highlighting these different styles, Lu Shaye, Director-General for African Affairs in China's Foreign Ministry, asserted, "China spends on average 95 per cent of the money on the project and on the recipient countries, while the West may spend 80 per cent on their own staff."[51]

Security Assistance

Some African governments look to China for military equipment, weapons, and training. Some seek Chinese materiel to supplement what they acquire from the West. However, a number of abusive regimes that have been sanctioned by the West rely more heavily on Chinese military cooperation.[52]

The United States provides little military hardware to African countries, with a few notable exceptions, through either sales or grants. In fiscal year 2011, for example, the United States provided a mere $18 million in Foreign Military Financing (FMF) grants to sub-Saharan Africa and about $91 million in "Section 1206" counterterrorism assistance.[53] However, when the United States does undertake substantial military engagement in Africa—whether with training or materiel—it typically does so to advance U.S. priorities, such as counterterrorism, African peacekeeping proficiency, or support to the internationally recognized Somali government. China, in contrast, considers military sales as just one more element of its trade with African countries, and it

---

50 Testimony of Deborah Brautigam in U.S. Senate, Committee on Foreign Relations, Subcommittee on African Affairs, "China's Role in Africa: Implications for U.S. Policy," Senate Hearing 112-203, November 1, 2011.

51 Terence McNamee, *Africa in Their Words: A Study of Chinese Traders in South Africa, Lesotho, Botswana, Zambia and Angola*, Brenthurst Foundation Discussion Paper 2012/03, April 2012, p. 20.

52 For a comprehensive overview of Chinese-African security cooperation, see Chris Alden, *China's Growing Role in African Peace and Security*, London: SaferWorld, January 2011.

53 Ted Dagne, *Africa: U.S. Foreign Assistance Issues*, Washington, D.C.: Congressional Research Service, Report RL33591, September 15, 2011, pp. 7, 9.

has proactively pursued African markets. It moved up the ranks of Africa's arms suppliers from #4 (with a 6 percent share by volume) in 1996–2000, to #2 in 2001–2006 (with a 9 percent share), to #1 in 2006–2010 (with a 25 percent share).[54]

Whereas the United States and other Western countries have imposed arms embargoes on several African countries because of their records of human rights abuses or political repression, China has been willing to sell weapons to such countries, arguing that refusing to engage in trade with a recognized government constitutes unacceptable interference in that country's internal affairs. Although Zimbabwe, for example, became subject to a European Union arms embargo in 2002 and to a U.S. embargo in April 2003, since that time China has become Zimbabwe's primary military supplier, even while vetoing a proposed UN arms embargo in July 2008.[55] Similarly, China continued selling conventional weapons and small arms to the Sudanese government throughout the period in which Sudanese forces and militias were undertaking extensive and highly publicized attacks against civilians in Darfur; even after the UN Security Council imposed an arms embargo on Sudan (specific to the Darfur conflict) in March 2005,[56] China sold Sudan as much as 90 percent of its imported small arms and light weapons (in 2006)[57] and blocked Security Council efforts to investigate the discovery of Chinese weapons in Darfur in 2011.[58] In the cases of Zimbabwe and Sudan, Chinese military assistance and materiel provided pariah governments with the resources needed to remain in power and to continue to oppress their populations.

[54] Pieter D. Wezeman, Siemon T. Wezeman, and Lucie Béraud-Sudreau, *Arms Flows to Sub-Saharan Africa*, SIPRI Policy Paper 30, Stockholm: Stockholm International Peace Research Institute, December 2011, p. 10.

[55] Samuel J. Spiegel and Philippe Le Billon, "China's Weapons Trade: From Ships of Shame to the Ethics of Global Resistance," *International Affairs*, Vol. 85, No. 2, 2009. Also, Lukas Jeuck, *Arms Transfers to Zimbabwe: Implications for An Arms Trade Treaty*, SIPRI Background Paper, Stockholm International Peace Research Institute, March 2011, pp. 1–2, 7.

[56] UN Security Council, *Resolution 1591*, March 29, 2005. See also United Nations Security Council, *Report of the Security Council Committee Established Pursuant to Resolution 1591 (2005) Concerning the Sudan*, S/2006/1045, December 28, 2006, p. 2.

[57] Human Rights First, "China's Arms Sales to Sudan," no date.

[58] Lynch, 2012.

CHAPTER THREE

How China-Africa Relations Have Developed

A Brief History

Starting in the late 1950s, Africa became central to China's ideologically driven campaign promoting revolution, anti-colonialism, and Third World solidarity.[1] This included moral and material support for liberation movements. Relations were further consolidated when Premier Zhou Enlai visited ten African countries in 1963–1964 and articulated the "Five Principles Governing the Development of Relations with Arab and African Countries" and "Eight Principles for Economic Aid and Technical Assistance to Other Countries" that would underpin China-Africa relations going forward.[2] These two documents laid out the principle that relations would be governed by "equality, mutual interest and non-interference," based on China's "Five Principals of Peaceful Coexistence."[3] These principals form the basis of China's present-day emphasis on "friendly relationships" devoid of political conditions or interference in the internal affairs of African countries.

The launch of the reform and opening program (改革开放) at the 11th Party Congress of the Chinese Communist Party in December 1978 fundamentally changed China's international and domestic priorities and, along with it, its Africa policy. The success of China's developmental progress and the unleashing of economic market forces resulted in the erosion of ideological leanings of the Chinese Communist Party. In its place was a singular desire to pull China out of poverty and improve the livelihoods of its citizens. Chinese state-owned enterprises (SOEs)—enjoying access to capital from China's centrally managed policy banks—began to look outward. Africa

---

1 For more on this period, see Domingos Jardo Muekalia, "Africa and China's Strategic Partnership, *African Security Review*, Vol. 13, No. 1, 2004, pp. 5–11.

2 These principles are listed in "Chinese Leaders on Sino-African Relations," China.org.cn, December 10, 2003.

3 The five principles of peaceful coexistence are mutual respect for sovereignty and territorial integrity; mutual non-aggression; non-interference in each other's internal affairs; equality and mutual benefit; and peaceful coexistence. See United Nations, "No. 4307: India and People's Republic of China," *United Nations Treaty Series*, Vol. 299, 1958, pp. 57–81.

quickly became the recipient of this "going out" strategy.[4] It wasn't until the late 1990s, however, that Chinese policymakers conceptualized a new framework of all-around engagement with Africa encompassing trade, cultural, and diplomatic ties.

The creation of an entity to centralize China-Africa relations—the Forum on China-Africa Cooperation (FOCAC)—marked the beginning of a period of unprecedented bilateral engagement. Initiated by the Ministry of Foreign Affairs (MFA) in October 2000, FOCAC was established to coordinate China's activities in Africa and has become the institutional vehicle for managing cooperation with Africa across a range of technical, economic, and political areas. Since 2000, five ministerial meetings have taken place—2000 in Beijing; 2003 in Addis Ababa, Ethiopia; 2006 in Beijing; 2009 in Sharm el-Sheikh, Egypt; and 2012 in Beijing.

Through the FOCAC framework, Beijing sets out three-year engagement plans toward the continent in the form of strategic initiatives and economic commitments. China's "state capitalist" approach—in which the state exercises control over leading companies through ownership, subsidies, and influence over corporate officials—enables the government to make sweeping pledges of capital and technical assistance.

According to its website, FOCAC was established as a "platform for collective dialogue and an effective mechanism for enhancing practical cooperation between China and African countries." It aims to "deepen mutual understanding, expand consensus, strengthen friendship and promote cooperation through equal consultation."[5] In a July 2012 op-ed in the *China Daily*, PRC Foreign Minister Yang Jiechi called FOCAC "the standard-bearer for China-Africa relations" and "an important engine driving practical cooperation between China and Africa."[6] While FOCAC summit meetings lay out broad policy objectives and aspirations that both China and African countries endorse, Beijing's interaction with African countries is generally executed on a bilateral basis.

FOCAC conferences provide a highly visible political and diplomatic platform upon which Beijing seeks to show respect to African leaders on the world stage. It is Beijing's way of "giving face" to African governments. African elites in turn appreciate the respect and lavish treatment granted by their Chinese counterparts. Beyond the pomp and circumstance, FOCAC meetings also make it logistically feasible for China to undertake high-level outreach to some 50 African countries. President Hu Jintao, for example, frequently met with dozens of African presidents before, during, and after the FOCAC conferences, which in some cases presented opportunities for China to unveil large bilateral trade deals with African nations.[7]

---

4 Linda Yueh, "China's 'Going Out, Bringing In' Policy: The Geo-Economics of China's Rise," presented at A New Era of Geo-economics: Assessing the Interplay of Economic and Political Risk International Institute of Strategic Studies (IISS) Seminar, March 23–25, 2012.

5 "About FOCAC," ChinAfrica.cn, no date.

6 Yang Jiechi, "Advance Friendly Cooperation" *China Daily*, July 17, 2012.

7 "President Hu Meets Five African Presidents in Beijing," Xinhua, November 3, 2006.

The publication of China's white paper on Africa in January 2006, titled "China's African Policy," further enhanced and consolidated China's strategic vision for in Sino-Africa relations. The white paper outlines China's four overarching principles in its engagement with Africa:[8]

> *Sincerity, friendship and equality.* China adheres to the Five Principles of Peaceful Coexistence, respects African countries' independent choice of the road of development and supports African countries' efforts to grow stronger through unity.
>
> *Mutual benefit, reciprocity and common prosperity.* China supports African countries' endeavor for economic development and nation building, carries out cooperation in various forms in the economic and social development, and promotes common prosperity of China and Africa.
>
> *Mutual support and close coordination.* China will strengthen cooperation with Africa in the United Nations and other multilateral systems by supporting each other's just demand and reasonable propositions and continue to appeal to the international community to give more attention to questions concerning peace and development in Africa.
>
> *Learning from each other and seeking common development.* China and Africa will learn from and draw upon each other's experience in governance and development, strengthen exchanges and cooperation in education, science, culture and health. Supporting African countries' efforts to enhance capacity building, China will work together with Africa in the exploration of the road of sustainable development.

China's policy objectives, as communicated through the FOCAC framework and 2006 white paper, make clear that China's central goal in increasing ties with Africa is rooted in a "win-win" approach that enhances Chinese trade and investment opportunities and brings economic opportunity to Africans without overly interfering in the internal affairs of African governments.

Political Engagement

Chinese policymakers and academics perceive their role in Africa as promoting principles of mutual respect, equality, and friendship, which China refers to as "all-round cooperation."[9] Chinese elites frequently draw on Chinese history and Europe's colonial past to highlight such principles. During a speech at the 2012 FOCAC, Chinese Ambassador to South Africa Tian Xuejun invoked memories of Admiral Zheng He's

---

[8] "China's African Policy," Chinese government paper, January 2006.

[9] The concept of "all-round cooperation" was put forward in "China's African Policy," 2006.

15th century naval diplomacy to the eastern coast of Africa, saying, "instead of establishing colonies or engaging in slave trade like Western colonists, Zheng traded goods with local people."[10]

In the political realm, China maintains that it has always upheld principles of mutual respect and equality with Africa, including not interfering in African countries' internal affairs and respecting their independent development path. In the economic realm, China sees itself as pursuing mutual benefit and common development. Chinese officials consistently highlight the fact that none of China's assistance to Africa is attached with political conditions.

These principles were most succinctly elucidated during a speech by Jia Qinglin, Chairman of the Chinese People's Political Consultative Conference, at the 18th summit of the African Union in January 2012:

> Throughout the development of China-Africa relations, we have always respected the sovereignty and development path of African countries and refrained from interfering in their internal affairs. We have always treated African countries on an equal footing and pursued mutually-beneficial and win-win cooperation with them. We have always regarded assistance and support between China and Africa as mutual, and have never attached political strings to our assistance to Africa.[11]

Despite its emphasis on non-interference, China does insist on one precondition for diplomatic relations with Beijing: It insists that African countries recognize the "One China" policy. Thus, while China consistently emphasizes its principle of de-politicization in its dealings with African countries, Taiwan remains the one clear exception to the rule.

China's focuses on non-interference in part because of its own concerns over sovereignty issues involving Xinjiang, Tibet, and Taiwan.[12] Due to these concerns, non-interference acts both as a means of deflecting international criticism of its own domestic policies as well as a policy that frees China from involving itself in the messy and complicated internal crises that continue to plague Africa. African leaders typically refrain from criticizing China in return.

Some scholars voice criticisms of China's principles of engagement, saying they "effectively legitimize human rights abuses and undemocratic practices under the guise of state sovereignty and 'non-interference.'"[13] China frequently counters such criticisms

---

[10] Tian Xuejun, Chinese ambassador to South Africa, "Friendship and Cooperation for a Better Future of China-Africa Relations," speech to the South African Institute of International Affairs (SAIIA), Johannesburg, July 4, 2012.

[11] Jia Qinglin, "Towards a Better Future with Stronger China-Africa Solidarity and Cooperation," speech to 18th summit of the African Union, Addis Ababa, Ethiopia, January 29, 2012.

[12] Rotberg, 2008, p. 12.

[13] Ian Taylor, "China's Oil Diplomacy in Africa," *International Affairs*, Vol. 82, No. 5, September 1, 2006.

with the notion that African problems "should be solved by Africans themselves," free from outside intervention and imposition of values, judgment, and ideology. On this point, Chinese scholars distinguish "intervention" from "involvement" or "diplomacy." The key difference, according to one Chinese scholar, is that the latter involves "consent from either Africans themselves or from international institutions such as the U.N. or AU [African Union]."[14]

This is not to say that China does not exercise influence to mediate conflicts. For example, in the run-up to the 2008 Beijing Olympics, China found itself under increased international pressure to use its influence in Sudan to resolve the crisis in Darfur. It did so not by voting for UN Security Council resolutions critical of Khartoum, but rather by pressing the Sudanese government to accept a UN–African Union peacekeeping missing in Darfur during a February 2007 visit by president Hu Jintao to Sudan. Five months later, the Security Council—with China holding the rotating presidency—passed a resolution establishing the peacekeeping mission that "commend[ed] . . . the agreement of Sudan that the hybrid operation shall be deployed in Darfur."[15] Thus, the Chinese ambassador to the United Nations could claim that China did not have to "twist arms" in Khartoum, but rather note that Sudan had given its consent to the peacekeeping mission through diplomatic dialogue.[16]

From China's perspective, non-intervention is intertwined with China's role in promoting human rights and economic development on the continent. Beijing perceives Western-led criticisms of Chinese human rights abuses in Africa as misguided and part of a larger effort to demonize Chinese policies abroad.[17] When asked about China's investment in nations with records of human rights abuses, Chinese Foreign Minister Li Zhaoxing famously retorted, "Do you know what the meaning of human rights is? The basic meaning of human rights is survival and development."[18] Such comments reinforce the notion that China sees human rights in economic development terms rather than in terms of individual liberties or political participation. Thus, applied to the context of economic development, China sees its role in Africa more as the *provider* of development opportunities for Africa and Africans, focusing on the *means* of development as opposed to the ends. To punish countries for their manage-

[14] Interview with Chinese scholar in Beijing, February 27, 2013.

[15] United Nations Security Council, S/RES/1769 (2007), July 27, 2007.

[16] David H. Shinn, "China and the Conflict in Darfur," *Brown Journal of World Affairs*, Vol. 16, No. 1, Fall/Winter 2009, pp. 91–94.

[17] "China-Africa Relations Based on Equality, Mutual Benefit and Common Development," *China People's Daily*, February 26, 2010.

[18] See Rukmini Callimachi, "China Courts Africa with Aid, Projects," Associated Press, January 4, 2007.

Chinese Government Agencies Involved in China's Africa Policy

Management and coordination of Sino-Africa relations is dispersed among a handful PRC governmental organs and agencies.

Ministry of Foreign Affairs (MFA)

MFA carries out China's foreign policy and represents the Chinese government in relations with foreign countries. Its main responsibility is to release the state's major foreign policy documents and issue statements responding to international events. The MFA, in particular the African Affairs Office, plays a central role in conceptualizing and shaping China's Africa policy. The MFA created FOCAC and continues to issue major long-term proposals and suggestions for the central government to use in formulating China's diplomatic strategy toward Africa. The 2006 white paper on Africa, for example, was written and publicized by MFA, with input for other government agencies.[1] In terms of aid, MFA plays an advisory role to the Ministry of Commerce (MOFCOM) and Ministry of Finance (MOF). Two MFA bureaus in the particular—the Bureau for Chinese Diplomatic Missions Abroad and the Department of External Security Affairs—have begun to play increasingly important roles in managing China's Africa policy. The former manages Chinese embassies overseas, which have become important conduits for transmitting feedback about Chinese policies back to Beijing. The latter's role has increased due to the increasing risk to Chinese nationals working near conflict zones in Africa.

Ministry of Commerce (MOFCOM)

MOFCOM is the main government agency charged with overseeing aid disbursements and government-to-government trade negotiations with Africa. For aid packages, this includes conceptualizing and monitoring grant aid, technical assistance, and all interest-free and concessional loans. MOFCOM, in consultation with MFA and MOF, negotiates intergovernment agreements, conducts feasibility studies for aid projects, chooses aid implementers, and conducts project reviews. It also coordinates with the China Exim Bank on concessional loans.[2] The department in charge of overseeing aid to Africa is the Department of Aid to Foreign Countries.[3] For economic and trade affairs, MOFCOM's Department of Western Asian and African Affairs and Department of Outward Investment and Economic Cooperation are the two advisory bodies charged with overseeing China's trade policy and strategy with Africa.[4]

---

[1] Interview with senior MFA official in Beijing, February 26, 2013.

[2] Brautigam, 2009, p. 108.

[3] Ministry of Commerce of the People's Republic of China, "Department of Aid to Foreign Countries," web page, no date.

[4] Ministry of Commerce of the People's Republic of China, "Department of Western Asian and African Affairs," web page, no date. Also, Ministry of Commerce of the People's Republic of China, "Department of Outward Investment and Economic Cooperation," web page, no date.

Ministry of Finance (MOF)

China's MOF is primarily a domestic government organ in charge of administering fiscal policy, economic regulations, and government expenditures for the state. Its role in implementing China's Africa policy is minor and limited to managing the budget for foreign aid expenditures, in cooperation with MOFCOM and MFA.

National Development and Reform Commission (NDRC)

Formerly called the State Development Planning Commission, the NDRC focuses primarily on formulating China's long-term strategy for domestic economic growth. It also has significant influence on China's foreign policy by coordinating Chinese "going out" strategy and approving overseas resource acquisition. The Department of Trade and the Office of Policy Studies, in coordination with departments within MOFCOM and MFA, are the two offices within the NDRC charged with formulating trade and investment policies related to Africa.

State-Owned Assets Supervision and Administration Commission (SASAC)

SASAC is administered by the State Council and manages the affairs of China's state-owned enterprises (SOEs). It is estimated that SASAC manages 120 state-owned firms and controls $3.7 trillion in assets.[5] SASAC wields significant influence over SOEs operating in Africa and elsewhere by appointing senior executives and the board of directors. China's three largest national oil companies—China National Petroleum Corporation, China Petroleum and Chemical Corporation (Sinopec), and China National Offshore Oil Corporation (CNOOC)—all have significant operations in Africa. SASAC's oversight and management role has a direct impact on their operations and strategy in Africa.

Export-Import Bank of China (China Exim Bank)

Established in 1994 and under the administration of the State Council, the China Exim Bank is China's largest lender for Chinese companies investing in Africa. Its portfolio is increasingly dominated by Africa, with between one third and one half of its activities devoted to financing projects on the continent.[6] Ratings agency Fitch estimates that $67.2 billion of China Exim Bank's loans were for African projects between 2001 and 2010, surpassing the World Bank's $54.7 billion over the same period.[7] It is also the primary lender for Chinese infrastructure projects in Africa, providing 92 percent of total Chinese investment from 2001 to 2007.[8]

---

5 "Of Emperors and Kings," *The Economist*, November 12, 2011.

6 Sébastien Le Belzic, *China's Exim Bank: Africa's Largest Financier Looks for an Even Bigger Role*, The Africa Report.com, October 25, 2012.

7 Le Belzic, 2012.

8 Le Belzic, 2012.

ment of their internal affairs by cutting off trade or imposing sanctions, Chinese officials argue, is therefore counterproductive.[19]

Economic Engagement

Much of Chinese engagement with Africa is centered on trade and investment. China's demand for energy resources coupled with Africa's need for investment and infrastructure development have allowed the Sino-African trade relationship to flourish over the past decade. At least one African official went so far as to suggest that Chinese support has been a key driver of Africa's success. Speaking at the January 2012 inauguration of the new African Union headquarters building in Addis Ababa—which China built, at a cost of $200 million, as a gift—Ethiopian Prime Minister Meles Zenawi stated, "China, its amazing re-emergence and its commitments for a win-win partnership with Africa is one of the reasons for the beginning of the African renaissance."[20]

Trade

China-Africa trade has shown astonishing growth over the past decade. Since 2000, China-Africa trade has increased twenty-fold, from approximately $10 billion in 2000 to $199 billion in 2012, representing an annual growth rate of almost 16 percent.[21] In 2012, China's imports from Africa stood at $113.17 billion and African imports from China at $85.32 billion.[22] (See Figure 3.1.)

Among the major trading blocs, China has emerged as a key trading partner for Africa. As Figure 3.2 indicates, while Africa imports the largest amount of goods from Europe in 2012, at 33 percent, Africa is importing comparatively more goods from China, increasing its share to 13 percent in 2012 from 2 percent in 1995. African imports from the United States have remained relatively stable, hovering around 5 to 8 percent between 1995 and 2012, while its imports from Japan fell to 3 percent in 2012 from 7 percent in 1995.

---

[19] One senior MFA official said, "By Western countries severing trade relations, how can that help human rights? Only development and trade helps human rights. China uses development and trade to improve people's livelihood, and improved livelihood is what improves human rights." Interview with senior MFA official in Beijing, February 26, 2013.

[20] Meles Zenawi, Ethiopian Prime Minister, "Remarks at the Inauguration of the New African Union Commission Conference Center and Office Complex," Addis Ababa, Ethiopia, January 28, 2012.

[21] "China-Africa Economic and Trade Cooperation (2013)," *People's Daily Online*, August 29, 2013.

[22] Trade and FDI statistics derived from IMF Direction of Trade (DOTS), website, no date; United Nations Comtrade Database, website, no date; United Nations Conference on Trade and Development, *Economic Development in Africa Report 2013—Intra-African Trade: Unlocking Private Sector Dynamism*, July 11, 2013; and Chinese Ministry of Commerce website, "Foreign Investment," no date.

Figure 3.1
China-Africa Imports and Exports, 2000–2012

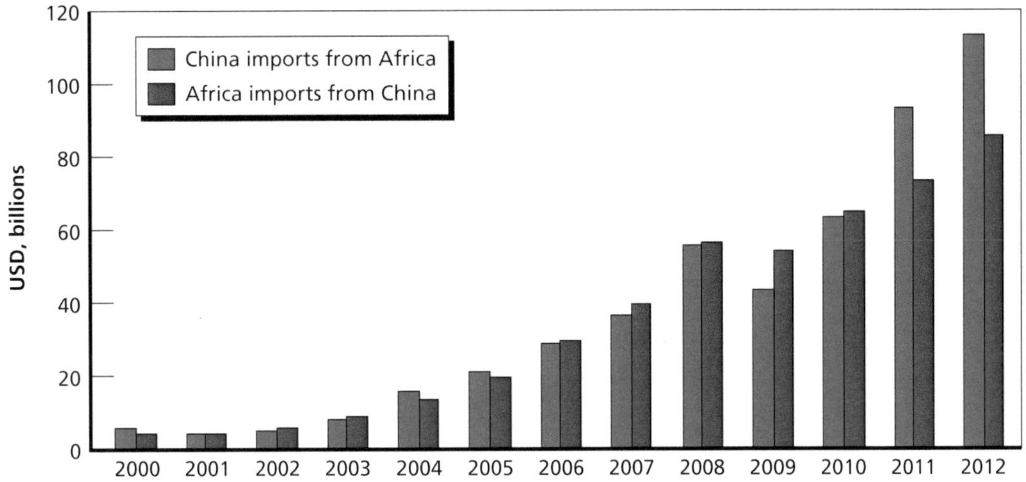

SOURCE: International Monetary Fund Direction of Trade Statistics; China-Africa Economic and Trade Cooperation (2013).
RAND *RR521-3.1*

Figure 3.2
Distribution of African Imports Among Major Trading Blocs

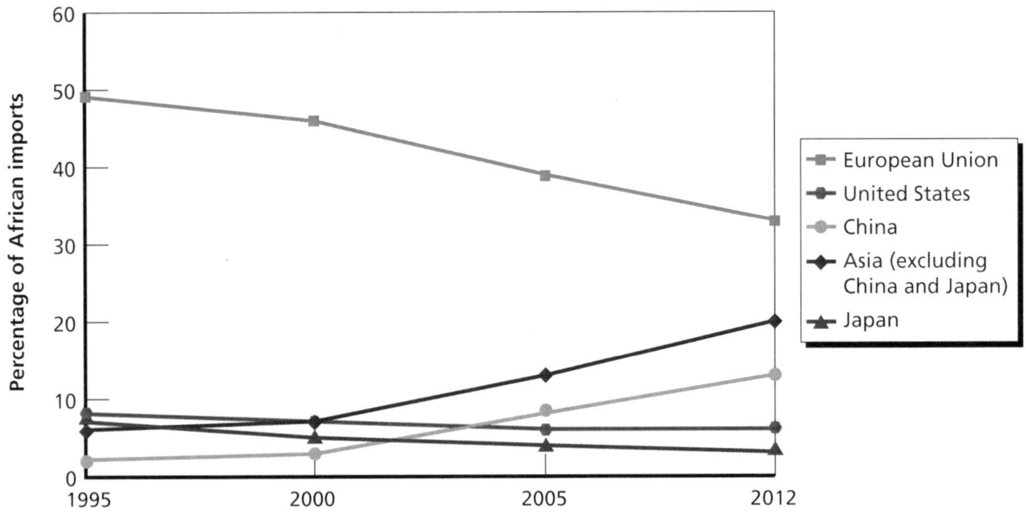

SOURCE: International Monetary Fund Direction of Trade Statistics.
RAND *RR521-3.2*

As Figure 3.3 illustrates, the European Union, Asia and the United States remain Africa's leading destinations for exports among the major trading blocs, China's share has grown significantly, from 1 percent in 1995 to 12 percent in 2012. It is very likely the growth in African imports from and exports to China and Asia will continue to increase, while those from traditional markets in the United States and Europe will remain either stable or decline.

From China's perspective, China-Africa trade is still relatively modest, comprising only 5.13 percent of the total Chinese imports and exports in 2012, up from 2.23 percent in 2000. China-Africa trade has had a comparably larger impact for Africa, at 16.13 percent of the continent's total cumulative exports and imports from 2012, up from 3.82 percent.[23]

Disaggregation of China-Africa trade data reveals that Africa's trade with China is highly concentrated in just a few countries (Figures 3.4 and 3.5). As of 2012, more than half of Chinese exports were concentrated in four countries: South Africa (21 percent), Nigeria (12 percent), Egypt (11 percent), and Algeria (7 percent). The overwhelming majority (87 percent) of Chinese imports in 2012 originated from five countries, all of which export primarily oil, gas, and minerals: South Africa (42 percent), Angola (32 percent), Libya (6 percent), Republic of Congo (4 percent), the Democratic Republic of Congo (3 percent).

Figure 3.3
Distribution of African Exports Among Major Trading Blocs

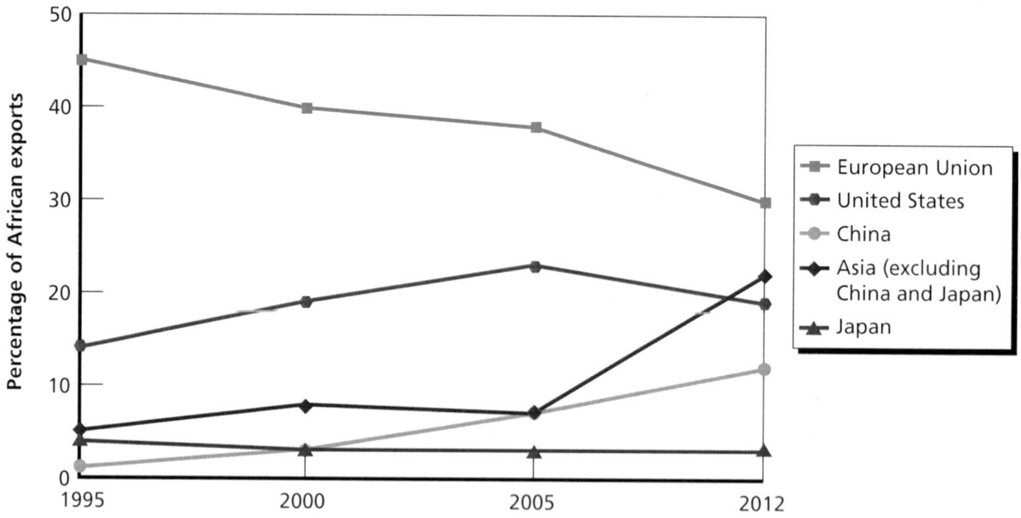

SOURCE: International Monetary Fund Direction of Trade Statistics.
RAND *RR521-3.3*

---

[23] "China-Africa Economic and Trade Cooperation (2013)," 2013, p. 2.

Figure 3.4
Chinese Exports to African Countries, 2012

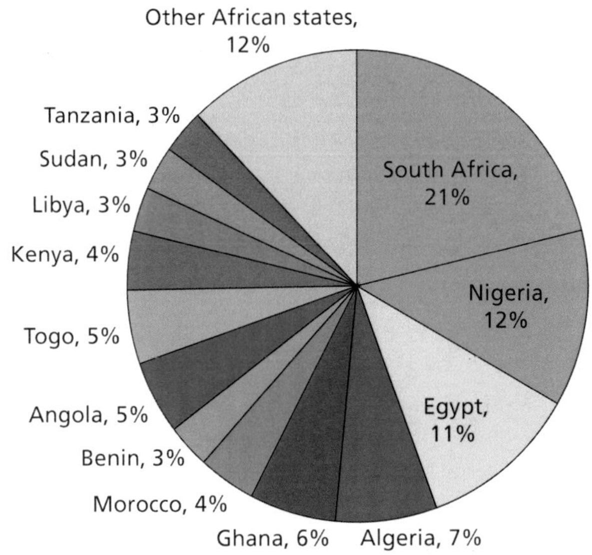

SOURCE: International Monetary Fund Direction of Trade Statistics.
RAND *RR521-3.4*

Figure 3.5
Chinese Imports from African Countries, 2012

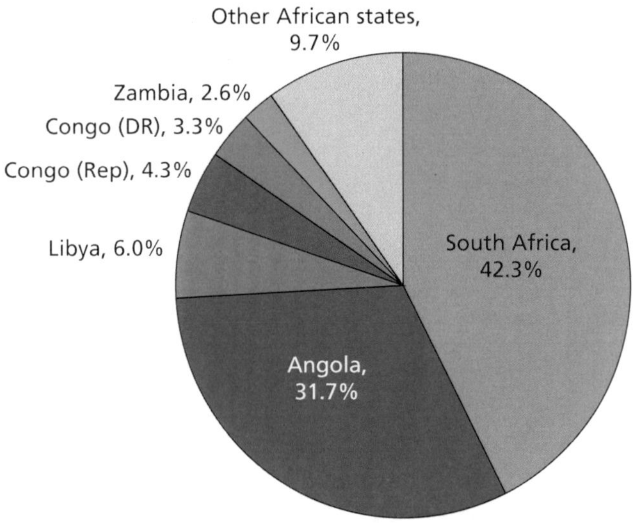

SOURCE: International Monetary Fund Direction of Trade Statistics.
RAND *RR521-3.5*

The high concentration of China-Africa trade is not just by country, but also by sector (Figure 3.6). In 2011, approximately 64 percent of registered Chinese imports from Africa consisted of petroleum; 16 percent iron and other metal ores; 8 percent manufactured goods; and 6 percent copper—figures which give credence to the claim that China's economic relationship with Africa is based largely on resource extraction. This specialization is accompanied by a very strong dependence on certain countries, since nearly all of Angola's and Sudan's exports are made up of crude oil.

Chinese exports to Africa are relatively more diversified, although three major types of products still dominant: machinery and transport equipment (38 percent), manufactured goods (30 percent), and miscellaneous articles (22 percent—mostly textiles) (Figure 3.7). Chemical products account for about 5 percent of the total. In general, Chinese products are considered to be well suited to African demand. Manufactured goods imports—electronic toys, textiles, etc.—have allowed Africans to expand their range of consumer products. Prices are often relatively inexpensive, making the products accessible to a larger number of people. Machinery and transport equipment imports are linked to the strong presence of Chinese firms in the infrastructure sector.

As China relies more heavily on oil imports from abroad, Africa's endowment of petroleum resources provides an increasingly important pillar of China-Africa trade. In 2011, Africa supplied China with 1.2 million barrels per day (bpd), or 24 percent

Figure 3.6
Chinese Imports from Africa, by Product, 2011

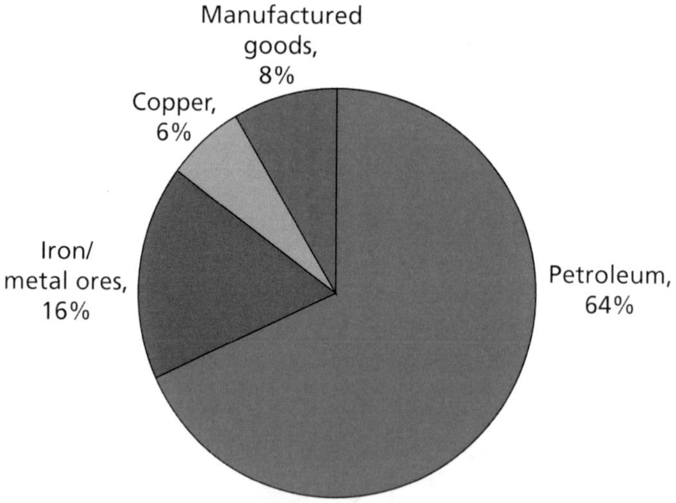

SOURCES: International Monetary Fund Direction of Trade Statistics; "China's Trade and Investment Relationship with Africa," United States International Trade Commission (USITC) Executive Briefings on Trade, April 2013.

RAND *RR521-3.6*

Figure 3.7
Chinese Exports to Africa, by Product, 2011

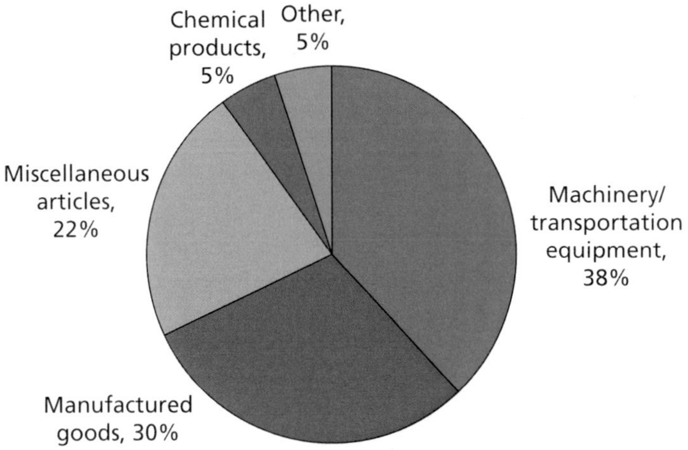

SOURCES: International Monetary Fund Direction of Trade Statistics; United Nations Comtrade.
RAND *RR521-3.7*

of China's total oil imports; Angola alone represented more than half that amount, or 12 percent of China's total crude oil imports.[24] Angola, Sudan, Congo, Libya, Algeria, and Nigeria together accounted for 90 percent of China's oil imports from Africa.[25]

Many African countries that do not have valuable raw materials to export to China—particularly oil and gas—have developed large trade deficits with Beijing. In such countries, trade with China leads to outflows of capital, competition for local manufacturers, and job losses in non-competitive industries while creating few, if any, new jobs. Eight of the ten countries with the largest bilateral trade deficits, according to the African Development Bank (AfDB), are non-oil producers.[26] Tiny Mauritius, for example, imported $433 million worth of goods from China in 2010 but exported only $10 million of its own products.[27]

In such countries, trade tends to become increasingly imbalanced as overall trade grows. Ghana, for example, had a trade deficit with China of $70 million out of $122 million in total trade in 2000; by 2006, the trade deficit grew to $474 million in 2006,

---

[24] U.S. Energy Information Administration, *China Country Report*, September 2012.

[25] Gamache, Hammer, and Jones, 2013.

[26] African Development Bank Group, "Chinese Trade and Investment Activities in Africa," Policy Brief, Vol. 1, No. 4, July 29, 2010.

[27] Shinn and Eisenman, 2012, p. 279.

even as Ghana's exports to China remained stagnant at a mere $29 million.[28] By 2012, despite Beijing's efforts to encourage Chinese investment and purchases of Ghanaian goods that yielded annual export growth of as much as 77 percent, Ghana's trade deficit with China reached $4 billion on $4.7 billion total bilateral trade.[29]

Chinese Investment

China's investment in Africa is the natural counterpart to increased China-Africa trade. Both form part of China's broader engagement strategy with Africa, albeit through different means and utilizing different institutional mechanisms.

Analyzing Chinese FDI in Africa is difficult for a variety of reasons. First, China does not publish data on FDI in Africa by sector. More importantly, according to experts, China's data on foreign direct investment have several limitations that affect their reliability, including problems associated with underreporting, inconsistencies between FDI flow and stock data, and different definitions of what constitutes FDI in Chinese statistical disclosures.[30]

This can lead to a wide range of estimates regarding China's FDI in Africa. For example, China's commerce minister, Chen Deming, announced in 2012 that Chinese FDI had "exceeded $14.7 billion in 2010, up 60 percent from 2009."[31] China's ambassador to South Africa, Tian Xuejun, commented in 2012 that "China's investment in Africa of various kinds exceeds $40 billion."[32] Regarding the discrepancy in the two figures, *The Economist* concludes, "Apparently, the first figure is for African investments reported to the government. The second includes estimates of Chinese funds flowing in from tax shelters around the world.[33]

Going by official Chinese statistics provided by the Ministry of Commerce, Chinese FDI flows in Africa have increased six-fold between 2005 and 2012, from $392

---

[28] African Center for Economic Transformation, *Looking East: China-Africa Engagements—Ghana Country Case Study*, December 2009, p. 5.

[29] Gao Wenzhi, Economic and Commercial Counselor, Embassy of China in Ghana, "Work by Mutual Efforts to Promote Trade And Economic Collaboration between Ghana and China," remarks to Standard Chartered Bank professional forum, Accra, Ghana, October 1, 2013.

[30] GAO, *Sub-Saharan Africa—Trends in U.S. and Chinese Economic Engagement*, GAO-13-199, Washington, D.C., February 2013, pp. 38–39.

[31] Chen Deming, Chinese Minister of Commerce, "China and Africa Poised to Embrace a Brighter Future for Economic Cooperation and Trade," speech to Fifth Ministerial Conference of FOCAC, Forum on China-Africa Cooperation, July 18, 2012.

[32] Tian Xuejun, Chinese Ambassador to South Africa, "Remarks at the South African Institute of International Affairs," Johannesburg, July 17, 2012.

[33] "Africa and China: More Than Minerals," *The Economist*, March 23, 2013.

million to $2.5 billion. Chinese FDI stock in Africa has increased thirteen-fold, from 1.5 billion in 2005 to 21.23 billion in 2012.[34]

Furthermore, according to the U.S. International Trade Commission, from 2003 to 2010, more than half of China's FDI in Africa was directed in oil, with Nigeria, Sudan, Angola, Egypt, Chad, and Niger as the major recipients.[35] Over 90 percent of the FDI came from China's large SOEs, which formed partnerships with African state oil companies and large multinationals. Some of the major state-owned firms with large holdings of FDI in Africa include the China National Offshore Oil Corporation (CNOOC), China National Petroleum Corporation, China Petroleum and Chemical Corporation (Sinopec), and China National Machinery Industry Corp (Sinomach).

Chinese FDI flows remain highly concentrated. In 2010, the top ten African recipients of Chinese FDI accounted for 76.3 percent of its total FDI to Africa (Table 3.1). Generally speaking, Chinese FDI in Africa is not correlated with total bilateral trade between China and African countries.

Table 3.1
Top Ten Destinations of Chinese Foreign Direct Investment in Africa, 2010

Country	Chinese FDI Flows in Africa (%)	Total China-Africa Trade (%)
South Africa	19.5	17.9
Democratic Republic of Congo	11.2	2.1
Niger	9.3	0.2
Nigeria	8.8	5.4
Algeria	8.8	4.1
Angola	4.8	19.6
Kenya	4.8	1.4
Zambia	3.6	2.0
Ethiopia	2.8	1.2
Ghana	2.7	1.6
Top 10's share of total	76.3	70.9

SOURCE: Sarah Baynton-Glen, *Beyond Trade—China-Africa Investment Trends*, Standard Chartered Global Research, February 22, 2012.

[34] Chinese Ministry of Commerce website, "Foreign Investment," no date; "China-Africa Economic and Trade Cooperation (2013)," 2013, p. 2.

[35] Gamache, Hammer, Jones, 2013.

The principal lenders responsible for administering Chinese investments in Africa are the China Development Bank and China Exim Bank. As state-owned banks, both have helped to promote the Chinese government's global interests, as well as those of China's state-owned and private companies. As opposed to directly financing African companies or governments, the two banks mainly offer lines of credit to assist Chinese companies in their overseas expansion. The China Development Bank's investment vehicle, the China Africa Development Fund (CADFund), has disbursed an estimated $1 billion in equity investment and aims to increase this to $5 billion by 2015. The bank claims to have "guided and supported" a total of $4 billion of investment by Chinese companies in Africa since 2007.[36]

Chinese Infrastructure Financing

Chinese financing of infrastructure in Africa has emerged as a major component unique to the China-Africa relationship. As Figure 3.8 illustrates, Chinese infrastructure investment in Africa increased from around $500 million in 2001 to $14 billion in 2011. Two-thirds of Chinese infrastructure investment during this period went to the power and transportation sectors;[37] in contrast, in 2010 non-Chinese official devel-

Figure 3.8
China's Infrastructure Finance Commitments

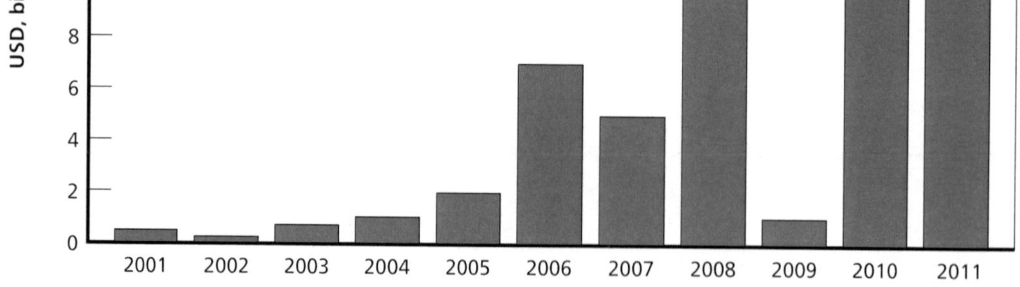

SOURCES: World Bank Report 2008; Standard Chartered Research 2012.
RAND *RR521-3.8*

[36] Sarah Baynton-Glen, *Beyond Trade—China-Africa Investment Trends*, Standard Chartered Global Research, February 22, 2012.

[37] Dollar, 2008.

opment infrastructure financing was divided primarily among water, sanitation, transportation, and energy, with only 3 percent allocated to communication.[38]

China's focus on infrastructure can be understood in terms of the economic complementarities that exist between the two countries. On the one hand, Africa remains perennially deficient in basic telecommunication, power, and transportation networks, while China has developed one of the world's largest and most competitive construction industries, with particular expertise in the civil works critical for infrastructure development. On the other hand, as a result of globalization, China's fast-growing manufacturing economy is generating major demands for oil and mineral inputs that are rapidly outstripping the country's domestic resources. Africa is already a major natural resource exporter, and infrastructure facilitates the extraction and transport of natural resources to markets abroad like China. Infrastructure can also enhance intra-African trade if built to connect manufacturing centers or sources of raw materials in one country to markets in another.

The vast majority of these infrastructure arrangements are financed by the China Exim Bank, which is devoted primarily to providing export seller's and buyer's credits to support the trade of Chinese goods. This deal structure is sometimes referred to as the "Angola model," in which repayment of the loan for infrastructure is made with future revenue from the sale of natural resources. In most cases, this arrangement is used for countries that cannot provide adequate financial guarantees to back their loan commitments and allows them to package natural resource exploitation and infrastructure development. It is no wonder that the majority of Chinese infrastructure finance is concentrated in resource-rich countries such as Nigeria, Angola, Sudan, and (as a legacy of the pre-independence period) South Sudan.[39] As will be discussed in the development aid and loans section, much of China's infrastructure construction activities in Africa and elsewhere are commercial transactions and have little to do with development assistance or FDI.

Chinese Development Aid and Loans

China gives development aid for a variety of reasons. Some are linked to China's trade and investment agenda. Others are tied to Chinese soft power objectives, in particular health and education aid. Beijing is keenly aware that development assistance has the potential to put a more positive face on Chinese engagement that can counter negative perceptions of Chinese activities on the continent.

Quantifying Chinese development aid to Africa has proven a difficult task for scholars and analysts. This is due to two factors. First, the Chinese government does not provide tailored statistics on its aid to African countries. Second, China defines

---

[38] OECD, *Mapping Support for Africa's Infrastructure Investment*, 2012, pp. 12–13.

[39] Vivien Foster, William Butterfield, Chuan Chen, and Nataliya Pushak, *Building Bridges: China's Growing Role as Infrastructure Financier for Sub-Saharan Africa*, Washington, D.C.: World Bank, 2008.

"aid" differently than the Organisation for Economic Co-operation and Development (OECD), of which China is not a member, making crosscut comparisons with other donors and among different countries challenging.

In April 2011, the Chinese State Council released its first white paper on foreign aid, giving analysts a more detailed account of Chinese aid worldwide broken down by loans, grants and concessional loans. The paper states that, "By the end of 2009, China had provided a total of 256.29 billion yuan [$37.7 billion] in aid to foreign countries, including 106.2 billion yuan [$15.6 billion] in grants, 76.54 billion yuan [$11.3 billion] in interest-free loans and 73.55 billion yuan [$10.8 billion] in concessional loans." It also revealed that aid had grown by 29.4 percent annually between 2004 and 2009, and 46.7 percent of total Chinese aid was committed to Africa in 2009.[40] As a basis of comparison, 32.8 percent went to Asia, 12.7 percent went to Latin America and the Caribbean, and 4 percent went to Oceania in 2009.[41] While helpful, the paper did not give detailed country-level aid figures and breakdowns, leaving scholars and analysts at the mercy of independent studies and analyses.

Deborah Brautigam, who has devoted significant scholarship to the issue, provides one of the more authoritative assessments of Chinese aid to Africa. She finds that "in 2008, China probably disbursed about $1.2 billion in Official Development Assistance (ODA)[42] to Africa, compared with the World Bank ($4.1 billion), the United States ($7.2 billion) and France ($3.4 billion)." She estimates that Chinese aid "probably rose to $1.4 billion in 2009."[43]

Other analysts offer much higher estimates, in part because they rely on a far broader definition of what counts as "aid." One 2009 report by the Congressional Research Service, for example, estimates that China gave almost $18 billion in aid to Africa in 2007 alone. A database published by the College of William and Mary in 2013 found that China committed $75 billion in aid and development projects to Africa from 2000 to 2011, and that the United States committed $90 billion over the same period. Finally, a recently released RAND report finds that between 2001 and 2011, 49 countries in Africa received approximately $175 billion in pledged assistance from China.[44]

---

40 Information Office of the State Council, People's Republic of China, "China's Foreign Aid," April 2011.

41 Information Office of the State Council, 2011.

42 ODA is one of the most widely used and cited indicators of international aid flows. It contains three key criteria: (a) undertaken by the official sector; (b) with promotion of economic development and welfare as the main objective; and (c) at concessional financial terms (if a loan, having a grant element of at least 25 percent). See Organisation for Economic Co-operation and Development, "Glossary of Statistical Terms, Official Development Assistance (ODA)," web page, August 28, 2003.

43 Brautigam, 2011b, p. 211. For a comprehensive analysis of China's aid to Africa, see Brautigam, 2009.

44 See Thomas Lum, Hannah Fischer, Julissa Gomez-Granger, and Anne Leland, *China's Foreign Aid Activities in Africa, Latin America, and Southeast Asia*, Washington, D.C.: Congressional Research Service, Report R40361, February 25, 2009; Mario Biggeri and Marco Sanfilippo, "Understanding China's Move into Africa: An Empiri-

The reason that the above estimates on Chinese "aid" to Africa vary so significantly from Brautigam's estimate is because most Chinese activity on the continent falls under "other official flows" (OOF), not the "official development assistance" (ODA) category.[45] The OOF category includes loans that are not concessional in character, but fall under the OECD definition of "official bilateral transactions." These can include strategic lines of credit and export buyers' credit and are typically financed through China's two policy banks, the China Exim Bank and China Development Bank. Since 2002, more than 70 percent of the China Exim bank's operational portfolio has consisted of export seller's credits, which are essentially loans for Chinese companies operating abroad offered at competitive commercial interest rates.[46]

However, these higher estimates of Chinese "aid" also include as "other official flows" inherently commercial investments made by Chinese companies that happen to be *state-owned* enterprises; because China's SOEs are typically large entities involved in large-scale projects, the dollar values of their projects tend to be sizable and thus inflate the amount counted as "aid." Similar types of investment made by OECD countries are typically made by private corporations, meaning they are not included in calculations of either "other official flows" or "aid." If General Electric built a power plant in an African country, for example, it would be counted as private investment, whereas if SinoHydro, a large Chinese SOE, did the same, it would, under this approach, be counted as Chinese OOF or "aid."

The topic of Chinese aid to Africa is large, complex, and ultimately beyond the scope of this report. However, three broad characteristics differentiate Chinese

cal Analysis," *Journal of Chinese Economic and Business Studies*, Vol. 7, No. 1, 2009, pp. 31–54; Claire Provost and Rich Harris, "China Commits Billions in Aid to Africa as Part of Charm Offensive—Interactive," *The Guardian*, April 29, 2013; and Charles Wolf, Xiao Wang, and Eric Warner, *China's Foreign Aid and Government-Sponsored Investment Activities: Scale, Content, Destinations, and Implications*, Santa Monica, Calif.: RAND Corporation, RR-118, 2013. The CRS report estimated Chinese aid to Africa as $17.96 billion in 2007. The *Guardian* article quotes statistics based on a newly released public database led by researchers at the College of William and Mary, Brigham Young University, and Development Gateway detailing almost 1,700 projects in 50 countries between 2000 and 2011. The database found that China committed $75 billion in aid and development projects to Africa from 2000 to 2011, and that the United States committed $90 billion over the same period. The RAND report characterizes aid and government investment under one methodological rubric it calls "foreign aid and government-sponsored investment activities," or FAGIA. It finds that between 2001 and 2011, 49 countries in Africa received approximately $175 billion in pledged assistance from China. As scholars have pointed out, however, many of these attempts to estimate China's aid to Africa suffer from methodological shortcomings, including relying on news reports that characterize investment as "aid," relying on second-hand sources that turn out to be incorrect or incomplete, and often counting the value of agreements that never come to fruition. See "Rubbery Numbers on Chinese Aid," from Deborah Brautigam's personal blog, "China in Africa: The Real Story," April 30, 2013.

45 The official ODA definition from OECD states that countries must fulfill one of two requirements for funding to be considered "ODA": (1) funds must be "concessional in character" and must be a genuine subsidy from the host government; or (2) loans must have a "grant element of at least 25 percent using a 10 percent discount rate" (Organisation for Economic Co-operation and Development, "Is It ODA?, Fact Sheet," November, 2008).

46 OECD, 2008.

aid practices from Development Assistance Committee (DAC) donors—a forum of selected OECD member states that have developed a framework on issues surrounding aid, development, and poverty-reduction strategies in developing countries.

First, Chinese aid is typically "tied" to the procurement of Chinese goods and services. For example, if the government of an African country seeks a Chinese loan for an infrastructure project, that loan will typically come from one of China's two state policy banks, the China Exim Bank and China Development Bank. These banks are export-promotion enterprises rather than development assistance agencies. Furthermore, contracts between African governments and Chinese policy banks typically stipulate preferential treatment for Chinese project contractors and goods. The China Exim Bank, for example, states that "no less than 50% of total procurement shall be made in China."[47]

Second, China emphasizes "local ownership," i.e., letting African countries decide how they wish to use the aid funding themselves. The benefit of this policy is that it empowers African governments in the decision process of how best to utilize the funds. The drawback, of course, is that this can lead to "prestige" projects of questionable value for poverty reduction or economic development value, such as government office buildings or sports stadiums.

Third, aside from a commitment to the "One China" policy, China does not attach conditions to its aid to Africa. DAC members have spent decades honing and researching what they consider to be the "best practices" of aid efficiency—tying aid with improvements in transparency, debt sustainability, and good governance in an effort to improve the overall capacity and efficiency of government institutions in Africa. For China, this constitutes an undue infringement in the internal affairs of other countries.

Chinese aid practices in Africa are tied to China's strategic objectives on the continent. China perceives itself as an "economic partner" first and "aid donor" second. This conception is derived in part from an identity of China as a "developing nation" that engages Africa on an equal footing without preaching or imposing standards. The concept of "aid donor" brings with it certain connotations of elitism and rich-poor status that China seeks to distance itself from. Perhaps more importantly, most Chinese "aid" is ultimately not conceived for purely *development assistance* purposes as envisioned by the OECD-DAC establishment. It is meant to support Chinese economic and strategic objectives, with the resultant effect of also benefiting Africans through infrastructure and other development projects. The fact that the majority of

---

[47] Deborah Brautigam, "Aid 'With Chinese Characteristics': Chinese Foreign Aid and Development Finance Meet the OECD-DAC Aid Regime," *Journal of International Development*, Vol. 23, 2011a, p. 760.

Chinese aid is tied to the procurement of Chinese goods and services further illustrates Chinese strategy in this regard.[48]

Special Economic Zones and the China-Africa Development Fund

China's foray into Special Economic Zones (SEZs) in Africa began in 2006, when the "Program for China-Africa Cooperation in Economic and Social Development" was launched at the FOCAC ministerial meetings. The program was conceived by China as a means to share with African countries its own experience in investment promotion and FDI growth. Seven SEZs are now in various stages of development in five countries: Egypt, Ethiopia, Mauritius, Nigeria, and Zambia. Some are developed through joint Chinese-African ventures, while others are entirely Chinese-owned.

SEZs are best understood as geographic areas designed and created to attract foreign investment by providing favorable commercial policies, such as tax breaks, along with infrastructure intended to lower transaction costs for investors and facilitate streamlined operations. They are also intended to help China's own economic restructuring, allowing less competitive and labor-intensive industries that are becoming increasingly more competitive in the Chinese domestic market, such as textiles, leather goods, and building materials, to move offshore.

The Zambia-China Economic and Trade Cooperation Zone was the first overseas economic and trade cooperation zone initiated by China. Since its inception, the zone has attracted several Chinese and multinational companies, who have reportedly invested more than $600 million and created employment opportunities for more than 6,000 Africans in the mining, engineering, and construction sectors.[49] The Lekki Free Trade Zone (LFTZ) in Nigeria, a joint venture between Lekki Worldwide Investment Limited and the Chinese government, is another venture that China and Nigeria hope will cultivate economic growth zone, attract FDI, promote exports, and create long-term employment opportunities for Africans.[50]

While most SEZs are in the beginning stage of development, challenges persist for many. For one, the geographical and political factors that led to success in the Chinese context are the not the same in Africa. One recent World Bank report concludes that country context is critical in the outcomes of many SEZ programs, which in some cases were not appropriate in the African context. The report concludes that China's one-size-fits-all model "seems plausible at the policy level, but implementation

---

[48] The "tying" of aid is not unique to China, of course. As recently as 2001, 92 percent of Italy's and 68 percent of Canada's official development aid was also tied to the procurement of donor goods and services. See Brautigam, 2009, p. 152.

[49] Embassy of the People's Republic of China in the Republic of Zambia, 2011.

[50] Roseline Okere, "Leveraging on Potential of Nigeria's Free Trade Zones for Economic Transformation," *The Guardian* (Nigeria), August 8, 2012.

and design are the critical factors determining success."[51] Furthermore, Africa's SEZs are not state-directed but are in the hands of private businesses to manage. In China, the SEZ model was implemented within a very specific political and economic context where the state was able to "direct" development, including marshaling the political will to carry it out. Unfortunately, most SEZs in Africa suffer from poor infrastructure, limited political support, and diffuse oversight mechanisms. However, as the majority of SEZs are still under construction, their eventual viability and success hinge on continued commitment from government officials and buy-in from the local people of Africa.

The China-Africa Development Fund (CADFund) forms part of the Chinese government's recent strategy for reorienting China's investment strategy in Africa in favor of investments that promote African industrialization. CADFund was established as part of the eight measures announced by President Hu Jintao at the 2006 FOCAC, but has received more attention from Chinese policymakers in recent years. CADFund's mandate is to facilitate China-Africa cooperation and to enhance capacity building of African economies through direct investment and advisory services.[52] CADFund is presented by its management as China's first fund that focuses on African investment and that encourages and supports Chinese enterprises' investments in Africa. According to its mandate, CADFund is to operate in line with market principles, deriving funding from the China Development Bank.[53] Up until 2012, CADFund has reportedly financed and supported 60 projects across 30 African countries.[54] In a July 2013 interview with the *China Daily* newspaper, CADFund chief executive officer Chi Jianxin announced that the fund plans to invest $2.4 billion on the continent in the coming years, mainly for investment in manufacturing and agriculture.[55] According to Chi, the fund has already benefited "about 700,000 people on the continent and contributed $1 billion in tax revenues to different African governments and $2 billion in goods for African countries to export annually."[56]

---

[51] Thomas Farole, *Special Economic Zones in Africa: Comparing Performance and Learning from Global Experience*, Washington D.C.: The World Bank, 2011.

[52] China-Africa Development Fund homepage, "Introduction," no date.

[53] China-Africa Development Fund homepage, no date.

[54] *The China-African Development Fund (CADFund) as a Sovereign Wealth Fund for Africa's Development?* Policy Briefing, The Centre for Chinese Studies, Stellenbosch University, July 2013.

[55] Mzwandile Jacks, "CADFund to Invest $2.4 Billion in Africa Projects," July 1, 2013.

[56] Jacks, 2013.

Security Engagement

Arms Sales

Since China reformed its defense industry from a military-operated to civilian-run system in 1999, the market-driven profit incentives of Chinese arms manufacturers have become the primary catalyst for increased Chinese arms sales abroad. Africa has become an increasingly important component of this expansion. According to the Stockholm International Peace Research Institute (SIPRI), as of 2011, China accounted for roughly 25 percent of the arms industry in Africa.[57] During the period from 2002 to 2009, China supplied $1.1 billion in conventional weapons to Sub-Saharan Africa and another $1.4 billion to North Africa.[58] China also is a key source of small arms and light weapons to Africa.[59]

No statistically significant correlation was found between Chinese FDI and arms sales. However, many of China's top destinations for FDI also receive a large proportion of China's total arms sales to the continent. For example, of China's top nine destinations for FDI in Africa in 2010 (excluding South Africa), five of those countries (55 percent) were also among China's top ten recipients of arms sales to Africa from 2006 to 2010.

Chinese arms transfers to Africa have been controversial, mainly due to reports of Chinese-made weapons turning up in conflict areas and in countries that are under UN-sanctioned arms embargos. In recent years, there is no evidence that China has provided these arms *directly* to rebel groups, though arms have been documented to fall into rogue hands through intermediary channels. Assistant Foreign Minister Zhai Jun said in 2006 that China always takes a "cautious and accountable" approach toward the export of small arms, light weapons, and other military hardware to Africa. He emphasized that China requires the recipient government to certify the end user and the ultimate purpose, and that the arms will not be transferred to a third party. Zhai also reiterated that China strictly abides by UN resolutions and does not export military equipment to countries and regions where the Security Council has imposed sanctions.[60]

Given these principles, it is easy to forget that a little more than a decade ago, China reserved the right for itself to object to arms exports by the United States, withdrawing from the United Nations Register of Conventional Arms (UNRCA) in pro-

---

[57] Lynch, 2012.

[58] Richard F. Grimmett, *Conventional Arms Transfers to Developing Nations, 2002–2009*, Congressional Research Service, Report R41403, September 10, 2010, pp. 52–58.

[59] Mitali Mirle, *The Question of Small Arms and Light Weapons (SALWs) in Africa*, General Assembly 1—Disarmament and International Security," Dubai International Academy Model United Nations 2012, fourth Annual Session, March 4, 2012.

[60] "Assistant Foreign Minister Zhai Jun Accepts an Exclusive Interview by Foreign Media concerning the Beijing Summit of the Forum on China-Africa Cooperation," Forum on China-Africa Cooperation (FOCAC) Summit, Beijing, October 26, 2006.

test of the United States' inclusion of arms sales figures to Taiwan.[61] China rejoined in 2007 after the UNRCA committee "affirmed the important principle that the Register should only include arms transfers among States Members of the United Nations."[62]

However, recent news reports indicate that Chinese officials have become more active in hampering UN-led investigations into accusations that Chinese arms are ending up in conflict zones. One *Washington Post* article, for example, alleges that China "routinely refuses to cooperate with U.N. arms experts and flexes its diplomatic muscle to protect its allies and curtail investigations that may shed light on its own secretive arms industry."[63]

Military Ties

China has been quietly increasing its military cooperation with many countries in Africa. The PLA's attaché program has seen extensive growth recently in Africa. It currently has attaché representation in one-third of African nations, and 75 percent of these countries have attachés in China.[64] High-level military visits are an important part of the security relationship. From 2009 to 2012, China sent a total of 12 high-level military delegations to Africa, while Africa sent a total of 13 to China.[65] These efforts are buttressed by an increase in the number of foreign military officers receiving scholarships and training on the mainland. For example, one- and two-star generals, chiefs of staff, and cabinet ministers from Africa are receiving training at China's National Defense University. President Joseph Kabila of the Democratic Republic of Congo has also received training there.[66] This is in addition to the African diplomats already receiving training at China's various foreign affairs academies, such as the China Foreign Affairs University.[67]

---

[61] In 1996, China had noted that arms transfers from the U.S. to Taiwan are "neither legitimate nor transfers between sovereign States'" and asked that such entries be deleted from future annual reports to the Register. Despite this protest, however, the U.S. included in its report to the Register in a footnote. See Malcolm Chalmers and Owen Greene, "The UN Register of Conventional Arms: A Progress Report," *Disarmament Diplomacy*, No. 35, March 1999.

[62] United Nations Disarmament Yearbook, Volume 31, 2006. See also Li Jun, "The Background of China Resuming Participation in the UN Register of Conventional Arms," *International Herald Leader*, September 10, 2007.

[63] Lynch, 2012.

[64] Jeniffer Parenti, "China-Africa Relations in the 21st Century," *Joint Forces Quarterly*, No. 52, 1st Quarter, 2009.

[65] RAND calculations based on Chinese-language news reports. China sent delegations to the following countries: Mozambique, Cameroon, Namibia, Angola, Ethiopia, Uganda, Seychelles, South Africa, Zambia (twice), and Tanzania (twice). Meanwhile, Africa sent delegations to China from the following countries: Namibia, Egypt, Mozambique, Sierra Leone, Rwanda, Algeria, Nigeria, Equatorial Guinea, South Africa, Ghana, Malawi, and Djibouti (twice).

[66] Horta Loro, *Defense and Military Education: A Dimension of Chinese Power*, Power and Interest News Report, September 29, 2006.

[67] "China Beefs Up Training of African Diplomats," China Radio International, November 25, 2013.

Generally speaking, Beijing seems to devote more attention to coastal states such as Djibouti and Tanzania, especially considering China's ongoing counter-piracy operations near the Gulf of Aden. Officials from Djibouti and Tanzania have visited or been visited by China twice from 2009 to 2012, with the vice chairman of China's Central Military Commission, Fan Changlong, recently meeting with the Tanzanian Minister of Defense in April 2013.[68] The Port of Djibouti has been identified as a possible "ship fuel and material replenishment point" for the PLA Navy in the future.[69] In May 2013, China agreed to assist Cape Verde—a coastal state off the west coast of Africa—with $210 million in military equipment and training over ten years.[70] Finally, starting in January 2009, Chinese naval forces were sent to the Gulf of Aden to participate in the ongoing multilateral counter-piracy effort, marking the first time the country's naval vessels have been operationally deployed in a multilateral setting outside of Chinese waters since the founding of the PRC in 1949.[71] As China's navy seeks to bolster its ability to safeguard its increasingly far-flung economic interests in that region of the world, it is inevitable that Chinese military leaders will seek to enhance military ties with African countries in key geostrategic areas.

To date, China has conducted regular defense consultations only with South Africa, beginning in 2003.[72] China's 2010 defense white paper also notes that China has established "mechanisms for defense cooperation meetings with Egypt"[73]

China has also increased military training and support for several African military forces. Citing "serious security challenges in the Gulf of Guinea" and Nigeria's "outdated military equipment," for example, PRC military attaché to Nigeria Colonel Kang Honglin announced in August 2012 that the PLA Navy had begun training exercises with the Nigerian Navy. Col. Kang also announced that China agreed to help Nigeria set up an ammunition assembly in Kaduna "in support of the federal government's desire for indigenous arms manufacturing."[74]

---

68 "Fan Changlong Meets with Tanzanian Guests," *PLA Daily*, April 18, 2013.

69 The other replenishment points identified were the Port of Aden in Yemen, and the Port of Salalah in Oman. See Hai Tao, "Is the Navy Establishing the First Batch of Overseas Strategic Support Points?" [海军建首批海外战略支撑点?] *Guoji Xianqu Daobao* (in Chinese), January 10, 2013.

70 Constanca de Pina, "China Assists Cape Verde with Military Equipment," *A Semana Online*, May 14, 2013.

71 Richard Weitz, "Operation Somalia: China's First Expeditionary Force?" *China Security*, Vol. 5, No. 1, Winter 2009, pp. 27–42; Andrew S. Erickson and Austin M. Strange, *No Substitute for Experience: Chinese Antipiracy Operations in the Gulf of Aden,* China Maritime Study No. 10, Newport, R.I.: U.S. Naval War College, 2013; Mark McDonald, "China Confirms Naval Role in Gulf of Aden," *New York Times*, December 18, 2008.

72 Chinese Foreign Ministry, "Relations with South Africa," June 14, 2006.

73 Government of China, "China's National Defense in 2010," no date.

74 Oghogho Obayuwana, "China Wants to Partner Nigeria on Gulf of Guinea," *The Guardian* (Nigeria), August 2, 2012.

UN Peacekeeping Operations

China's stance toward international peacekeeping has evolved from outright rejection in the 1970s to reluctant participation in the 1980s and then to prolonged involvement starting in the mid-1990s.[75] This shift reflects recognition on the part of policymakers in Beijing that peacekeeping conforms to Beijing's policy of non-intervention while giving Chinese security and military personnel the opportunity to gain valuable experience with overseas deployments. Since UN peacekeeping operations are carried out under the authority of a multilateral institution (i.e., the UN) and in most cases with the consent of the hosting state, UN peacekeeping operations are viewed as legitimate means for China to contribute to peace and stability in Africa.

Since 2001, the number of peacekeepers that China has sent to participate in UN peacekeeping operations worldwide has rapidly increased. In January 2001, China contributed 27 military personnel to Africa, all of whom were observers. At the time, China ranked 42nd among contributors worldwide. As of 2012, China has well over 1,800 military, police, and civilian personnel in UN peacekeeping operations in Africa, the largest contributor among UN Security Council permanent members and constituting 75 percent of China's total number of deployed peacekeepers worldwide.[76] Chinese peacekeeping operation deployments are concentrated in Darfur, South Sudan, Liberia, and the Democratic Republic of the Congo, though it also has small contingents in Côte d'Ivoire and the Western Sahara.

In June 2013, China agreed to commit 395 peacekeeping troops to Mali. The most notable aspect of this decision was that combat troops would be sent as part of the contingent, marking the first time China has sent combat troops on a peacekeeping mission. Chen Jian, head of the UN Association of China, a Chinese think tank, called the move a "major breakthrough in our participation in peacekeeping," adding, "With this, our contribution will be complete. We will have policemen, medical forces, engineering troops and combat troops."[77] According to Xinhua, the Mali contingent will include engineers, medical personnel, and guard teams to be sent in two batches at the end of July and the beginning of September 2013.[78] The peacekeepers will be tasked with "repairing roads and bridges, safeguarding peace and stability as well as providing medical assistance."[79]

---

75 For more on this history, see Ayenagbo et al., 2012, pp. 22–32; and Bates Gill and Chin-hao Huang, *China's Expanding Role in Peacekeeping: Prospects and Policy Implications*, SIPRI Policy Paper No. 25, November 2009.

76 Ton Dietz, Kjell Havnevik, Mayke Kaag, and Terje Oestigaard, eds., *African Engagements: Africa Negotiating an Emerging Multipolar World*, Leiden and Boston: Brill Publishers, 2011, p. 214.

77 Kathrin Hille, "China Commits Combat Troops to Mali," *Financial Times*, June 27, 2013.

78 "China to Send Peacekeeping Forces to Mali," Xinhua, July 12, 2013.

79 "China to Send Peacekeeping Forces to Mali," 2013.

CHAPTER FOUR

The Impact of Chinese Engagement on African Countries

China's impact on Africa has been mixed. Its investments have created jobs, developed critically needed infrastructure, and contributed to economic growth, particularly in sectors or geographic areas in which international financial institutions and Western governments and companies have been unwilling to engage. Its expenditures on education, training, and economic development have contributed positively to Africans' standard of living and economic opportunities. Beijing's participation in UN peacekeeping missions in Africa has contributed in concrete ways to peace and security on the continent.

That said, China's engagement has had deleterious effects as well. Its investments and political and military support have helped a number of nondemocratic regimes cling to power. Its emphasis on investing in natural resources has reinforced many African countries' dependence on raw materials and unskilled labor. Growing trade between China and Africa has contributed to the loss of hundreds of thousands of manufacturing jobs in industries such as textiles that could not compete with less expensive Chinese imports. And the nature of many Chinese investment deals has contributed to high levels of debt, economically unviable decisions, and official corruption.

Political and Military Impact

China sends frequent signals that its engagement with Africa is of great political importance. Senior Chinese officials visit frequently and travel much more extensively throughout the continent. As president, Hu Jintao visited 18 African countries in four separate trips to the continent. Recent Chinese foreign ministers have made their first foreign trip anywhere in the world to Africa, while also traveling to Africa annually since 1991.[1] In 2006, the Chinese president, premier, and foreign minister visited a total of 17 countries in Africa, an unprecedented level of engagement unmatched even

1 Testimony by David H. Shinn in U.S. Senate, Committee on Foreign Relations, Subcommittee on African Affairs, November 1, 2011.

by the president of South Africa, Thabo Mbeki.[2] Newly installed President Xi Jinping, in his first overseas trip as head of state, traveled to Africa in March 2013, sending a clear signal regarding China's commitment to the continent. Senior American officials, in contrast, have made far fewer African trips.[3] Two out of the three countries President Obama visited in June and July 2013 had just been visited by Chinese President Xi Jinping three months earlier, creating the impression that Obama was following in Xi's footsteps and playing "catch-up" to China.[4]

In the political sphere, it is clear that Chinese engagement has helped legitimize, or at least support, a number of autocratic regimes. China's willingness to invest in mining, form costly (but lucrative) oil/gas ventures, and sell weapons and military materiel to Sudan, Zimbabwe, and other states regardless of their human rights records has provided these governments with the resources needed to remain in power and to continue to oppress their populations. From 2001 to 2009, for example, China provided $143 million in heavy weapons, plus small arms, to Sudan, and also helped Sudan build indigenous weapons factories, all at a time when government-backed militias were engaged in violent attacks on civilians in Darfur.[5] (Despite this support, when negative publicity about Chinese support to Sudan threatened to undermine the 2008 Beijing Olympics, political pressure from Beijing was critical in getting Sudan to accept the deployment of an AU/UN peacekeeping mission in Darfur.[6]) Similarly, China has sold fighter jets, heavy military vehicles, and military communications equipment to the government of Zimbabwe despite President Robert Mugabe's use of the armed forces to silence political opponents.[7] Beijing also provided political support to the Sudanese and Zimbabwean regimes that has insulated them from international isolation; China prevented the UN Security Council from sanctioning Zimbabwe in July 2008, for example,[8] and it long defended Khartoum from Security Council action.

---

2 Andrew Nathan and Andrew Scobell, *China's Search for Security*, second edition, New York: Columbia University Press, 2012b, p. 184.

3 Each U.S. president since George H. W. Bush has made one trip to sub-Saharan Africa per term. (Thus, Bill Clinton and George W. Bush visited twice overall.) Secretary of State Hillary Clinton visited Africa independently four times in her four-year tenure; her predecessors, Condoleezza Rice and Colin Powell, made three and four independent trips to the continent, respectively, some of them to attend a specific event in a single country (such as the swearing-in of Liberian President Ellen Johnson Sirleaf or the signing of the Sudanese Comprehensive Peace Agreement). See U.S. Department of State, Office of the Historian, "Travels of the President," web page, no date. See also U.S. Department of State, Office of the Historian, "Travels of the Secretary," web page, no date.

4 Ross Anthony, "Obama 'Playing Catch-Up' as Africa Looks to China," CNN, June 26, 2013.

5 Alden, 2011, p. 51.

6 Shinn, 2009, pp. 91–94.

7 Rotberg, 2008, p. 15.

8 Rotberg, 2008, p. 13.

China is not actively working to prop up tyrants who have expressed hostility to the West, argues Chris Alden of the London School of Economics, but rather maintains relations with such states in order to pursue economic opportunities, whether that means making money from Zimbabwean arms sales or protecting its significant investments in Sudan's oil infrastructure. Alden notes, however, that Chinese leaders have recognized that "tying their economic fortunes to the fate of a particular illegitimate regime" generates potential political costs, leading them to take steps to distance themselves from some of their pariah partners.[9]

That said, China is not alone in providing support to African despots. While the United States and other Western countries have drawn the line at working with repressive regimes like those in Sudan and Zimbabwe, they have cooperated with many African governments that lie somewhere on the spectrum between Jeffersonian democracy and dictatorship. Among the countries that receive Foreign Military Financing (FMF) from the United States, for example, are Chad, the Democratic Republic of the Congo, and Guinea, which Transparency International ranks as the 11th, 17th, and 23rd most corrupt countries in the world.[10] U.S. partners in the Trans-Sahara Counterterrorism Partnership (TSCTP) include four countries ranked "not free" by Freedom House (Chad, Mali, Mauritania, and Algeria).[11] Nevertheless, these countries receive extensive security assistance from the United States and participate in an annual multinational military exercise led by AFRICOM.[12]

Western corporations also engage numerous African countries governed by despotic regimes. The government of Equatorial Guinea, for example, is arguably one of the most corrupt and cruel regimes on the continent, yet the State Department notes that "U.S. oil companies are one of Equatorial Guinea's largest investors, and they have a lead role in oil and gas exploration and extraction,"[13] and the State Department reopened the American Embassy there in 2006 after an 11-year hiatus, primarily to facilitate these commercial activities.[14] Corrupt but resource-rich governments such as those in Angola and Nigeria have had little trouble getting money from Western aid agencies and banks, particularly when they could guarantee loans with future revenues from oil and other natural resources. Scholar Deborah Brautigam states that

---

[9] Chris Alden, *China in Africa*, London: Zed Books, 2007, p. 66.

[10] Transparency International, *Corruption Perceptions Index 2012*, December 5, 2012; U.S. Africa Command, "Fact Sheet: Foreign Military Financing," October 2012.

[11] U.S. Department of State, *Country Reports on Terrorism 2012*, May 2013, pp. 8–9.

[12] Freedom House, *Freedom in the World 2013*, 2013, pp. 14–18; U.S. Africa Command, "Fact Sheet: Exercise Flintlock," October 24, 2012.

[13] U.S. Department of State, "U.S. Relations with Equatorial Guinea: Fact Sheet," web page, April 1, 2013.

[14] U.S. Department of State, Office of the Historian, "A Guide to the United States' History of Recognition, Diplomatic, and Consular Relations, by Country, Since 1776: Equatorial Guinea," no date. Also, Voice of America, "US to Open 'Mini Embassy' in Equatorial Guinea," November 19, 2002.

few American or European oil companies or banks "apply any general democracy or human rights litmus test to their investment decisions" and notes that "Beijing fits in with these other amoral financiers quite comfortably."[15]

A potentially more positive development is China's enhanced involvement in UN African peacekeeping missions and international anti-piracy efforts. Though few Africans are likely to have firsthand exposure to the Chinese forces involved, Beijing has made significant contributions to peace and security on the continent through these collaborative security initiatives.

Economic Impact

In April 2013, China's Foreign Ministry assessed that Chinese aid and investment directly led African economies to grow by more than 20 percent since 2000.[16] A study by two Canadian economists reported notable, though more modest, impacts, claiming that in the few years before and after the 2008 global financial crisis (2005–2009), Chinese investment alone contributed as much as a half-percent per year to individual countries' GDP growth, suggesting that "a significant, even if in some cases small, portion of the elevated growth in sub Saharan Africa in the three years before the Financial Crisis and also in the two years afterwards (2008–2009) can be attributed to Chinese inward investment."[17]

Chinese companies have indeed created thousands of jobs in mining, construction, manufacturing, and other sectors, though most of them are unskilled. The vast majority of managers and foremen are Chinese, and Africans have little to no chance of advancing to such positions. Even for unskilled positions, however, Chinese firms import thousands of laborers from China rather than hire local workers,[18] and Chinese workers are widely reported to be paid more than their African counterparts.[19]

---

[15] Brautigam, 2009, p. 285.

[16] "China-Africa Cooperation Contributes to African Growth: FM Spokeswoman," *People's Daily Online*, April 19, 2013.

[17] Aaron Weisbrod and John Whalley, *The Contribution of Chinese FDI to Africa's Pre Crisis Growth Surge*, National Bureau of Economic Research Working Paper 17544, October 2011, p. 2.

[18] See, for example, Sautman and Hairong, 2008, pp. 109–110; and also *African Studies Review*, 2007, p. 91. See the assertion that Angola has admitted 250,000 Chinese workers since President Jose Eduardo dos Santos's election in 2002 (Rafael Marques de Morais, "Growing Wealth, Shrinking Democracy," *New York Times*, August 29, 2012). Deborah Brautigam points out that small numbers of Africans do gain entrepreneurial experience from participating in joint ventures with Chinese investors, and that others acquire technical skills from their employment at Chinese factories that allow some to launch their own ventures. See Brautigam, 2009, pp. 225–227.

[19] Marc Howe, "South African Report Highlights Chinese Labor Abuses in the Sub-Sahara," mining.com, November 9, 2012.

Moreover, some Chinese investment ends up undercutting local businesses, which are forced to close and/or eliminate jobs because of the competition. The "flood of cheap goods" from China, according to Robert Rotberg, has put "hundreds of thousands of Africans out of work"[20] as local manufacturers could not compete on price with less-expensive Chinese imports; the import of inexpensive Chinese fabrics alone forced the closure of hundreds of textile factories, and the loss of thousands of jobs, in Nigeria, South Africa, Lesotho, Swaziland, Mauritius, and other countries.[21] Chinese exports, Ian Taylor writes, have therefore had "the unintended consequence of eroding what little is left of Africa's manufacturing base, which is relatively labor intensive."[22] In 2005, a federation of southern African textile and garment industry trade unions denounced Chinese imports as "a fundamental challenge for the industry, its workers and their jobs."[23]

A 2006 study of Chinese clothing exports to South Africa demonstrates the ways in which the lower prices of Chinese goods have benefited African consumers while harming African manufacturers. From 1996 to 2005, prices in several categories of clothing declined by as much as 15 percent per year as Chinese products entered the market in greater amounts.[24] While South African consumers benefited from falling prices, clothing manufacturers in neighboring African countries lost South African market share as Chinese clothing exports grew. In one clothing category (HS61, knit apparel), Chinese products grew from 19 percent of total South African imports in 1996 to 76 percent in 2005; during this time, Malawi's share of the South African market for the same item declined from 31 percent to 3 percent despite the absence of duties on Malawian products.[25]

Chinese-built infrastructure has undoubtedly contributed to African GDP growth. A 2010 study by the World Bank's Africa Infrastructure Country Diagnostic program claimed in late 2011 that infrastructure has been responsible for "more than half of Africa's recent improved growth performance and has the potential to contribute even more in the future."[26] Given that Chinese investments represent about one-

---

20 Rotberg, 2008, p. 11.

21 Rupp, 2008, p. 70; see also "The Chinese in Africa: Trying to Pull Together," *The Economist*, April 20, 2011.

22 Taylor, 2009, p. 71.

23 Taylor, 2009, p. 63.

24 Ron Sandrey, *The Trade and Economic Implications of the South African Restrictions Regime on Imports of Clothing from China*, TRALAC Working Paper No. 2006/16, Stellenbosch, South Africa: Trade Law Center, 2006, pp. 2, 10.

25 Sandrey, 2006, pp. 8–9.

26 Foster and Briceño-Garmendia, 2010, p. 1.

eighth of external support to African infrastructure,[27] China is a significant driver of this growth.

Continued reliance on raw material exports for revenues and growth has created concern, however, that African countries will remain dependent on the sale of natural resources to outsiders rather than diversify their economies, develop a manufacturing sector focused on higher-value production, and expand intra-regional trade. Some oil-rich countries in which China has invested, write academics Kweku Ampiah and Sanusha Naidu, demonstrate that "the economies of the African states are quickly becoming overly dependent on commodity exports to China, while at the same time ignoring the need to devise robust and coherent national industrial policies."[28] South African Trade Minister Rob Davies highlighted this concern at the World Economic Forum on Africa in May 2011, stating, "The building of the domestic market and consumer industries is fundamental if we're going to move further forward. We cannot live on just a mineral boom and a growing market which is serviced by imports. We have to occupy that productive space as African countries."[29]

As noted, Chinese-built SEZs have generated little additional trade and few jobs beyond those related to the actual construction of the zone, despite the significant investment of resources. For the most part, African countries have agreed to pay for the construction work—which was almost entirely undertaken by Chinese firms—by committing future revenues from natural resource extraction. Thus, despite generating little near-term benefit, the SEZs will drain future income from these nations' coffers in order to repay China for the construction.

Corruption

The vast amount of money involved in infrastructure and construction projects is an invitation to official corruption. Government officials have the authority to sign off on the expenditure of state funds and the commitment of state resources, and the general absence of independent oversight creates opportunities to solicit kickbacks. Moreover, unlike American companies, which are prevented by the Foreign Corrupt Practices Act from offering bribes to foreign officials to secure business deals, Chinese firms are widely believed to engage in such practices.

When China and the Democratic Republic of the Congo signed a $6 billion mining and infrastructure construction deal in 2007, the deal was negotiated in secret

[27] Schiere, Ndikumana, and Walkenhorst, 2011, p. 96.

[28] Kweku Ampiah and Sanusha Naidu, "Introduction: Africa and China in the Post–Cold War Era," in Sanusha Naidu and Kweku Ampiah, eds., *Crouching Tiger, Hidden Dragon? Africa and China*, Scottsville, South Africa: University of KwaZulu-Natal Press, 2008, p. 11.

[29] Justine Gerardy, "Africa Must Raise Quality of Trade with China: WEF," Agence France Presse, May 6, 2011.

and without competition, according to the watchdog group Global Witness, despite the potential to generate as much as 11 times the country's GDP in revenues. The Congolese negotiating team included figures close to the president who held no government positions but excluded several relevant government ministries. Just before receiving its large signing bonus from the Chinese side, a Congolese parliament inquiry found, the state mining company paid $24 million into an offshore bank account.[30] The suspicious payments, combined with the extreme secrecy surrounding a large-scale deal, which, as explained below, is highly advantageous to the Chinese side, strongly suggest that corruption was a factor.

In Angola, political promises and almost certain official corruption led the government to waste billions of dollars on a fiscally unsound effort, using Chinese financial assistance and labor, to build towns from scratch. During the campaign for Angola's 2008 parliamentary elections, President José Eduardo Dos Santos promised to address the shortage of adequate housing for the nation's poor by building 1 million state-funded housing units that citizens could purchase at low rates. Angola contracted with the Chinese company CITIC (China International Trust and Investment Corporation) to build 2,000 residential buildings, as well as 41 schools, water and sewage treatment plants, electrical networks, a traffic signal system, a power system, a communication system, roads, and other supporting infrastructure in the area. At the time, CITIC declared that the $3.5 billion "Angola Social Housing project is currently the biggest EPC [engineering, procurement and construction] project amongst similar overseas projects undertaken by Chinese contractors." CITIC announced the project would use 12,000 Chinese workers at its peak.[31] The government tasked a subsidiary of the notoriously corrupt[32] state oil company, in which several senior government officials held investments, to manage the project.[33] Once completed, apartments were

---

30 Global Witness, *China and Congo: Friends in Need*, March 2011, pp. 4–8, 17–19.

31 CITIC Construction Co., Ltd., "Angola Social Housing: Project Overview," web page, March 17, 2009.

32 According to anti-corruption group Transparency International, "Analysts regard Sonangol—which is the biggest company in the country and the largest source of revenue—as an important factor in ensuring the survival of the current regime as well as a major source of personal enrichment for state officials. . . . A significant proportion of Sonangol's income is diverted to the ruling elite through complex offshore financial systems and/or used to weaken the political opposition." See Marie Chêne, "U4 Expert Answer: Overview of Corruption and Anti-Corruption in Angola," Anti-Corruption Resource Center Expert Answer No. 257, February 25, 2010. See also Human Rights Watch, *Transparency and Accountability in Angola: An Update*, April 2010. See also "The Queensway Syndicate and the Africa Trade," *The Economist*, August 13, 2011. A 2010 U.S. Senate report asserted that "Angola's ongoing corruption problem [is] a problem so severe that it led Citibank to close all accounts associated with the Angolan government and Sonangol [the state oil company] in 2003." See U.S. Senate, Committee on Homeland Security and Governmental Affairs, Permanent Subcommittee on Investigations, *Keeping Foreign Corruption Out of the United States: Four Case Histories, Majority and Minority Staff Report, Permanent Subcommittee on Investigations,* Washington, D.C., February 4, 2010, p. 320.

33 Rafael Marques de Morais, "The Ill-Gotten Gains Behind Angola's Kilamba Housing Development," *Pambazuka News*, No. 552, October 12, 2011.

selling for between $120,000 and $200,000—which, given that two-thirds of Angolans live on less than $2 per day[34]—hardly qualifies it as a "social housing" project meant to alleviate the conditions of the nation's poor.[35] As a result, the 750-building Nova Cidade de Kilamba development was reported in July 2012 to be a virtual ghost town.[36] Construction was funded with future sales of Angolan oil, so the government is paying the cost whether the apartments sell or not.

Some analysts of Chinese engagement in Africa caution that the structure of Chinese loans and grants actually makes it difficult for African officials to embezzle funds. *The Economist* points out that money typically goes straight to Chinese companies, giving African leaders little control over the funds and little opportunity to illicitly take a cut.[37] Similarly, a British consulting group examining international business risks believes "China's threat to governance has been overstated"—especially since actual cash rarely changes hands.[38] David Shinn, a professor at George Washington University and former U.S. ambassador to Ethiopia and Burkina Faso, notes that opportunities for corruption in Chinese-African business deals usually manifest themselves during the negotiation phase, as Chinese enterprises maintain firm control over projects after agreements have been signed.[39] Nevertheless, as the above examples demonstrate, ample opportunities remain for African officials who are so inclined to use Chinese resources for their personal enrichment or political advancement.

Wasted Public Resources

Even when African officials are not enriching themselves personally, central governments' involvement in many large-scale aid, infrastructure, and investment deals can easily lead to waste, as leaders have political incentives to approve projects that generate high-profile results regardless of their long-term economic viability or fiscal efficiency. African leaders can take credit for high-profile facilities or infrastructure built by Chinese firms regardless of whether the projects were cost-effective or even necessary.[40] Among such "vanity projects" are soccer stadiums (Cameroon, Mozambique, Tanzania, Malawi, Ghana, Angola, Zambia, Equatorial Guinea, Guinea-Bissau,[41]

---

[34] Lesley Wroughton, "IMF Finds Most of Angola's Missing $32 bln," Reuters, January 25, 2012.

[35] Louise Redvers, "Angola's Chinese-Built Ghost Town," BBC News, July 2, 2012.

[36] Mamta Badkar, "Check Out the Massive Chinese-Built Ghost Town in the Middle of Angola," *Business Insider*, July 3, 2012.

[37] "The Chinese in Africa: Trying to Pull Together," 2011.

[38] "China-Africa: Much More Than Resources," *Emerging Markets Monitor*, Vol. 17, No. 32, November 21, 2011.

[39] David H. Shinn, correspondence with authors, September 2, 2013.

[40] Rupp, 2008, p. 75.

[41] "Guinea Bissau Takes Delivery from China of Refurbished National Stadium," Macauhub.com, March 7, 2013.

and Gabon);[42] parliament buildings (Republic of Congo,[43] Lesotho,[44] Sierra Leone,[45] Mozambique,[46] Malawi[47]); presidential palaces (Burundi,[48] Togo,[49] Sudan,[50] Guinea-Bissau,[51] and Angola[52]); and airports (Sierra Leone,[53] Ghana,[54] Nigeria,[55] Sudan,[56] South Sudan,[57] Tanzania,[58] Zimbabwe,[59] Mauritius,[60] Republic of Congo[61]).

---

42 "China's 'Stadium Diplomacy' in Africa and Its Top Beneficiaries," *Ventures Africa* (Nigeria), March 29, 2013. See also Frank Kandu, "China to Build New Malawi Stadium," BBC Sport.com, October 31, 2012.

43 Ministry of Foreign Affairs of the People's Republic of China, "Xi Jinping Delivers a Speech at the Parliament of the Republic of Congo Calling for Writing New Chapters in Friendship between Chinese and African People," web page, March 30, 2013.

44 "The Chinese Are Everywhere," *The Economist*, August 5, 2010.

45 "Chinese Investment in Africa Examined; Stalemate in Middle East Peace Discussed," transcript, *CNN's Amanpour*, March 28, 2013.

46 Jorge Njal, "The 'Chinese Connection' in Mozambique's Hosting the 2011 Maputo All-Africa Games," *African-East Asian Affairs: The China Monitor*, No. 72, June 2012, p. 14. Also, Judith van de Looy, "Africa and China: A Strategic Partnership?" ASC Working Paper 67/2006, Leiden, The Netherlands: African Studies Center, 2006, p. 10.

47 "You Can't Stay Aloof Forever: The Political Economy of Chinese Investment in Africa," *The East African* (Kenya), February 11 2012. Also, Ministry of Foreign Affairs of the People's Republic of China, "China and Malawi," web page, August 22, 2011.

48 "China to Begin Constructing Burundi's Presidential Palace in Early 2011," Xinhua, November 12, 2010.

49 "New Palace for Togo's New Leader," BBC News.com, April 25, 2006.

50 "Chinese Leader Boosts Sudan Ties," BBC News, February 2, 2007. Also, Joanne Wagner, "'Going Out': Is China's Skillful Use of Soft Power in Sub-Saharan Africa a Threat to U.S. Interests?" *JFQ*, No. 64, 1st Quarter 2012.

51 Loro Horta, *Guinea-Bissau: China Sees a Risk Worth Taking*, Washington, D.C.: Center for Strategic and International Studies, no date. Also, "Guinea-Bissau: Possibilities and Pitfalls Following President's Death," IRIN, UN Office for the Coordination of Humanitarian Affairs, January 20, 2012.

52 "East Africa Branch Co. of CJI," China Jiangsu International Economic and Technical Cooperation Group, Ltd., web page, no date.

53 "Sierra Leone Signs $190mn Agreement with China for Airport Construction," StarAfrica.com, December 14, 2012.

54 Lawrence Quartey, "China to Construct Ghana's Second International Airport," *The Africa Report*, October 15, 2012.

55 Ismail Adebayo, "Nigeria: China to Build Four Airport Terminals in the Country," *The Daily Trust* (Nigeria), September 23, 2012. Also, Chinedu Eze, "Nigeria: Chinese Firm to Build Four Airport Terminals in Nigeria," *This Day* (Nigeria), March 12, 2013.

56 "China to Build $1.2 Billion Airport in Sudan," Associated Press, February 15, 2011.

57 "China to Help Build South Sudan Airport," *Ventures Africa*, August 21, 2012.

58 Beibei Yin, "Chinese Investment in Tanzania Bears Bitter Fruit," *The Guardian*, March 2, 2012.

59 "Zimbabwe Overhauls Major Tourist Airport on Chinese Loan," *People's Daily Online*, April 12, 2012.

60 "China Signs $260m Airport Deal with Mauritius," *China Daily*, February 17, 2009.

61 China Jiangsu International Economic and Technical Cooperation Group, Ltd., no date.

Leaders also have incentives to use Chinese assistance and investment for the benefit of key political constituencies whose support is needed to keep them in power. After floods left hundreds of Ethiopians homeless, for example, China pledged $4 million to build housing for displaced families. Once construction was completed, however, the Ethiopian government transferred the eight apartment buildings to the Ministry of Defense—a key power base—for use as military housing. An official of the Chinese company hired by Beijing to build the complex said, "We don't really care who uses it. It was a political task for us and so long as Ethiopia officials are happy, our goal is fulfilled."[62]

African leaders have even less incentive to worry about expenses when payments are made by committing revenues from future economic activity (e.g., mineral extraction), as is the case with many Chinese investments.[63] For example, Zimbabwe engaged a Chinese company (Anhui Foreign Economic Construction Group) to build a new National Defense College; the $100 million cost was covered by a Chinese loan that would be paid back by Zimbabwean diamond revenues over 20 years.[64] Similarly, the $6 billion Congolese-Chinese mining deal guaranteed Chinese investors a 19 percent rate of return regardless of global copper prices, and it obliged the Congolese government to pay the Chinese entities any investment it fails to recoup after 25 years—an agreement that shifted all of the deal's economic risk onto the Congolese government.[65]

Summary

Overall, Chinese engagement has generated some significant benefits for Africa, including development of much-needed physical infrastructure and investment that has created thousands of jobs in construction, mining, and other sectors. Nevertheless, while many Africans benefited from Chinese activities, many others have had negative experiences or have failed to see their expectations of concrete economic gains materialize. Others have had frustrating dealings with Chinese economic migrants to Africa—individuals who have nothing at all to do with China's pursuit of its political and economic objectives but who are often seen as symbols of Chinese intervention. The next section will examine perceptions of Chinese engagement by both African governments and African publics, as well as the social tensions that often exist between African communities on the one hand and the Chinese enterprises and individual economic migrants on the other.

---

[62] Karby Leggett, "Staking a Claim: China Flexes Economic Muscle Throughout Burgeoning Africa," *Wall Street Journal*, March 29, 2005.

[63] Howard W. French, "The Next Empire," *The Atlantic*, May 2010.

[64] "Chinese Labour Practices Haunt Zim Factory Workers," *Mail & Guardian* (South Africa), January 6, 2012. Also, Inyasha Chivara, "Construction of Chinese-Built Zim Defense College Under Scrutiny," *Mail & Guardian* (South Africa), February 8, 2013.

[65] Global Witness, 2011, pp. 5–6, 16.

CHAPTER FIVE

African Reactions to Chinese Engagement

Africans themselves have had a range of reactions to Chinese engagement in the region. African leaders and governments generally portray Chinese engagement as positive. Many have praised Chinese contributions to their nations' infrastructure, pointing out very visible improvements that contribute to expanded economic activity, create jobs for local workers, and, in many cases, result in tangible improvements to roads, rails, bridges, and other transportation networks that benefit ordinary citizens engaged in their daily activities. Others draw attention to Chinese aid projects to highlight the ways in which their governments, thanks to Chinese cooperation, have enhanced basic services and quality of life. For the most part, African government officials have voiced little criticism of Chinese engagement, David Shinn asserts, because they have "no desire to kill the goose that is laying the golden egg."[1]

Not all African leaders view Chinese involvement favorably, however. A handful of officials have taken a pessimistic tone, warning that the terms of Chinese economic and commercial engagement in Africa perpetuate a neo-colonial dynamic in which Africa exports raw materials to a growing economy, which provides finished goods in return. At least one African political leader, Zambia's Michael Sata, ran presidential election campaigns in 2006 and 2011 that centered on the economic and social dangers of Chinese economic dominance, and he promised to expel Chinese companies if elected—though he quickly reversed himself after he was elected in 2011.[2]

African popular opinion has been more mixed. As Barry Sautman and Yan Hairong have explained, "African views are not nearly as negative as Western media make out, nor as positive as official Chinese sources imply."[3] Opinion polls have found that Africans generally view Chinese engagement as a positive development. However, opposition to certain aspects of Chinese activities—such as poor labor practices at factories and mines, occasionally shoddy workmanship, and low-quality imported

1 David H. Shinn, correspondence with authors, September 2, 2013.

2 Kristin Palitza, "Why Zambia's Elections Will Be All About China," *Time*, September 19, 2011.

3 Barry Sautman and Yan Hairong, "African Perspectives on China-Africa Links," *China Quarterly*, Vol. 199, September 2009, pp. 728–759.

goods—has often become particularly vehement and occasionally even violent. Such negative popular perceptions have created obstacles to Chinese investment and business operations and posed often significant challenges to China's strategy of building long-term political and economic relationships with some African countries.

Generally speaking, ordinary Africans are influenced primarily by the economic aspects of China's economic engagement. Their opinions of China and their willingness to mobilize in some way in response to Chinese engagement are based on the extent to which China's investments create jobs, the quality of working conditions for such jobs, the existence of tensions between Chinese managers and local laborers, the quality of Chinese imported goods, their perceptions of local Chinese merchants' business practices, and similar dynamics related to quotidian economic and commercial activities. There is little information to suggest that ordinary citizens hold strong views on the political issues associated with Chinese involvement in Africa, such as its treatment of African governments as equals on the world stage, the absence of conditions on Chinese aid and investment, and the willingness to provide military assistance regardless of government behavior. These dynamics resonate primarily with African political and economic elites, who use Chinese support on strategic political and macroeconomic issues to legitimize their roles.

It can be presumed that these arguments resonate to some extent with the general public, at least on a rhetorical level, as some African leaders reference these characteristics of Chinese engagement in positive, nationalistic ways in political campaigns and speeches. Moreover, polls have shown that ordinary citizens' opinions regarding China are indeed shaped by perceptions of Chinese intentions and a sense that China is contributing to their country's national development.[4] People in six African nations surveyed by Pew Research in 2013, for example, overwhelmingly indicated that China is a partner of their countries rather than an enemy.[5] However, while Africans have rioted over poor working conditions, they have not been similarly motivated to assemble en masse to celebrate China's egalitarian approach or the lack of conditionality on Chinese aid.

Official Responses

Leaders from many African countries praise China's contributions to job creation, development, and, most notably, infrastructure.

---

[4] Sautman and Yan, 2009, pp. 728–759.

[5] Pew Global Attitudes Project, *America's Global Image Remains More Positive Than China's*, Washington, D.C.: Pew Research Center, July 18, 2013.

Political Issues

After decades of dominance by European colonial powers, followed by additional decades of Western aid and investment provided under conditions that are often viewed as paternalistic, many African leaders have expressed appreciation for China's "no strings attached" approach. In pledging not to interfere in African countries' internal affairs, whether through political pressures or conditionality, China's approach is seen as less condescending than the West's insistence on imposing requirements related to transparency, human rights, democratization, and other Western priorities on their aid and investment. Senegalese president Abdoulaye Wade, for example, wrote in 2008 that "China's approach to our needs is simply better adapted than the slow and sometimes patronising post-colonial approach of European investors, donor organisations and non-governmental organisations."[6] President Festus Mogae of Botswana put it more concisely: "I find that the Chinese treat us as equals. The west treats us as former subjects."[7] These political figures thus not only welcomed Chinese investment and assistance, but saw in such efforts a political legitimization that were often perceived as absent from their interactions with the West.

Many African leaders have particularly appreciated the lack of political pressures, lectures on good governance, and close oversight associated with China's engagement, particularly when compared with Western aid and investment. Consistent with China's policy of non-interference, Chinese infrastructure and investment projects generally involve less up-front oversight in the form of planning meetings and impact assessments.[8] Sierra Leonean Ambassador to China Sahr Johnny said in 2005, "We like Chinese investment because we have one meeting, we discuss what they want to do, and then they just do it. . . . There are no benchmarks or preconditions, no environmental impact assessment."[9] Senegalese President Abdoulaye Wade expressed his preference for working with China by citing the absence of project planning and management procedures prevalent in Western-funded efforts:

> I have found that a contract that would take five years to discuss, negotiate and sign with the World Bank takes three months when we have dealt with Chinese authorities. I am a firm believer in good governance and the rule of law. But when bureaucracy and senseless red tape impede our ability to act—and when poverty persists while international functionaries drag their feet—African leaders have an obligation to opt for swifter solutions. I achieved more in my one hour meeting with President Hu Jintao in an executive suite at my hotel in Berlin during the

---

[6] Abdoulaye Wade, "Time for the West to Practise What It Preaches," *Financial Times*, January 23, 2008.

[7] Lindsey Hilsum, "Africa's Chinese Love Affair," *Channel 4* (UK), November 3, 2006. Also see "Why Beijing Succeeds in Africa," *Washington Times*, editorial, January 7, 2007.

[8] Rupp, 2008, p. 75.

[9] Lindsey Hilsum, "The Chinese Are Coming," *The New Statesman* (UK), July 4, 2005.

> recent G8 meeting in Heiligendamm than I did during the entire, orchestrated meeting of world leaders at the summit—where African leaders were told little more than that G8 nations would respect existing commitments.[10]

As Wade suggests, planning and oversight requirements typical of World Bank (and Western) projects exist to ensure good governance and the effective use of aid and investment funds. China's willingness to proceed without going through such evaluations may enable faster decisions, but it also increases the likelihood that funds could be used inefficiently or to promote projects that generate few tangible results.

Economic Issues

Other African leaders have warned that China's approach to Africa amounts to a second "scramble for Africa" that echoes the inherently unequal dynamics of the colonial era, in which rich outside powers acquired resources while creating markets for their manufactured goods and preventing the emergence of local value-added production. In 2007, Thabo Mbeki, then president of South Africa, warned that Africa's continued export of raw materials and China's export of consumer goods to Africa would lead to a "colonial relationship with China."[11] More recently, the governor of Nigeria's Central Bank, Lamido Sanusi, wrote in a 2013 *Financial Times* editorial, "So China takes our primary goods and sells us manufactured ones. This was also the essence of colonialism. . . . Africa is now willingly opening itself up to a new form of imperialism."[12]

At least one African leader believed nefarious intentions, rather than just unequal economic dynamics, characterized Chinese economic goals in Africa. During his unsuccessful 2006 campaign for the Zambian presidency, Michael Sata called Chinese "infesters" rather than "investors," threatened to kick out Chinese workers, and pledged to implement foreign exchange controls that would prevent Chinese firms from repatriating their profits.[13] He also took the provocative step of pledging to recognize Taiwan if elected, provoking condemnation from the Chinese ambassador to Zambia.[14] In 2010, he accused Chinese mining companies of using Zambians as "slave labor" in harsh working conditions.[15] In 2011, when he ran a successful presidential campaign, he complained that "Zambia has become a province of China, and the

---

10 Wade, 2008.

11 "Mbeki Warns on China-Africa Ties," BBC News.com, December 14, 2007.

12 Lamido Sanusi, "Africa Must Get Real About Its Romance with China," *Financial Times*, March 26, 2013. The author is the governor of the central bank of Nigeria.

13 Erin Conway-Smith, "Zambian Election Results Check Chinese Influence in Africa," *GlobalPost*, September 25, 2011.

14 Brautigam, 2009, p. 151.

15 Ed Cropley, "Zambia Opposition Slates China, Malaysia Investors," Reuters, January 20, 2010.

Chinese are the most unpopular people in the country because no one trusts them. The Chinaman is coming just to invade and exploit Africa."[16] Observers proclaimed that Sata's 2011 election would lead to a decline in China's influence throughout the continent.

Few other African leaders have leveled such strident criticism at Beijing, however, as Chinese contributions to African countries' economies are simply too great to walk away from. Even as strident an opponent of China as Sata changed his tune after taking office in September 2011. Sata's first official meeting after his inauguration as president was with the Chinese ambassador.[17] One month later, Sata told the Chinese ambassador to Zambia and a group of Chinese businessmen, "My dear sisters and brothers from China, you are very welcomed in Zambia because we are all-weather friends."[18] During a one-week visit to China in April 2013, Sata signed several investment agreements and requested that Chinese companies invest in railways, agriculture, and mining.[19] On his return, he proudly announced to residents of a rural district that Chinese companies would develop Zambian wetlands for rice production.[20] Sata even asked China to help Zambia reestablish a state airline—a cliché of a vanity project often sought by developing countries regardless of their profitability.[21] Though Sata showed signs of softening his rhetoric toward China in the last months before the election,[22] his eagerness to seek Chinese investment once in office marked a remarkable about-face for a leader whose campaign was marked by populist anti-Chinese vitriol.

African Popular Perceptions of Chinese Engagement

Certainly, when national-level figures such as a presidential candidate draw attention (either positive or negative) to Chinese engagement in a country, public opinion is often swayed.[23] Not surprisingly, for example, Michael Sata's virulent anti-China platform created considerable popular hostility toward China among the Zambian popu-

---

16 Howard W. French, "In Africa, an Election Reveals Skepticism of Chinese Involvement," *The Atlantic*, September 29, 2011.

17 Andrew England, "Sata Gives Chinese Investors Guarded Welcome," *Financial Times*, September 26, 2011.

18 Han Wei and Shen Hu, "Zambian President Embraces Chinese Investment," Caixin Online, October 30, 2011.

19 Teddy Kuyela, "Sata Back from China," *Zambia Daily Mail*, April 13, 2013.

20 Kaiko Namusa, "Chinese to Engage in West Rice Production," *Times of Zambia*, April 15, 2013.

21 Newton Sibanda, "We Want Own Airline," *Zambia Daily Mail*, April 11, 2013.

22 Aislinn Laing, "Zambia's President Rupiah Banda Congratulates Rival Michael Sata, Bows Out in Tears," *The Telegraph*, September 23, 2011.

23 Max Rebol, "Public Perceptions and Reactions: Gauging African Views of China in Africa," *Alternatives: Turkish Journal of International Relations*, Vol. 9, No. 4, Winter 2010, pp. 149–186.

lace. Sata's rhetoric is a clear illustration of Sautman and Yan's hypothesis that national political discourse is the leading determinant of how Africans view China; "no generalized 'Chinese problem' exists," they write, "until politicians decide to create it."[24]

Africans Hold Generally Positive Views of China

In the absence of such widespread attention, opinion polls show generally positive views of China as a whole but mixed and even critical views regarding specific aspects of Chinese engagement in Africa. A 20-country January 2010 survey by Afrobarometer (a research project that measures the social, political, and economic atmosphere in Africa) found that twice as many Africans view China favorably as unfavorably.[25] A 2007 Pew Global Attitudes Project poll of people in ten sub-Saharan African countries found very similar results, reporting that respondents in nine of the ten countries viewed China favorably (as opposed to non-favorably) by a two-to-one margin or more.[26] Overwhelming majorities in the same nine countries also believed that China's own economic growth is good for their own country's economy.[27] In 2013, Pew found that substantial majorities in six sub-Saharan African countries believed that China had a good influence on their countries' and their economies,[28] and Africans believed to a far greater extent than people from other parts of the world that China considers their countries' interests when making foreign policy decisions.[29]

Deborah Brautigam suggests that China likely attracts popular support in part because its experience as a developing country is more similar than the industrialized West's to that of African countries, and its success at transforming its own economy offers hope that African countries can accomplish the same through a comprehensive partnership.[30]

Africans' Views Are Primarily Influenced by Chinese Economic/Commercial Activities

Beyond these general perceptions, however, Africans' views are largely determined by their experience or exposure to Chinese economic and commercial activities. Afrobarometer reported, for example, that the drivers of opinion for ordinary Africans

---

[24] Sautman and Yan, September 2009, p. 730.

[25] Gadzala and Hanusch, 2010, p. 18.

[26] Pew Global Attitudes Project, *Global Unease with Major World Powers: 47-Nation Pew Global Attitudes Survey*, public opinion survey, Washington, D.C.: Pew Research Center, June 27, 2007, pp. 39–41.

[27] Pew Global Attitudes Project, 2007, p. 43.

[28] Pew Global Attitudes Project, 2013, p. 40.

[29] Pew Global Attitudes Project, 2013, p. 31.

[30] Brautigam, 2009, p. 11.

removed from the political process are "discernible Chinese activities . . . as well as their perceived economic and political repercussions."[31]

That said, the political and macroeconomic implications of Chinese engagement are of little import to ordinary Africans. Even Africans who expressed a belief that democracy and human rights are important had no better or worse view of China than those who expressed no such belief, although such respondents did tend to hold higher opinions of the United States than of China.[32]

Similarly, in the economic realm, Chinese investment in infrastructure and industry has little to no impact on popular views of China. Afrobarometer found that higher levels of Chinese investment coincide with higher approval ratings of China only to a "statistically insignificant" degree, in part, the survey authors hypothesize, because "Chinese FDI in Africa is not sufficiently pronounced so as to influence African attitudes towards the bourgeoning Chinese presence across the continent."[33] In other words, the returns on Chinese investment are sufficiently abstract and intangible to the ordinary "man in the street" that they have little impact on popular opinion. This dynamic may not hold when Chinese business operations are themselves the subject of high-profile controversy, as in Zambia; indeed, though Michael Sata lost the 2006 presidential election, he won majorities in regions with significant Chinese investment, suggesting that Chinese businesses had such a widely perceived negative social impact that they drove even those who benefited from their presence (by getting jobs, for example) to support a candidate who argued for their expulsion.[34]

To the extent that Chinese FDI does affect popular perceptions of China, it is likely to generate some degree of disappointment; expectations of demonstrable improvements in economic health and quality of life promised by local leaders have gone largely unmet, as Chinese enhancements to infrastructure and industry have directly impacted the daily lives of few ordinary Africans—particularly since they create few jobs for local nationals.

A country's trade balance with Beijing plays a far more important role than FDI in shaping Africans' views toward China, in part because of the more tangible nature of goods that are exported and imported. As the share of African exports (as a percentage of total bilateral trade) rises, African perceptions of China rise—perhaps because of the belief that Chinese purchases of African goods are good for the local economy or because many Africans can attribute jobs and income (their own or their countrymen's) to the manufacturing of goods or extraction of resources sent to China. Similarly, as imports of Chinese goods rise (as a percentage of total trade), African percep-

---

[31] Gadzala and Hanusch, 2010, p. 7.

[32] Gadzala and Hanusch, 2010, pp. 16–17.

[33] Gadzala and Hanusch, 2010, p. 14.

[34] Rebol, 2010, p. 171. Also, Sautman and Yan, 2009, p. 750.

tions of China declines. In essence, economic issues that have visibility and relevance to ordinary people affect public opinion of China more noticeably.[35]

Cheap Chinese consumer goods, for example, are widespread in African stores and markets. Though poorer Africans appreciate the low prices such products command,[36] many Africans are frustrated by their omnipresence[37] and their poor quality.[38] Inexpensive Chinese imports have also forced less competitive local manufacturers to close, eliminating thousands of jobs.[39] These perceptions may contribute to Afrobarometer's finding that "African support of the Chinese declines as the percentage of Chinese imports increases."[40]

African publics are often aware of Chinese-backed large-scale infrastructure and construction projects, particularly high-profile ones such as stadiums, government buildings, major hospitals, and major physical infrastructure. However, many such Chinese projects have been criticized for poor quality work that deteriorates quickly. For example, a Chinese-built hospital in Luanda that was opened ceremonially by Prime Minister Wen Jiabao in 2006 had to be closed four years later because of structural weaknesses.[41] Similarly, Chinese-built roads in Angola "washed away after one rainy season,"[42] according to the pan-African media outlet Pambazuka News, as did a new road connecting Lusaka to southeastern Zambia.[43] Host governments may bear some responsibility, however, for setting poor quality requirements. In Angola, for example, the Chinese may have been following the local government's directives to build roads quickly (and cheaply) in order to show results in the run-up to an election.[44] President Ian Khama of Botswana made clear in early 2013 that the country's power shortages were due to delays by Chinese construction companies. "Right now, as we speak today, we should be totally self-sufficient if we hadn't been let down by the Chinese," Khama told a South African news outlet. "We have had some bad experiences with Chinese companies in this country. . . . We are going to be looking very

35 For example, one study finds that levels of Chinese imports and African exports have a statistically significant effect on African perceptions of China, where increases in Chinese imports have a negative effect on overall African favorability and increases in African exports have a positive effect. See Gadzala and Hanusch, 2010, p. 15.

36 Rebol, 2010, p. 149.

37 Rupp, 2008, pp. 69–70.

38 "The Chinese in Africa: Trying to Pull Together," 2011.

39 Rupp, 2008, p. 70.

40 Gadzala and Hanusch, 2010, p. 15.

41 Nathan William Meyer, "China's Dangerous Game: Resource Investment and the Future of Africa," Foreign Policy Association Blogs, October 12, 2012. See also "The Chinese in Africa: Trying to Pull Together," 2011.

42 Marques de Morais, 2012.

43 "The Chinese in Africa: Trying to Pull Together," 2011.

44 David H. Shinn, correspondence with authors, September 2, 2013.

carefully at any company that originates from China in providing construction services of any nature."[45]

Such high-profile failures may well be the exception rather than the rule, and some stories of Chinese incompetence—like claims regarding the extent of damage to the Luanda hospital and the Lusaka-Chirundu road, according to scholar Deborah Brautigam—may be exaggerated. Regardless, a plethora of visible and widely publicized examples of poor-quality Chinese work (exaggerated or not) have created the perception that Chinese construction is sub-standard. These impressions, in turn, have created somewhat of a backlash against Chinese infrastructure projects and generated a widely held view that government spending on large-scale Chinese projects is wasted.[46]

China Invests Little in Social Infrastructure

Some Chinese business ventures—particularly those focused on natural resources—are located in remote or rural areas where the government provides few social services. In such places, locals often hoped that the newly arrived foreigners—who were visibly spending a great deal of money on facilities and equipment—would also provide housing, schools, clinics, and other services, just as many state-owned mines had done.[47] In fact, however, Chinese enterprises typically invested little in such social infrastructure, as they sought mostly unskilled labor, which was in ample supply, from surrounding communities.[48] Since the privatization of mines in Zambia, for example, the Chinese mine operator in Chambishi stopped providing health care to all dependents of its workers, reduced preventative health care programs, and greatly reduced its contributions to municipal water, sewage, and trash collection.[49]

As will be discussed in detail in Chapter Six, China has recently begun to change its approach, seeing that its business operations have an interest in being seen as responsible corporate actors in areas where they have operations.[50]

---

45 Nicholas Kotch, "News Analysis: Khama Wants Fewer Chinese Firms to Receive State Contracts," *Business Day Live* (South Africa), February 20, 2013.

46 Rebol, 2010, pp. 158–159.

47 Barry Sautman and Yan Hairong, "Trade, Investment, Power and the China-in-Africa Discourse," *Asia-Pacific Journal,* Vol. 9, No. 52, December 28, 2009.

48 Rupp, 2008, p. 76.

49 Alastair Fraser and John Lungu, *For Whom the Windfalls? Winners and Losers in the Privatisation of Zambia's Copper Mines*, Lusaka: Civil Society Trade Network of Zambia and the Catholic Centre for Justice, Development and Peace, no date (2006 or after), pp. 48–51.

50 Ding Rijia, "Mining for Growth," *China Daily*, March 8, 2013.

African Opinion of China Is Negatively Influenced by Perception That China Enables Waste, Inefficiency, and Corruption

Public opinion of China is also negatively affected by perceptions that Chinese aid and investment contribute to corruption and waste. China is certainly not the only source of money for dishonest officials who seek to enrich themselves, but the lack of transparency or independent scrutiny of many Chinese-funded projects—a corollary of Beijing's no-strings-attached, non-interference policy—makes such initiatives particularly ripe for personal enrichment.[51] Moreover, extractive industries—which represent a large share of Chinese investment on the continent—are particularly susceptible to corruption because of the enormous amounts of money involved and because governments often hold exclusive rights and powers regarding land, licensing, regulations, and exports of commodities.[52]

Outright corruption, however, is often the target of popular ire (though there is no evidence to suggest that Africans are any more angry about corruption when it involves China). In one notable example, in 2009, China granted Namibia a below-market-rate loan so it could buy airport security equipment, without competitive bidding, from a Chinese company headed by President Hu Jintao's son. The inflated $55 million price—about double the market value of the equipment—included $12.8 million in kickbacks to be paid to a member of Namibia's Public Service Commission through a front company she operated[53] despite lacking authorization to engage in commercial activities while she served in her position.[54] The Namibian official, her business partner, and a representative of the Chinese company were arrested in 2009.[55] The incident attracted widespread attention in Namibia, at least in part because of the links to China's president. (In China, in contrast, coverage of the incident was censored.[56]) Namibians also reacted negatively to reports that China secretly awarded scholarships to study in China to the children of top government officials, including the president, defense minister, justice minister, and three senior officials at the Ministry of Mines and Energy. Even officials from the ruling party criticized the affair, and one Namibian

---

[51] Rupp, 2008, pp. 74, 82. Also, Gadzala and Hanusch, 2010, p. 6.

[52] Schiere, Ndikumana, and Walkenhorst, 2011, p. 9.

[53] Sharon LaFraniere and John Grobler, "China Spreads Aid in Africa, with a Catch," *New York Times*, September 21, 2009.

[54] See Werner Menges, "Finance Scanners Trial in the Starting Blocks," *The Namibian*, April 16, 2013.

[55] Michael Wines, "Graft Inquiry in Namibia Finds Clues in China," *New York Times*, July 21, 2009. See also John Grobler, "Nuctec 'Corruption' Spreads to Namibia," *Mail & Guardian* (South Africa), July 18, 2009. Also, Werner Menges, "Lameck and Co. Turn Charges Against ACC," *The Namibian*, April 19, 2013.

[56] Simon Elegant, "Could Corruption Probe Be Linked to Son Hurt Hu?" *Time*, July 22, 2009. See also Jo-Mare Duddy, "China Blocks Nam on Internet," *The Namibian*, July 30, 2009.

civil society leader asserted, "People are thinking China is making secret deals with the government here and they are having all kinds of suspicions."[57]

Negative Perceptions of China Have Led to Social Unrest

One of the most notable influences of African public opinion of China is the perception that working conditions at Chinese-managed mines, factories, and facilities are dangerous and that African workers are abused, underpaid, and prevented from assuming managerial positions. There is some debate about whether conditions at Chinese-operated facilities are any worse than at similar facilities operated by Western or local entities, and in some cases blame must be laid on African governments for failing to enforce their own labor laws as well as on the Chinese companies that violate them. In any case, it is clear that Chinese investment projects have often failed to generate the benefits that people expected, and poor working conditions have led to multiple high-profile violent protests, some of which generated further anti-Chinese backlash.

Chinese companies are widely reported to pay less than comparable non-Chinese operations and, in some cases, less than the required minimum. Chinese textile factories in South Africa, for example, pay less than local minimum wage,[58] and Zimbabwean construction workers employed by Anhui Foreign Economic Construction Company struck in 2011 over salaries that were less than half the minimum wage for the construction sector.[59] Workers at Chinese mines in Zambia complained bitterly (as described in detail below) that they were paid lower salaries than similar employers in the area.[60]

Chinese companies created an estimated 20,000 jobs in Zambia alone,[61] many (if not most) of them unskilled jobs in factories and mines. While some workers acknowledge, as *The Economist* points out, that "a poorly paid job is better than none,"[62] others disagree. "We are badly in need of work," a Zambian miner told Chinese journalists in 2011, "but just because you give us work doesn't mean you can exploit us like slaves. Why would we want a job that doesn't pay enough to support ourselves?"[63]

---

57 Sharon LaFraniere, "Uneasy Engagement: China Helps the Powerful in Namibia," *New York Times*, November 19, 2009.

58 "The Chinese in Africa: Trying to Pull Together," 2011.

59 Stanley Kwenda, "Zimbabwe: Chinese Become Unwelcome Guests," *China in Africa*, August 15, 2012.

60 Ching Kwan Lee, "Raw Encounters: Chinese Managers, African Workers and the Politics of Casualization in Africa's Chinese Enclaves," *The China Quarterly*, 199, 2009, p. 659.

61 Nicholas Bariyo, "Chinese-Owned Miner in Zambia Fires 1,000 Striking Workers," *Wall Street Journal*, October 21, 2011.

62 "The Chinese in Africa: Trying to Pull Together," 2011.

63 Shen Hu and Han Wei, "China's Harsh Squeeze in Zambia's Copper Belt," Caixin Online, November 10, 2011.

Low wages and poor working conditions in Chinese-operated mines and factories in Zambia have contributed to violent labor protests. Human Rights Watch documented dangerous working conditions and extensive abuses in a 2011 report:

> Human Rights Watch found that while Zambians working in the country's Chinese-run copper mines welcome the substantial investment and job creation, they suffer from abusive employment conditions that fail to meet domestic and international standards and fall short of practices among the copper mining industry elsewhere in Zambia. . . .[64]

Although the Zambian public largely blamed Chinese companies for the problems, Human Rights Watch attributed responsibility to both the Chinese entities and the Zambian government. On the one hand, it reported, "The troubling situation stems largely from the attitude of Chinese-owned and run companies in Zambia, which have tended to treat safety and health measures as trivial."[65] However, on the other hand, "Primary responsibility for ensuring that Zambia's copper mines operate in accordance with international standards rests with the Zambian government, which has largely failed to enforce the country's labor laws and mining regulations."[66]

Given these safety shortcomings in a sector that is hazardous under even the best of circumstances, Chinese-operated mines and factories in Zambia have not surprisingly been the scene of several high-profile workplace tragedies that led to violent protests. In 2005, an explosion at the Beijing General Research Institute of Mining and Metallurgy explosives factory in Chambishi killed roughly 50 workers, all of them Zambian.[67] During a July 2006 strike at Chambishi Mine, operated by Non-Ferrous Corporation Africa, over payment disputes, Chinese supervisors shot a half-dozen local employees.[68] "The incident confirmed in the popular imagination the idea that Chinese bosses were uniquely brutal and exploitative."[69] Anti-Chinese sentiment was so strong in the area that Hu Jintao had to cancel a February 2007 planned visit to Chambishi,

---

[64] Human Rights Watch, *"You'll Be Fired If You Refuse": Labor Abuses in Zambia's Chinese State-Owned Copper Mines*, November 2011, p. 1.

[65] Human Rights Watch did point out that Chinese firms do not necessarily treat African laborers any worse than they treat similar workers back in China, noting that Chinese mining firms' African operations demonstrated the same health and safety shortcomings that they did at home. See Human Rights Watch, 2011, pp. 1–2. Deborah Brautigam echoes this assertion, writing that labor conditions at Chinese-run facilities in Africa are "roughly at the level that they are in China." See testimony of Deborah Brautigam in U.S. Senate, Committee on Foreign Relations, Subcommittee on African Affairs, 2011, p. 33.

[66] Human Rights Watch, November 2011, p. 1.

[67] Lee, 2009, p. 664. Also see Fraser and Lungu, no date, p. 48. Also see Human Rights Watch, 2011, p. 4. The number killed varies in different accounts, from 46 to 52.

[68] Nicholas Bariyo, 2011.

[69] Fraser and Lungu, no date, p. 48.

where he was expected to inaugurate construction of a new copper smelting plant.[70] Chinese managers fired shotguns at protesting miners at the Collum coal mine in southern Zambia in 2010, injuring several of them;[71] though the Chinese were charged with attempted murder, the government dropped the charges the following year.[72] In August 2012, workers at the same mine killed a Chinese supervisor while protesting salaries that were lower than a newly established minimum wage.[73] In February 2013, the Zambian government took over a Chinese-run coal mine over labor abuses and poor environmental conditions[74] in the wake of a Human Rights Watch follow-up report, despite the fact that the report cited modest improvements.[75]

Clashes with Local Chinese Populations

Negative opinions of Chinese companies have affected many Africans' views of individual Chinese—both the workers sent to Africa to work on large-scale industrial initiatives and the hundreds of thousands of Chinese in Africa who work as merchants, traders, restaurateurs, and small businesspeople. Quite simply, individual Chinese people are visible targets of anti-Chinese sentiment ginned up by opposition to labor abuses, competition, poor quality goods, and other economic elements of China's engagement on the continent. As the South African Brenthurst Foundation noted:

> With their increasingly visible presence in Africa's towns and cities, Chinese traders have become the whipping boy for Africa's politicians, merchants, consumers and unions angered by the effects of Beijing's growing ties to the continent. They become targets of popular discontent even when it springs directly from the activities of large Chinese-owned enterprises.[76]

"Social relations between ordinary Africans and Chinese," writes cultural anthropologist Stephanie Rupp, "are marked by a tension between mutual admiration and mutual loathing."[77] Chinese are admired for their work ethic yet simultaneously disdained for being demanding bosses, remaining separate and aloof, and offering stiff competition to local traders. For example, though "most respondents" in a survey in

---

[70] Lee, 2009, p. 664. Also, Peter Hitchens, "How China Has Created a New Slave Empire in Africa," *Daily Mail* (UK), September 28, 2008.

[71] "The Chinese in Africa: Trying to Pull Together," 2011.

[72] "Zambian Miners Kill Chinese Manager During Pay Protest," BBC News.com, August 5, 2012.

[73] "Zambian Miners Kill Chinese Manager During Pay Protest," 2012.

[74] Nick Kotch, "Zambia Seizes Chinese Mine over Safety," *Business Day Live* (South Africa), February 21, 2013.

[75] Human Rights Watch, "Zambia: Safety Gaps Threaten Copper Miners: Government, Chinese State-Owned Subsidiaries Make Uneven Progress," news release, February 20, 2013.

[76] McNamee, 2012, pp. 40–41.

[77] Rupp, 2008, p. 77.

five African countries "see the presence of Chinese small merchants as *both* a help and a source of problems for local people" (emphasis added), roughly 10 percent think Chinese small businesses actively harm African merchants by competing with them.[78] Similarly, despite the fact that 92 percent of Cameroonians polled in 2007 believed that China helped their country's overall economy, 70 percent were "disturbed" by the "influx" of Chinese workers and merchants.[79]

Reliable numbers are difficult to come by, but the Chinese government estimated in early 2013 that 1 million Chinese nationals are living and working in Africa.[80] However, some analyses raise questions about the reliability of statistics derived from African countries and estimate the number to be in the range of 580,00 to 800,000.[81] The majority of them are laborers who come to work on a project managed by a large Chinese enterprise and who return to China after several years.[82] These workers are often the focus of local ire because they are perceived as taking jobs that should go to local nationals or taking all of the management jobs and then abusing local laborers working under their authority.

Tensions also exist between Africans and the far smaller numbers of Chinese nationals who have set down roots in African countries and generally operate small businesses. Many of them migrated to Africa in search of economic opportunity, though some—particularly those with few skills or education—came to Africa to work on large construction projects and decided to make their future on the continent rather than return to uncertain job and marriage prospects back in China. While some of these economic migrants open legitimate businesses (stores, import-export businesses, etc.), others engage in unofficial economic pursuits that create conflicts with locals.[83] Though several large Chinese enterprises engage in legal gold mining in Ghana[84] (Africa's second-largest gold producer[85]), thousands of Chinese immigrants operated local mining businesses despite laws prohibiting foreigners from acquiring small-scale mining licenses.[86] After occasionally violent conflicts with locals over land,

---

78 Sautman and Yan, September 2009, p. 733.

79 Sautman and Yan, September 2009, pp. 738–739.

80 Obulutsa and Ng'wanakilala, 2012, p. 222.

81 Yoon Jung Park, "Chinese Migration in Africa," Occasional Paper No. 24, China in Africa Project, South African Institute of International Affairs (SAIIA), January 2009, p. 3.

82 Shinn and Eisenman, 2012, p. 222.

83 Shinn and Eisenman, 2012, pp. 222–226.

84 Heng He, "Ghana Gold Mines Suggest Larger Crisis for China," *Epoch Times*, June 12, 2013.

85 "Easy Riches Draw Chinese to Ghana," *News 24* (South Africa), June 12, 2013. Also, Peter Robison and Ekow Dontoh, "Losing Faith in Gold from Ghana to Vancouver Proves Rout," Bloomberg, August 14, 2013.

86 Liu Dong, "Chinese Miners Lured by Ghana's Gold Rush Hit Rock Bottom After Crackdown," *Global Times*, June 13, 2013.

money, and pollution resulting from the mining activities,[87] the Ghanaian government cracked down, arresting more than 200 Chinese miners in mass roundups in which local residents and security officials alike were accused of beating and robbing the Chinese.[88] After the arrests, more than 1,000 Chinese nationals returned to one county in China alone.[89]

Both groups of Chinese in Africa—those working for a few years on specific projects and those that have set up their own businesses in Africa—have failed to assimilate into their communities, which exacerbates tensions with local residents. Few Chinese workers on large construction or industrial projects speak a local language or stay long enough to learn one. They typically live in walled compounds,[90] and their infrequent interactions with local residents—one Chinese manager in Tanzania stated that they are advised "not to go downtown or mingle with the locals, for their own safety"[91]—often create impressions that they are aloof and unfriendly.[92] In part because many Chinese laborers (like economic migrants and job-seekers in other parts of the world) have come to Africa to save money or to support families back home, they often live frugally; in some cases, their salaries are sent directly to families back in China, giving the workers little disposable income.[93] They thus contribute little to the local consumer economy[94]—another source of tension.

University of California, Los Angeles, sociologist Ching Kwan Lee shows how isolated Chinese laborers are from local communities by painting a vivid portrait of compound life at two mine facilities in Zambia (in Chambishi and Kitwe) and at the Tanzania–China Friendship Mill (known in Swahili as "Urafiki") in Dar es Salaam, Tanzania:

> The Chinese management teams in both firms lead segregated lives from the local workforce. The "China houses" in Chambishi and Kitwe (a major town on the Copperbelt about 15 miles from Chambishi) and the "Chinese compound" across

---

[87] See Adam Nossiter and Yiting Sun, "Chasing a Golden Dream, Chinese Miners Are on the Run in Ghana," *New York Times*, June 10, 2013. See also Adam Nossiter and Bree Feng, "Ghana Arrests Chinese in Gold Mines," *New York Times*, June 6, 2013. For reports of violence in October 2012 that led to the death of a 16 year-old Chinese boy, see "Police in Ghana Detain Illegal Chinese Miners Killing One in the Process," *African Globe*, October 16, 2012.

[88] Dan Levin, "Ghana's Crackdown on Chinese Gold Miners Hits One Rural Area Hard," *New York Times*, June 29, 2013.

[89] "1,072 Chinese Gold Miners Return from Ghana," *People's Daily Online*, June 14, 2013. See also "More Than 1,000 Chinese Gold Miners Return from Ghana," UPI.com, June 14, 2013.

[90] Rupp, 2008, pp. 76–77.

[91] Lee, 2009, p. 655.

[92] Rupp, 2008, pp. 76–77.

[93] Lee, 2009, p. 653.

[94] Rupp, 2008, p. 78.

> the street from Urafiki are secluded residential quarters for Chinese personnel, complete with their own security guards, cooks, satellite dishes, television and karaoke rooms, videos and DVDs from China, ping-pong tables and basketball courts. Inside the Chinese compound for the 25 Urafiki managers, engineers and office staff, there is a huge vegetable garden where African caretakers grow Chinese vegetables, and raise pigs, ducks and chickens. They rarely buy food from the local market. They even dug their own wells.... The Chinese are chauffeured every day from the factory to the canteen in the compound for lunch and dinner, even though they are only half a mile apart. The China house in Kitwe, Zambia is also a spacious compound, with basketball fields, large areas of greenery and low-rise staff quarters, and it is more heavily guarded than the one in Dar.[95]

Though Chinese shopkeepers are more likely to live in the communities they serve, they do not assimilate any better. A study by the South African Brenthurst Foundation reported that "almost without exception, Chinese traders seal themselves in cocoons, completely cut off from local communities. Their experience suggests that, at least for now, it is pointless to even speculate on the prospects for deeper integration of Chinese migrants into African society. In some countries, just halting the rise of mutual suspicion and tension could prove a colossal task."[96] Their isolation is potentially reinforced (or perhaps even caused) by the fact that majority of Chinese migrant traders surveyed do not want to stay in Africa.[97] Of the traders interviewed by Brenthurst Foundation, "nearly all longed for the day they could return to China. Nowhere within the global Chinese diaspora are migrants seemingly less keen to settle than in Africa."[98]

Chinese merchants have penetrated retail-level markets in ways that foreigners have not done before,[99] often with cheaper goods and lower prices,[100] and the resulting perception that Chinese are undercutting African vendors creates severe resentment. In the wake of nationwide protests against Chinese merchants in Malawi, the Malawian government passed a law banning foreigners from operating small businesses anywhere except in four major cities.[101] The minister of trade made clear that the measure was intended specifically to protect local business owners from Chinese competition, stating, "We will not accept foreigners to come all the way from places like China and

95 Lee, 2009, p. 653.

96 McNamee, 2012, p. 5.

97 McNamee, 2012, p. 19.

98 McNamee, 2012, p. 42.

99 Rupp, 2008, pp. 72–73.

100 Keet, 2008, p. 80. Also Laribee, 2008.

101 Claire Ngozo, "Malawi's New Law Targeting Chinese Traders in Rural Areas Draws Criticism," *The Guardian* (UK), August 9, 2012. See also Andrew Bowman, "Africa's Chinese Diaspora: Under Pressure," *Financial Times*, August 8, 2012.

open small businesses and shops in the rural areas of this country and compete with local traders."[102]

Some African governments have made clear that the only Chinese who are welcome in their countries are ones who create jobs for local nationals. In Tanzania, for example, Chinese sellers were ordered to vacate Dar es Salaam's Kariakoo Market in early 2011, with a deputy Cabinet minister stating that Chinese were welcome as investors but not as "vendors or shoe-shiners"—jobs which could be performed by Tanzanians.[103] A Nigerian immigration official was equally blunt in announcing the arrest of 45 Chinese textile merchants in May 2012. He made a distinction between Chinese investors, who would be "welcomed and supported by the federal government," and Chinese traders, whose engagement in "lowly-rated" economic pursuits is "depriving [Nigerians] of job opportunities." Explaining the distinction, the official informed local media that "only quality expatriates would be allowed into the country, not those who are economic scavengers."[104]

China's Ministry of Foreign Affairs (MFA) is aware of the tensions between Chinese nationals and local African populations. While acknowledging that the MFA "cannot keep tabs on all Chinese living in Africa at all times," one senior MFA official said that the MFA, through diplomatic and media channels, tries to encourage Chinese businessmen "not to be so competitive," to "be aware of their social responsibility," and to "make efforts to mingle with the local population."[105]

Overall, African perceptions of China are decidedly mixed. A general sense that Chinese engagement is good for African countries is tempered by negative impressions of Chinese goods, working conditions at Chinese enterprises, and links to corrupt officials, as well as by wide-ranging tensions with Chinese laborers and emigrants and by unmet expectations regarding the benefits of Chinese investment to individual Africans. Beijing has clearly become aware that Africans' myriad frustrations with the Chinese presence have the potential to undermine its broader political and economic objectives. As a result, in recent years the Chinese government has increasingly taken steps to promote its largesse, build a wider range of cultural ties, and ensure that its commercial activities are seen as "win-win" ventures that generate long-term economic benefits for Africans rather than as one-sided resource grabs. While many of the steps Beijing has taken include substantive development initiatives and reforms to the ways Chinese enterprises do business, it has also launched a robust continent-wide public diplomacy campaign to improve its image.

---

[102] Ngozo, 2012.

[103] "Tanzania Orders Chinese Out of Dar es Salaam Market," BBC News.com, January 7, 2011.

[104] "Nigeria Accuses Chinese Traders of 'Scavenging' in Kano," BBC News.com, May 22, 2012. See also "Nigeria 'Frees Chinese Traders,'" BBC News.com, May 25, 2012.

[105] Interview with senior MFA official in Beijing, February 26, 2013.

CHAPTER SIX

China Modifies Its Approach

Recent actions and policy proposals issued by senior Chinese officials suggest a subtle but important shift occurring in China's approach to the continent. The shift highlights a reality that economics and trade, long the bedrock of Sino-Africa relations, are insufficient in promoting the kind of long-term, sustainable relationship that both Africa and China desire. It also reflects an acknowledgement by Chinese elites that certain Chinese policies are producing negative perceptions among Africans and require attention from policymakers in Beijing. Going forward, issues such as soft power (media, culture, and people-to-people exchanges), health aid, sustainability, and security will occupy larger components of China's engagement strategy with Africa. These policies form what Hu Jintao referred to at the 2012 FOCAC as a "new type of China-Africa strategic partnership."[1]

"Soft Power": Media, Culture, and People-to-People Exchanges

In recent years, the government of China has begun to pay more attention to soft power as a tool of its engagement strategy abroad. In 2010, the *People's Daily* published an article in which Premier Wen Jiabao stated that China would more actively engage in "culture promotion," highlighting the notion that soft power had become a key concept in contemporary international relations.[2] In the context of Africa, this involves disseminating a positive narrative to Africans through media, culture, and people-to-people exchange.

In recent FOCAC ministerial meetings, Beijing has placed a greater emphasis on strengthening personal bonds and civilizational ties that serve as the underpinning for stronger political, economic, and commercial relations. To develop such connections,

1 Hu Jintao, president of the People's Republic of China, "Open Up New Prospects for a New Type of China-Africa Strategic Partnership," speech at the opening ceremony of the Fifth Ministerial Conference of the Forum on China-Africa Cooperation, Beijing, July 19, 2012.

2 Yu-Shan Wu, *The Rise of China's State-Led Media Dynasty in Africa*, South African Institute of International Affairs Occasional Paper 117, June 2012.

China has expanded people-to-people contacts, cultural exchange programs, and educational and training initiatives that enable Africans to spend time in China, learn Chinese language and culture, and engage Chinese counterparts. Over the past few years, China has greatly expanded the number of Chinese-owned news outlets operating in Africa as means of presenting a "Chinese face" in a media environment historically dominated by the West.

Media

China's media push began in earnest after January 2009, when China's central government unveiled plans to allocate 45 billion yuan ($6.6 billion) to fund the global expansion of Chinese state media in Africa.[3] Although Xinhua—the official news agency of China—has long had a presence on the continent, the media conglomerate expanded the number of bureaus to more than 20 by late 2009.[4] Xinhua's television station, "CNC World," began broadcasting to African satellite and cable viewers at the beginning of 2011. In January 2012, the state-run Chinese Central Television (CCTV) established "CCTV Africa." The state broadcaster chose Nairobi to be its first ever broadcast hub outside its own headquarters in Beijing, marking a turning point in China's television expansion overseas.[5] On December 14, 2012, *China Daily*, China's largest English-language newspaper, launched its first African edition.[6] The presence of Xinhua and *China Daily* allows China to compete directly with other well-established news agencies like Reuters, AP, and Bloomberg for reporting on events in Africa.[7]

China's robust media expansion efforts can be viewed in the context of Chinese dissatisfaction with the monopoly of Western media outlets. Beijing has long perceived bias in their reporting, negatively affecting Sino-African relations. Chinese rebuttals to critical news stories usually center on a perception that Western news agencies are extensions of Western government policies, which aim to "contain" China abroad and are derived from outdated "neo-colonialist" attitudes.[8] In this sense, China's media expansion can be seen as an attempt to manage overseas and African perceptions of China's role in Africa. Rather than simply refuting Western media reports, China's state-led media can now produce their own content for African consumption and let Africans decide for themselves.

---

3 Joost Akkermans, "China Plans 45 Billion Yuan Media Expansion, Morning Post Says," Bloomberg.com, January 12, 2009.

4 For an overview of Xinhua's history in Africa, see Shinn and Eisenman, 2012, pp. 196–99; on Xinhua's recent push into Africa, see Xiaoling Zhang, "China Makes Voice Heard Above Din," *China Daily*, January 21, 2013.

5 David McKenzie, "Chinese Media Making Inroads Into Africa," CNN, September 25, 2012.

6 "China Daily Newspaper Launches Africa Edition," BBC News.com, December 14, 2012.

7 "China Daily Newspaper Launches Africa Edition," 2012.

8 Hu Yihan, "China Has No Colonial Designs on Africa," *China Daily*, December 9, 2011.

Such sentiment was expressed by Liu Guangyuan, PRC Ambassador to Kenya, in a speech on China-Africa media cooperation in Nairobi, Kenya, when he said,

> In this era of fast development of information and globalization, media play a crucial role in the transformation of international relations and foreign policies. Unfortunately, in today's setting, dominant information mainly flows from the few developed countries to the developing countries. Stories and information from developing countries are often edged out. This reality creates a serious gap that affects how developing countries view themselves and the rest of the world.[9]

China clearly intends to use its state-run media to advance its policy goals in Africa. As Ambassador Liu continued in his speech:

> To realize the dreams of both China and Africa, our media must play a significant role. First, our media must break the monopoly of the current international discourse. . . . Second, our media should report China-Africa friendship positively . . . to nurture greater cooperation, friendship and partnership among our people. . . . Third, our media should serve common development interests shared between China and Africa.[10]

Chinese television dramas have recently shown signs of success among African viewers. The Chinese television show "Doudou and Her Mothers-in-Law," about the domestic life of two ordinary Chinese families set in contemporary China, has been a huge commercial and popular success in Tanzania since it first aired in 2011. Complete with Swahili dubbing, the show has expanded broadcasts to other countries, such as Kenya and Uganda. During his recent trip to Africa, President Xi Jinping reportedly told a Tanzanian audience that the show helped Africans "learn about the joys and sorrows of an ordinary Chinese family."[11]

Policymakers are also promoting media exchange through official bureaucratic channels and auspices. In August 2012, the first high-level official forum on China-Africa media cooperation was held in Beijing. More than 200 delegates from 42 African countries attended the forum. Leaders from China's communications industry who attended the forum expressed the hope that it would help China and Africa play a larger role on the global media stage. Cai Fuchao, Minister of State Administration of Radio, Film and Television, said, "By means of filing more reports on China and Africa, we hope to promote mutual understanding, and correct some of the biased

---

[9] Liu Guangyuan, H.E. Ambassador, "Deepen China-Africa Media Cooperation and Enrich the China-Africa Community of Shared Destinies," speech at the seminar on China-Africa Media Cooperation on 18th November 2013, Chinese Embassy in Kenya, November 19, 2013.

[10] Liu Guangyang, 2013.

[11] Xu Ming, "Daily Life of Chinese Family Is TV Hit in Africa," *Global Times*, April 12, 2013.

opinions about us in the West."[12] The 2012 FOCAC also called for the establishment of the China-Africa Press Exchange Center to host African journalists in China and offer training and education.[13]

Finally, China has begun to make inroads in the publishing industry in Africa. In 2012, China launched a publishing house in South Africa called CHINAFRICA Media and Publishing Ltd. In addition to assuming operations of *ChinAfrica* Magazine, which ran in English and French from 1988 to 2001, and then again in English only beginning in 2009,[14] Xinhua reported that the publishing house aims to "introduce China's culture, opinions, economic and social development, including the challenges during its development," with special attention to "hearing African voices in a bid to understand their needs to develop relations with China."[15]

Culture and People-to-People Exchanges

During his March 2013 trip to Africa, President Xi Jinping called people-to-people exchanges "an important pillar for the new type strategic partnership between China and Africa," adding that it provides a "soft propellant" and "spiritual impetus" for the entire relationship.[16] Chinese scholars and officials view cultural exchange, and in particular people-to-people ties, as an important and under-utilized mechanism to counteract a predominantly government-to-government and trade-oriented relationship.

People-to-people exchanges have always been a part of China's engagement in Africa. However, it is clear that Beijing sees them increasingly as an important component of China's soft power strategy to engender good will among the people of Africa. For example, relative to the past, the 2012 FOCAC included a strong civil society/people-to-people theme, calling for greater interaction between non-official Chinese and African actors, such as universities, think tanks, and nongovernmental organizations (NGOs). Between 2011 and 2012, a variety of programs were launched, including the China-Africa People's Forum to enhance exchange between African and Chinese NGOs; the Forum on Local Government Cooperation to create formal linkages between subnational Chinese governments and African counterparts; the China-Africa Think Tank Forum to promote academic exchange; and the China-Africa Young

---

[12] "China and Africa Join Hands in Media Cooperation," CCTV News in English, August 23, 2012.

[13] "China and Africa Join Hands in Media Cooperation," 2012.

[14] "Re-Launch of 'ChinAfrica' Magazine to Strengthen China-Africa Friendly Exchanges," Xinhua, October 31, 2009.

[15] "Beijing Review Launches China's First Africa-Oriented Print Media Company in South Africa," Xinhua, May 8, 2012.

[16] "China Will Be Africa's All-Weather Friend and Partner: Chinese President," *People's Daily Online*, May 30, 2013.

Leaders Forum to promote exchange among young intellectuals and aspiring leaders.[17] The programs build on previous successful people-to-people initiatives, such as the China-Africa Joint Research and Exchange Program, launched on March 30, 2010, to promote exchanges between scholars, think tanks, and intellectuals. So far, that initiative has reportedly completed 64 projects, including research programs, seminars, academic exchanges, and book publishing.[18]

One initiative linked to the China-Africa Think Tank Forum is the Think Tank 10+10 Partnership Plan, which aims to link ten think tanks in Africa with ten from China to form long-term academic and exchange partnerships. The plan is supported by the Chinese Ministry of Foreign Affairs and organized under the auspices of the Beijing Action Plan of the 5th ministerial meeting of FOCAC, which was held in Beijing in 2012.[19] According to the Chinese-issued communiqué, the thinking behind the plan is to create new "theoretical thinking" on Sino-African relations and contribute to "uplifting the discourse power of developing countries in international affairs."[20] Due to the fact that very little discourse and research on China-Africa relations originates from Africans themselves—only 7 percent, according to some reports[21]—China and Africa have reason to foster greater academic partnerships in the future.

China has also steadily increased the scope and scale of training and scholarships to Africans. At the 2012 FOCAC, Hu Jintao promised to train 30,000 Africans, offer 18,000 scholarships, and build cultural and vocational skills training facilities by 2015.[22] For comparison, the 2009 FOCAC Action Plan offered 5,500 scholarships and promised to train 20,000 Africans by 2012.[23] In total, China claims to have offered more than 20,000 government scholarships to African students, trained more

---

[17] "Declaration of the First Meeting of the China-Africa Think Tank Forum," Forum on China-Africa Cooperation, November 23, 2011; People's Republic of China Ministry of Foreign Affairs, "Implementation of the Follow-Up Actions of the Fourth Ministerial Conference of the Forum on China-Africa Cooperation," July 18, 2012; "China Attaches Importance to Africa's Concerns, Interests: FM," Forum on China-Africa Cooperation, January 6, 2012; "The First Forum on China-Africa Local Government Cooperation Closes in Beijing; Dai Bingguo Attends and Addresses the Closing Ceremony," PRC Ministry of Foreign Affairs, August 28, 2012.

[18] Lu Shaye, *Seizing Opportunities and Overcoming Difficulties to Promote the Development of China-Africa Relations*," China Institute of International Studies, April 19, 2013.

[19] South African Institute of International Affairs, "SAIIA Attends China-Africa Think Tanks 10+10 Partnership," November 3, 2013.

[20] "Initiative for the China-Africa Think Tanks 10+10 Partnership Plan," Beijing, China, October 2103.

[21] Yu-Shan Wu and Chris Alden, "BRICS' Public Diplomacy and the Nuances of Soft Power," South African Institute of International Affairs (SAIIA), January 16, 2014.

[22] "Hu Jintao Proposes Measures in Five Priority Areas to Boost China-Africa Ties," Xinhua, July 19, 2012.

[23] "Forum on China-Africa Cooperation Sharm El Sheikh Action Plan (2010–2012)," Forum on China-Africa Cooperation, November 12, 2009.

than 30,000 African professionals, and sent to Africa more than 350,000 technicians, young volunteers, and agricultural experts.[24]

Policymakers in Beijing are hoping that improved awareness of Chinese language and culture will orient Africans increasingly toward China. As of 2012, China has built 31 Confucius Institutes and five Confucius classrooms in 26 African countries[25] in an attempt to spread Chinese culture and language. At a 2012 Conference of Confucius Institutes in Africa, Chinese Ambassador to South Africa Tian Xuejun noted that Confucius Institutes are "more than a place for African people to know Chinese language and culture"; instead, describing Confucius Institutes as "the 'cultural business card' of China," he made clear that they are intended to "promote Chinese culture so as to present a comprehensive, dynamic and vivid picture of China to the whole world, at the same time, showcase the image of the Chinese nation and people as open, peace-loving and hardworking."[26] Confucius Institutes are clearly a central element of Beijing's efforts to cultivate young Africans who, according to Ambassador Tian, "know China, enjoy Chinese culture and are willing to carry forward China-Africa friendship."[27]

For the first time, culture ministers from China and Africa held their own forum at the 2012 FOCAC, in which ministers from 45 African countries participated.[28] 2012 marked the year of "African Culture Focus" in China, with African exhibits and performances taking place around the country.[29] From 2012 to 2015, China and Africa will expand cultural exchange under the "Sino-African Cultural Partnership Program." The program aims to build 100 cultural institutions in China and Africa and establish a human resources and cultural business development component to help African nations develop their cultural industries.[30]

Although Chinese soft power is growing, Chinese officials recognize the challenges ahead. As one MFA official put it, "Right now, cultural attraction and awareness is lacking, like a stool that is missing a leg. Chinese weak soft power in Africa is a function of weak soft power influence globally." Time, according to the official, is on China's side: "As China's soft power increases globally, so will our soft power increase

---

24 "Remarks by H.E. Ambassador Tian Xuejun at the South African Institute of International Affairs (SAIIA)," Forum on China-Africa Cooperation, July 4, 2012.

25 "China-Africa Economic and Trade Cooperation (2013)," 2013.

26 Tian Xuejun, Chinese Ambassador to South Africa, "Address at the Joint Conference of Confucius Institutes in Africa," Stellenbosch, South Africa, September 13, 2012c.

27 Xuejun, 2012c.

28 People's Republic of China Ministry of Foreign Affairs, 2012.

29 "African Culture Promoted in China," Xinhua, May 25, 2012.

30 Zhang Rui "Culture Forum Hosts African Officials in Beijing," China.org.cn, June 19, 2012.

in Africa."[31] There are likely limitations to China's soft power, however, as European football and American pop music are tough competitors for influence among African youth; as David Shinn noted, "Chinese opera just does not cut it in Africa."[32]

Health Aid

Medical cooperation between China and Africa began in 1963, when the Chinese government dispatched a medical team to provide supplies and medical assistance to the Algerian government.[33] Since then, Chinese medical aid in Africa has expanded substantially to include medical teams, anti-malaria campaigns, medical training and cooperation, and financing for clinics and hospitals. In general, China views medical aid as an important component of South-South relations and of China's broader soft power goals on the continent.

China's approach to health aid in Africa is distinct from the model followed by most Western countries. Beijing's emphasis has been on vertical interventions initiated by the Chinese government that focus on health care infrastructure and "medical diplomacy"—sending Chinese volunteers to poverty-stricken countries in Africa to administer care and supplies. Estimates of the extent of Chinese health aid to Africa vary. Since 1964, more than 20,000 Chinese medical personnel have reportedly provided services in Africa.[34] Among the 1,700 current Chinese aid projects in Africa identified by U.S.-based AidData, more than one-tenth are health-related, consisting mostly of medical staff, infrastructure projects, and medicine donations.[35] Another report estimates that the Chinese government had given 5.3 billion renminbi (roughly $864 million) in medical aid over the past five years.[36]

One of those projects is China's anti-malaria campaign. During the 2006 FOCAC, President Hu Jintao announced that China would provide 300 million renminbi ($49 million) in grants for the construction of 30 malaria-prevention and treatment centers in Africa. Staffed primarily by Chinese doctors, such centers have not only played a role in diagnosis and treatment, but also have contributed to communication, capacity-building, and research. By integrating into the local health infrastructure, the centers have provided immunizations and other treatment to patients in the most at-risk areas

---

[31] Interview with senior MFA official in Beijing, February 26, 2013.

[32] Shinn, correspondence with authors, September 2, 2013.

[33] Li Anshan, *Chinese Medical Cooperation in Africa*, Discussion Paper 52, Uppsala, Sweden: Nordiska Afrikainstitutet, 2011, p. 9.

[34] Beibei Yin, "Reality Check Casts Doubts on Chinese Health Aid to Africa," *The Guardian*, June 10, 2013.

[35] Yin, 2013.

[36] Victoria Fan, "Sizing Up China's Role in Global Health Aid to Africa," Center for Global Development blog, March 29, 2013. Based on the date of the article, the five-year period is estimated to be between 2007 and 2012.

in Africa.[37] Some centers, however, have faced challenges operating in local communities, including accusations that they have provided Chinese-manufactured counterfeit drugs.[38]

China is also employing academic exchanges and medical training programs to a greater extent than in the past. Under the FOCAC framework, it has established the Ministerial Forum of China-Africa Health Development, an annual meeting for discussing the expansion of health cooperation mechanisms between China and Africa. In addition, the China's Center for Disease Control and Prevention launched five training workshops over the past three years on such topics as "Infectious Diseases Prevention and Control" and "Prevention and Control of Malaria and Schistosomiasis."[39] The "International Roundtable on China-Africa Health Cooperation"—a Chinese government-sponsored forum on China-Africa health cooperation—recently completed its fourth conference in Botswana. The roundtable brings African and Chinese leaders together to "share experiences, discuss progress and lessons learned, and make recommendations on how China-Africa health cooperation could be strengthened."[40] Ren Minghui, director-general of the Department for International Cooperation within the National Health and Family Planning Commission of China, said at the Botswana conference that China considers research and development—in particular "building capacity for research" and "technology transfer" in Africa—as priorities.[41]

China has also focused its African health diplomacy on the construction of clinics and the training of African medical students. Among its most recent initiatives, Beijing plans to begin trial operations of Chinese-built "container hospitals" in either Cameroon or Namibia by the end of 2013.[42] Each hospital consists of ten containers with rooms for "general clinics, waiting patients, treatments, a pharmacy and back-up power supply."[43] These portable hospitals were developed for long-term service use near suburban villages with limited access to medical care. Developers say the contain-

---

37 National Institute of Parasitic Diseases; Chinese Center for Disease Control and Prevention (China CDC), Shanghai; and World Health Organization China Representative Office, Beijing, *China-Africa Collaborative Project on Malaria Control and Elimination*, May 2013.

38 Kathleen E. McLaughlin, "'Malaria Is Not Going Away Because We Are Getting Fake Treatment'," *The Guardian*, December 23, 2012. See also Kathleen E. McLaughlin, "Counterfeit Medicine from Asia Threatens Lives in Africa," *The Guardian*, December 23, 2012.

39 National Institute of Parasitic Diseases; Chinese Center for Disease Control and Prevention (China CDC), Shanghai; and World Health Organization China Representative Office, Beijing, 2013.

40 "Africa: Fourth International Roundtable on China-Africa Health Cooperation 6–7 May 2013, Gaborone, Botswana," press release, May 16, 2013.

41 Ochieng Ogodo, "China-Africa Joint Medical Research to Deepen," SciDev.Net, July 5, 2013.

42 Li Jiao, "Africa: Chinese 'Container Hospitals' Ready to Deploy in Africa," allAfrica.com, June 13, 2013.

43 Li Jiao, 2013.

ers can be used for decades if properly maintained. The clinics are expected to reach Kenya, South Africa, Tanzania, and Egypt in the near future.

Finally, in late 2010, China's recently unveiled "Peace Ark" hospital ship made its maiden voyage to Africa, visiting Djibouti, Kenya, Tanzania, and the Seychelles. The ship reportedly provided medical services for local African residents as well as for Chinese military personnel participating in the anti-piracy mission off the Gulf of Aden.[44]

While China's focus on infrastructure and training has made tangible contributions to African health care needs, China's state-centric approach for the most part operates outside the framework of many international health organizations, such as the World Health Organization. There are signs that China seeks greater cooperation with these institutions, however: China recently began working with organizations such as The Gates Foundation and the World Health Organization on malaria and HIV/AIDS treatment.[45] Calls for China to align its efforts with those of the global health organizations may prompt Beijing to augment its top-down, bilateral approach to Africa with multilateral efforts in the coming years.

Sustainability

China's recent emphasis on enhancing the "sustainability" of its engagement in Africa—during Hu Jintao's speech at the 2012 FOCAC, for example, and among Chinese officials more generally—suggests that China seeks to redress the trajectory of Sino-Africa trade in favor of investments that provide long-term economic benefits to Africans. A more sustainable approach, Chinese officials have stated, would include the provision of training and new skills to African workers, technology transfer to African businesses, services for communities in which African enterprises operate, greater Chinese purchases of African manufactured goods, and a greater emphasis on promoting intra-Africa trade networks.

Criticism has grown in recent years related a China-Africa trade pattern that benefits China more than Africa. During the 2012 FOCAC ministerial meetings, South African President Jacob Zuma was unusually blunt in his assessment of current trends, saying, "[T]his trade pattern is unsustainable in the long term. Africa's past economic experience with Europe dictates a need to be cautious when entering into partnerships with other economies."[46] A March 2013 editorial published in the *Financial Times* by Nigerian Central Bank Governor Lamido Sanusi was harshly critical of China for exploiting the continent's mineral wealth while undermining its manufacturing indus-

---

[44] Shinn and Eisenman, 2012, p. 190.

[45] Neil Ungerleider, "Bill Gates and the Chinese Government Want to Take on World Hunger, " Fast Company.com, October 31, 2011.

[46] Leslie Hook, "Zuma Warns on Africa's Trade Ties to China," *Washington Post*, July 19, 2012.

tries. Sanusi wrote, "We must see China for what it is: a competitor. We must not only produce locally goods in which we can build comparative advantage, but also actively fight off Chinese imports promoted by predatory policies."[47]

In response to these and other criticisms, the 2012 FOCAC featured "African integration" as one of China's key policy proposals for the 2012–2015 period. The third point of Hu Jintao's Five Point Proposal expanded on the concept:

> China will establish a partnership with Africa on transnational and trans-regional infrastructural development, support related project planning and feasibility studies and encourage established Chinese companies and financial institutions to take part in transnational and trans-regional infrastructural development in Africa. China will help African countries upgrade customs and commodity inspection facilities to promote intra-regional trade.[48]

Hu called for special attention to cross-border interconnection of roads, water, electricity, and telecommunications networks as a means of promoting intra-African trade and regional development, and he gave priority status for joint project financing ventures. This marked a departure from FOCAC's traditional role as a site for largely bilateral deal-making. It also reflected a new responsiveness on the part of Chinese officials, given that barriers to intra-African trade are a principal concern of African leaders themselves.

Chinese ministers and diplomats are reinforcing the message of "sustainability" in a bid to change the perception of Chinese businesses and entrepreneurs. Vice Foreign Minister Zhai Jun, for example, told participants at an African business seminar in March 2013 that Chinese companies should work to benefit their African host economies by investing in industries, such as power generation, agriculture, textiles, and communications, that "create jobs and generate tax revenues." Zhai noted that "making quick money and leaving is a myopic action, and 'catching fish by draining the pond' is unethical."[49] Similarly, Lu Shaye, Director-General of the Africa Affairs Department of the MFA, gave a speech in May 2010 emphasizing the need to adjust China's investment strategies to accommodate African needs in manufacturing and agriculture, saying, "There are very broad investment areas in Africa. Chinese companies can explore more opportunities in sectors like agriculture and manufacturing, apart from the current focus on infrastructure and energy resources."[50] Chinese efforts to invest in local manufacturing and purchase local products—which would

---

[47] Sanusi, 2013.

[48] "President Hu Proposes New Measures to Boost China-Africa Ties," Chinese government official website (gov.cn), July 19, 2012.

[49] "Chinese Firms Urged to Invest in Africa," Associated Press, March 18, 2013.

[50] "Chinese Firms Told to Invest More in Africa," Chinese government official website (gov.cn), May 29, 2010.

help reverse the trade imbalances that exist between China and non-oil producers in Africa—could help mitigate the increased hostility toward China engendered by a high proportion of Chinese imports to local exports, as noted in Chapter Five.

Africans have long called for China to make greater efforts at training Africans in technical skills and managerial expertise that will contribute to higher value-added industrial output. At the 2012 FOCAC meetings, the PRC Minister of Commerce seemed to acknowledge this need, saying, "We will continue to expand investment cooperation with Africa, and migrate to Africa industrial chains with which China enjoys a comparative edge, so as to extend the value-added chain for 'Made in Africa' products and create more job opportunities for African people."[51] He was quoted in a Xinhua article a few days later as saying that China "will adjust its cooperation with Africa . . . to include providing more technique teaching and strengthening subregional cooperation in Africa."[52]

Security and Diplomacy

Historically, China has been reticent to engage too actively in African security affairs. There are signs, however, that China might be considering some adjustments in light of its increasing economic and political interests on the African continent. At the 2012 FOCAC, President Hu Jintao announced a program to bolster African security capacity, entitled the Initiative on China-Africa Cooperative Partnership for Peace and Security.[53] According to the statement, the initiative will "promote peace and stability in Africa and create a secure environment for Africa's development." Specifically, China will "deepen cooperation with the African Union (AU) and African countries in maintaining peace and security in Africa, provide financial support for AU peacekeeping missions and the development of the African Standby Force, as well as train more security officials and peacekeepers for the AU."[54]

Although couched in multilateralist terms, the initiative marks a clear break from Beijing's aversion to military or security intervention in Africa. Chinese officials have stated in the past that socioeconomic development in African countries is dependent on peace and stability. Yet China has been wary to get involved in the complicated and messy conflicts in Africa in part because doing so would contradict Beijing's central principle of non-interference. Due to persistent feedback from African leaders for a

[51] Chen Deming, Chinese Minister of Commerce, "China and Africa Poised to Embrace a Brighter Future for Economic Cooperation and Trade," speech to Fifth Ministerial Conference of Forum on China-Africa Cooperation, July 18, 2012.

[52] "China Industrial Relocation Boosts "Made in Africa" Products" Xinhua, July 20, 2012.

[53] "President Hu Proposes New Measures to Boost China-Africa Ties," 2012.

[54] "President Hu Proposes New Measures to Boost China-Africa Ties," 2012.

greater role in peacemaking on the continent, however, Beijing added "security cooperation" as one of China's new policy initiatives.[55] The announcement suggests a rethinking of Chinese priorities on the continent and marks recognition that China's participation in conflict resolution will be an unavoidable byproduct of increased Chinese engagement with Africa.

China's mediation of the South Sudan split in 2011–2013 offers a window into Beijing's more proactive diplomatic approach to conflict in Africa. In 2011, South Sudan seceded from Sudan, taking roughly 75 percent of the country's oil reserves with it. In December 2011, disputes over transit fees between the North and South led to a halt in oil production, directly impinging on China's significant oil interests in the country. China imports approximately 82 percent of the oil produced in South Sudan and about 70 percent of that production in the North.[56] It was under these circumstances that China began its intervention by dispatching its envoy for African affairs, Liu Guijin, to the region—first representing Chinese interests and later accepting a lead role in the UN Security Council—to seek resolution to the conflict. In late December 2011, Liu managed to break the deadlock, warning that "the repercussions would be very serious" for all involved if the situation were not resolved.[57] The fragility of the truce between the two sides—including several instances in 2012–2013 in which the North shut down oil flows from the South, forcing China to shut down operations in some areas—required successive trips by Ambassador Zhong Jianhua, China's special envoy to Africa, and China's Foreign Minister, Wang Yi, to mediate the conflict.[58]

While still ongoing, the dispute illustrates China's willingness to exert influence over the conflicting parties to promote peace. As Ambassador Zhong noted on China's role in the conflict: "The diplomatic efforts made by China in solving the Sudan–South Sudan issue have been productive, not only easing the regional tension and promoting the two sides' reaching an agreement in oil revenues sharing, but also consolidating China's relations with both countries."[59] The South Sudan case also highlights China's changing calculus of national interest versus non-intervention. When the conflict quickly evolved into a crisis, China, in concert with African and U.S. cooperation, imposed its diplomatic clout to mediate the situation. This reflects the reality that Bei-

[55] Interview with Chinese scholar in Beijing, February 27, 2013. Also see "News Analysis: African Scholars Call on China to Participate in Continent's Security," Xinhua, August 9, 2012.

[56] "Sudan-South Sudan Oil Conflict Brings New Role for Beijing" *Future Directions*, May 29, 2013.

[57] "Sudan: China Urges Govt and South Sudan to Break Oil Deadlock," *All Africa*, December 11, 2011.

[58] Sudarsan Raghavan, "With Oil at Stake, South Sudan's Crisis Matters to Its Customers," *Washington Post*, January 20, 2014.

[59] Zhong Jianhua, "The Sudan-South Sudan Reconciliation: More Patience and Efforts Needed," *Global Review*, Winter 2012, Special Issue, pp. 1–2.

jing's ever-widening economic stake on the continent will increasingly involve greater diplomatic intervention.

Finally, the June 2013 announcement that China would commit 395 peacekeeping troops to Mali—the first time China has sent combat troops on a peacekeeping mission—further underscores Beijing's commitment to security engagement on the continent.

Chinese scholar Pang Zhongying has coined this shift in security policy "constructive engagement"—which he defines as "constructively and comprehensively participating in the peace, security and stability in Africa" by "providing initiatives, solutions, rules and arrangements."[60] Noting Chinese support for the AU, Pang emphasizes the fact that the principle is based on multilateralism that supports "African solutions to African problems." Thus, Pang differentiates this policy from that of previous Western powers with its emphasis on non-coercive and non-unilateralist approach to engagement.

However, as the Director-General of the Department of African Affairs of the MFA explained recently, China is keen to manage African expectations about the scope of scale of Chinese involvement in security affairs, saying, "In recent years, with the rise of China's comprehensive national strength and international influence, African countries have greater expectations that China will engage in peace and security affairs in Africa. There is a gap between China's actual capabilities as a developing country and the expectations of African countries towards China."[61]

Threats to Chinese Nationals

A mix of anti-Chinese sentiment, social tension, and militant rebel groups within certain African countries has produced an increasingly hostile environment for Chinese civilians in Africa. Tensions over wage disputes and perceptions of unscrupulous labor practices at Chinese-run SOEs are on the rise. Kidnappings occur with more regularity. Since 2004, for example, Chinese nationals have been the victims of four kidnapping incidents in Sudan alone; the most recent involving the kidnapping of four Chinese road workers in Northern Darfur in January 2013.[62] In 2012, rebels kidnapped

---

60 Pang Zhongying, "From Non-Interference to Constructive Intervention? Defining the Good Intervention," in *African Security and External Interference: Exploring the Role of a Newcomer, China*, London School of Economics, Department of International Relations and Africa Talks Public Debate, January 29, 2013.

61 Shaye, 2013.

62 Khalid Abdelaziz, "Four Abducted Chinese Workers Released in Sudan's Darfur," Reuters, January 16, 2013.

29 Chinese road workers in South Kordofan, Sudan.[63] Just two weeks later, 24 Chinese cement workers were kidnapped by armed gunmen in Sinai, Egypt.[64]

Regime instability in several African countries further complicates Chinese policy in the region and challenges China's principle of non-interference in domestic affairs. China reportedly lost around $4 billion in Libyan investment following the toppling of the Gaddafi regime in 2011.[65] Moreover, the Libya conflict presented China with one of its biggest security challenges yet on the continent—the evacuation of 36,000 Chinese nationals who were trapped in the war zone as a result of the ongoing civil war.[66]

These developments serve as a reminder that with increasing engagement come increasing complexity and risk—a phenomenon Beijing has only recently come to grips with. China has begun to devote more attention to the issue, however, with scholars and policymakers beginning to publish on the issue of how to protect Chinese citizens from kidnappings and acts of terrorism in Africa.[67] One of the options discussed is an effort to enhance a private security presence, including private security personnel and bodyguards, for individuals working in high-risk zones and conflict areas.[68]

In interviews with Chinese scholars and officials, there is broad acknowledgement of the challenges faced by Chinese civilian employees in Africa. One scholar called instability and kidnappings of Chinese citizens "one of the biggest challenges for China going forward," while emphasizing that Beijing "will not use military force to deal with the problem."[69] One senior MFA official said that China is still trying to use "diplomatic channels" to deal with the kidnapping issue and "not involve the Chinese military." However, the official acknowledged that China has "stepped up cooperation with African militaries and governments to do more to ensure worker safety."[70]

---

63 "Kidnapped Chinese Workers Freed in Sudan," Al Jazeera.com, February 7, 2012.

64 Peter Ford, "Why Chinese Workers Are Getting Kidnapped Abroad," *Christian Science Monitor*, February 1, 2012.

65 Gavin du Venage, "China, Africa Show Lessons Learnt with $20 bn Pledge," *Asia Times Online*, August 9, 2012.

66 Shinn and Eisenman, 2012, p. 182.

67 See, for example, Yang Mian and Song Fei, "Further Reminding the Chinese Enterprises and Workforces in Africa of the Risks and Necessary Safety Measures" [进一步提升驻非企业和员工的风险意识和安全措施], *Asia & Africa Review*, Vol. 2, 2012.

68 Mian and Fei, 2012.

69 Interview with Chinese scholar, Beijing, February 25, 2013.

70 Interview with senior MFA official, Beijing, February 26, 2013.

Summary

In sum, to a greater extent than in the past, China seems to be taking seriously feedback and criticism of certain Chinese policies that negatively affect the lives and interests of Africans. For decades, China's engagement in Africa was transactional in nature and premised on the market complementarities that existed between China's need for natural resources and Africa's need for manufactured goods and infrastructure development. Nowadays, China's footprint and influence have quickly outpaced its ability to manage and control the situation on the ground. At the same time, African leaders and media outlets have become more vocal in their criticisms of Chinese policies, with many calling for a more equal relationship based the needs and desires of Africans. Recent policy adjustments and statements issued by Chinese elites seem to suggest that Beijing is responding more proactively to calls for change as well as reflect a long-term strategy to engender personal ties between Africans and Chinese.

CHAPTER SEVEN

Implications for U.S. Interests

Implications of China's Expanding Influence in Africa for U.S. National Security Interests

The United States and China actually have similar strategic interests in Africa. China, as discussed in the Chapter Two, has four overarching strategic interests in Africa: access to natural resources, particularly oil and gas; export markets; political support, particularly in international fora and adherence to its "One China" policy; and sufficient security and stability to ensure the safety of its investments and the continuation of its commercial activities.

With the exception of the "One China" policy, the United States shares these interests; it seeks access to natural resources, export markets for U.S. products, and support for policy initiatives at the United Nations and other international arenas. It also has an interest in promoting security and stability on the continent, although U.S. security concerns extend to a wider range of issues, such as the mitigation of terrorism, narcotics trafficking, and international crime. The United States also seeks access for U.S. military forces, including ground troops and both air and naval assets, to both train African counterparts and directly engage threats to U.S. national security—a strategic military interest that goes far beyond the military diplomacy in which China engages as a means of fostering overall diplomatic ties.[1]

However, for the most part, the United States and China have pursued different policy objectives and priorities in Africa in virtually every arena—political, military, economic development, economic and commercial engagement, and cultural outreach. The United States has emphasized good governance, foreign aid focused on human development, and private sector–led investment, whereas China has stressed political independence and state-backed investment in infrastructure and natural resource extraction.[2] As Senator Richard Lugar, former chairman of the Senate Foreign Rela-

[1] The authors are grateful to David H. Shinn for emphasizing that the United States and China have common strategic interests in Africa even if their policy objectives differ greatly.

[2] Testimony of Deborah Brautigam in U.S. Senate, Committee on Foreign Relations, Subcommittee on African Affairs, 2011, p. 18.

tions Committee, stated, "They are investing in infrastructure and building potential for economic growth. We are investing in people and health care."[3] AFRICOM Commander General Carter Ham stated more bluntly in November 2012, "We don't focus much on building stuff. We've chosen a different path, which is primarily investment in human capital."[4] With China's recent decision to increase its people-to-people engagement, however, Beijing, too, will increasingly be investing in Africa's human capital.

As a result of these very different approaches to advancing their interests, Washington and Beijing are not competing directly against each other for strategic access or influence in Africa; unlike the competition between the United States and the Soviet Union during the height of the Cold war, when relations with individual African countries were more or less a zero-sum game, Washington and Beijing are each unilaterally pursuing their own goals and priorities in Africa, and competition exists in those areas where specific policy or commercial objectives differ.

To the extent that Chinese activities conflict with U.S. policy goals, Washington is likely to do little to address the discrepancy, as it has far more strategically important interests to advance in its bilateral relations with Beijing. Furthermore, though many observers have looked for areas in which Washington and Beijing can collaborate in Africa, the absence of significant overlap in U.S. and Chinese policy objectives means that few opportunities exist for the two countries to partner in pursuit of shared regional interests. While shared strategic interests might prompt discussions among bureaucrats from both governments on how the two countries might cooperate, such consultations rarely create government-led initiatives in which both sides devote resources and manpower to achieve policy deliverables.

The Political Arena

In a speech to Ghana's parliament in 2009, President Obama stated that "good governance is the ingredient that can unlock Africa's enormous potential." In the belief that transparent, democratic political processes are necessary for success in other arenas, Assistant Secretary of State for African Affairs Johnnie Carson said in March 2013 that democracy and good governance are the United States' "top priority in Africa."[5] Indeed, their promotion is one of the four "pillars" of the White House's June 2012 *U.S. Strategy Toward Sub-Saharan Africa*; President Obama's preface to this strategic

---

[3] Remarks by Senator Richard Lugar in U.S. Senate, Committee on Foreign Relations, Subcommittee on African Affairs, 2011, p. 41.

[4] Carter Ham, "Transcript: General Ham at the Chatham House, London," November 21, 2012.

[5] Johnnie Carson, "Remarks to Panel Discussion on 'Consolidating Democratic Gains, Promoting African Prosperity,'" U.S. Institute of Peace, Washington, D.C., March 29, 2013.

plan notes that U.S. efforts will prioritize these political goals, along with the promotion of economic growth, above other U.S. objectives on the continent.[6]

China does not share the American goal of strengthening democratic institutions, and it has little interest in promoting the elements that make up this "pillar" of the U.S. strategy: accountable and transparent government, democratic processes, human rights, civil society, and independent media. To the contrary, arguing that it has the right to enter into agreements with sovereign states, Beijing has pursued political and economic ties with African countries irrespective of whether or to what extent they promote transparency, democracy, or political rights. In essence, whereas the United States seeks to transform African politics to promote a democratic ideal, China believes firmly that outsiders have no right to interfere in the inner workings of a sovereign African government.

The Security Sphere

China and the United States also have very different security interests in Africa. Certainly, China wants to prevent instability that would hinder or threaten its investments, though its emphasis on non-interference means that as a policy matter it is willing to tolerate far greater political unrest than the United States, which sees such developments as potential threats to democracy, human rights, and economic growth. China and the United States do share an interest in combating piracy, which both see as a threat to commercial shipping.

One of the core elements of U.S. security objectives in Africa, according to the *U.S. Strategy*, is countering al-Qa'ida and other terrorist groups, which concerns Beijing minimally, if at all. China would view most of the other U.S. security goals listed in the *U.S. Strategy*—preventing conflict, mitigating atrocities, and reforming defense institutions—as unmerited interference in African countries' internal affairs.

U.S. policy priorities in Africa are more heavily dominated by military and security concerns than are China's. Indeed, some Chinese observers note somewhat critically that U.S. relations with Africa have become heavily militarized since the September 11, 2001, terrorist attacks.[7] Though AFRICOM is perhaps the most visible manifestation of this dynamic, U.S. engagement in many African countries has been dominated by

---

[6] The White House, *U.S. Strategy Toward Sub-Saharan Africa*, June 2012, introductory letter by President Barack Obama and p. 2.

[7] One Chinese academic expressed concern about the U.S.-Africa relationship becoming overly "militarized," adding, "China does not hope for a militarily-driven relationship in Africa." Interview with Chinese academic in Beijing, February 27, 2013. The academic was responding to the announcement that AFRICOM would send additional troops to 35 African countries to support anti-terrorism activities. See Miles Yu, "After Policy Disasters, U.S. AFRICOM to Deploy Troops to 35 countries," *World Tribune*, January 21, 2013.

cooperation regarding terrorism, piracy, and other transnational threats.[8] Among the myriad U.S. military initiatives in Africa are the following:

- *Counterterrorism and Counter-Piracy:* The United States now maintains a permanent military presence of roughly 2,500 troops, government civilians, and contractors in Djibouti,[9] which serves as a hub for counterterrorism and counter-piracy missions in the Horn of Africa and Yemen.[10] The deployment of U.S. military unmanned aerial vehicles (UAVs), or drones, to various locations around the world has been widely reported, with UAV deployments to Djibouti, Niger, Ethiopia, and the Seychelles acknowledged by U.S. and foreign officials.[11] The

---

[8] David H. Shinn, "The Impact of China's Growing Influence in Africa," *The European Financial Review*, April–May 2011, p. 18.

[9] U.S. Combined Joint Task Force—Horn of Africa, "CNIC//Camp Lemonier, Djibouti," web page, no date.

[10] Thom Shanker, "Djibouti Outpost Behind Somalia Rescue Is Part of New Defense Strategy," *New York Times*, January 25, 2012.

[11] The U.S. Congress referred to drone operations in Djibouti in a House Armed Services Committee report accompanying the National Defense Authorization Act for Fiscal Year 2014. The report states,

> the committee is aware that the Government of Djibouti mandated that operations of remotely piloted aircraft (RPA) cease from Camp Lemonnier, while allowing such operations to relocate to Chabelley Airfield, Djibouti. To date, the committee has received notification of approximately $13.0 million in investments made to ensure that appropriate infrastructure and equipment is in place to support the relocation of RPA operations to Chabelley Airfield. (U.S. House of Representatives, Committee on Armed Services, *Report on H.R. 1960, National Defense Authorization Act for Fiscal Year 2014,* H.Rpt. 113-102, 113th Cong., 1st sess., June 7, 2013, p. 326).

The president of Niger, Issoufou Mahamadou, acknowledged the presence of U.S. UAVs in his country, telling the *Washington Post* in early 2013, "We welcome the drones" (Craig Whitlock, "Drone Base in Niger Gives U.S. a Strategic Foothold in West Africa," *Washington Post,* March 21, 2013).

According to *Stars and Stripes*, an AFRICOM spokesperson, Vince Crawley, announced in August 2009 that the United States planned to deploy MQ-9 Reaper UAVs to the Seychelles for intelligence, surveillance, and reconnaissance purposes (Mark Abramson, "U.S. Plans Land-Based UAV Patrols to Combat Piracy," *Stars and Stripes*, August 29, 2009). The Seychelles foreign minister, Jean-Paul Adam, acknowledged the deployment to the *Washington Post*, writing "The operation of the drones in Seychelles for the purposes of counter-piracy surveillance and other related activities has always been unarmed. . . . This was agreed between the two governments" (Craig Whitlock and Greg Miller, "U.S. Assembling Secret Drone Bases in Africa, Arabian Peninsula, Officials Say," *Washington Post*, September 20, 2011). In December 2011, a U.S. Air Forces in Europe (USAFE) spokesperson disclosed that a Reaper had recently crashed in the Seychelles (Jennifer H. Svan, "Air Force Investigating Cause of Drone Crash in Seychelles," *Stars and Stripes*, December 13, 2011). After several similar crashes, AFRICOM spokesperson Tom Saunders told the *Washington Post* that drone flights in the Seychelles stopped in April of 2012 (Craig Whitlock, "Drone Crashes Mount at Civilian Airports," *Washington Post*, November 30, 2012).

The *Washington Post* reported on October 27, 2011, that a spokesperson for the 17th Air Force, Master Sgt. James Fisher, disclosed the deployment of MQ-9 Reaper UAVs to Arba Minch airport in Ethiopia (Craig Whitlock, "U.S. Drone Base in Ethiopia is Operational," *Washington Post,* October 27, 2011). State Department spokesperson Victoria Nuland confirmed this deployment in her daily press briefing on October 28, 2011, stating,

> our colleagues in the Pentagon made clear this morning that the United States does have an unarmed reconnaissance aircraft, does have some of these at an Ethiopian facility as part of our partnership with the Government of Ethiopia to promote stability in the Horn of Africa and to combat terrorism. . . . These drones are not

United States has provided extensive and repeated military training under the auspices of the Trans-Sahara Counterterrorism Initiative (TSCTI), East African Counterterrorism Initiative (EACTI), and funding provided under section 1206 (training and equipment for forces involved in counterterrorism and stability operations), Section 1207(n)(1)(A) (support to counterterrorism operations in Djibouti, Ethiopia, and Kenya), and Section 1208 (aid to forces supporting U.S. counterterrorism initiatives). The U.S. military is actively working with East African countries to counter piracy off the coast of Somalia and with West African countries to counter piracy, smuggling, and other threats through the Gulf of Guinea maritime security initiative and the Africa Partnership Station.

- *Peacekeeping:* The United States trains African militaries to participate in international peacekeeping efforts through the African Contingency Operations Training and Assistance (ACOTA) initiative[12] and supports African forces that are participating in the African Union Mission in Somalia (AMISOM).
- *Regional Threats:* Congress has given the U.S. military authorities and funding to support African militaries that are working to counter the Lord's Resistance Army (LRA). The United States has deployed roughly 100 troops to provide training, logistics support, and intelligence to Uganda, South Sudan, the Central African Republic, and the Democratic Republic of the Congo.[13]

The United States has made a point of not selling weapons to parties to armed conflict or to autocratic governments accused of human rights abuses (such as Sudan and Zimbabwe). It has frequently contrasted its restraint in this regard to China's willingness to sell weapons to virtually any government. This comparison has enabled U.S. officials to highlight Washington's commitment to democracy and human rights.

In practice, however, whereas China has been a far more prolific seller of arms to Africa than the United States, the United States has been less discriminating regarding the nature of the regimes buying its weapons. From 2006 to 2010, according to the research group SIPRI, China provided 25 percent of African conventional weapons imports, while the United States sold only 3 percent.[14] Interestingly, however, a 2012 analysis of U.S. and Chinese arms sales to Africa in the 17-year period from 1989 to 2006 showed that "the United States tends to transfer conventional arms to authori-

---

equipped with offensive capability. These are ISR aircraft. (Victoria Nuland, State Department Daily Press Briefing, October 28, 2011).

12 U.S. Department of State, "Fact Sheet: African Contingency Operations Training and Assistance (ACOTA) Program," February 6, 2013.

13 Karen Parrish, "U.S. Supports Pushback Against Lord's Resistance Army," American Forces Press Service, April 25, 2012.

14 Wezeman, Wezeman, and Béraud-Sudreau, 2011.

tarian regimes to a greater extent than does China" and that "Western (European and US) arms sales do not systematically prefer democracies."[15]

China's military engagement in the region, aside from arms sales, is quite limited. It participates in seven UN peacekeeping missions on the continent, but it provides no bilateral assistance to African governments through such initiatives. China has engaged in military diplomacy, hosting African military leaders in Beijing and sending senior defense officials to meet with counterparts in Africa, but such initiatives have generally served to enhance China's overall bilateral relations with its African partners rather than to advance any specific military-related policy objectives.[16]

One of China's most robust military diplomacy initiatives on the continent is with South Africa. Soon after South Africa switched its diplomatic recognition from Taiwan to the mainland in 1998, China's defense minister visited South Africa, and the two countries' senior defense officials have met regularly since then. China conducts formal defense policy discussions with South Africa through the biennial China-South Africa Defense Committee, China's only regularized senior-level defense policy discussions in the region, which has met five times since 2003. South Africa has also sold artillery, UAVs, and other military materiel to China.[17]

Beijing's close defense ties with Pretoria are a key part of the two countries' bilateral relationship. China and South Africa formed a strategic partnership in 2008, which they elevated to a Comprehensive Strategic Partnership in 2010. They have a wide-ranging economic relationship; South Africa is China's largest trade partner on the continent, and Beijing is Pretoria's largest overall trading partner. China has advocated for a greater South African role on the international stage; as South Africa's Deputy Minister of International Relations and Cooperation, Marius Fransman, said in a September 2013 speech commemorating the 15th Anniversary of Sino–South African diplomatic relations,

> when South Africa was lobbying for membership of the then BRIC [Brazil, Russia, India, and China], it was China in the forefront of this campaign. When we became a non-permanent member of the UNSC [United Nations Security Council], it was because of the role played by China in championing its support for our membership. . . . Advancing South-South Cooperation and the African Agenda through the multilateral structures such as the G77+ China, BRICS and FOCAC, as well

---

[15] Paul Midford and Indra de Soysa, "Enter the Dragon! An Empirical Analysis of Chinese Versus US Arms Transfers to Autocrats and Violators of Human Rights, 1989–2006," *International Studies Quarterly*, Vol. 56, 2012, p. 844.

[16] Jonathan Holslag, "China's New Security Strategy for Africa," *Parameters*, Summer 2009, p. 32.

[17] Shinn and Eisenman, pp. 347–348. Also, David H. Shinn, "Military and Security Relations: China, Africa, and the Rest of the World," in Robert I. Rotberg, ed., *China into Africa: Trade, Aid, and Influence*, Washington, D.C.: Brookings Institution Press, 2008, pp. 169–170. Also, "Fifth Meeting of China-South Africa Defense Committee Held in South Africa," *PLA Daily*, July 23, 2012.

as the UN will remain some of the fronts at which China's support will always be appreciated and cherished.[18]

Because Washington is interested in a far wider spectrum of security threats than Beijing is, and because Washington and Beijing pursue such dramatically different security activities there, the United States and China do not really "compete" in the security arena. Indeed, Chinese engagement with African countries has only minimally affected U.S. security policy in Africa. The primary impact on U.S. security interests has been to provide support that enabled "pariah" regimes (such as those in Sudan and Zimbabwe) to resist U.S. and Western sanctions, embargoes, and other forms of political pressure designed to push these governments to reverse objectionable policies. Continued Chinese military assistance, trade, and investment in mining activities (oil in Sudan, diamonds in Zimbabwe) provided these regimes with resources that enabled them to cling to power without changing course. Critics of Beijing argue that the Sudanese regime was free to continue its genocide in Darfur only because China blocked efforts to establish a UN peacekeeping mission, continued purchasing much of Sudan's oil output, and persisted in selling weapons, helicopters, and other military materiel to Khartoum.[19]

Economic Development

In accordance with the 2010 Quadrennial Diplomacy and Development Review, the United States focuses its development initiatives "in six development areas where the U.S. government is best placed to deliver meaningful results: food security, global health, global climate change, sustainable economic growth, democracy and governance, and humanitarian assistance."[20] A wide range of economic challenges facing Africa are included in the category of "sustainable economic growth," including

> promoting entrepreneurship, growing both the hard and soft infrastructure needed for increased trade, developing broad-based agricultural economies, educating their peoples, formalizing vast numbers of small- and medium-sized businesses, strengthening broad-based agricultural economies [sic], and investing in clean energy technologies to reduce greenhouse gas emissions.[21]

In Africa, however, the vast majority of U.S. development aid is focused on basic needs (food security, health, humanitarian assistance), peace and security, and the pro-

---

[18] Marius Fransman, "Keynote Address to the Ambassadorial Forum on China—South Africa Diplomatic Relations at 15 Years," Pretoria, South Africa, September 19, 2013.

[19] See Danna Harman, "How China's Support of Sudan Shields a Regime Called 'Genocidal,'" *Christian Science Monitor*, June 26, 2007.

[20] U.S. Department of State, *Quadrennial Diplomacy and Development Review (QDDR)*, 2010, p. 76.

[21] U.S. Department of State, 2010, p. 76.

motion of democracy and good governance. Of the $6.368 billion in aid requested for Africa in FY2013, 16.7 percent ($1.064 billion) was slotted for economic growth, but two-thirds of this amount ($691 million, or 65 percent) was dedicated to agriculture and slightly more than one-eighth ($144.7, or 13.6 percent) was dedicated to environmental initiatives such as conservation, pollution control, and adaptation to climate change. Thus, only 3.6 percent ($228 million) of the total FY2013 U.S. aid request for Africa was dedicated to economic growth initiatives other than agricultural and environmental programs, such as trade, investment, finance, infrastructure, and private-sector competitiveness.[22]

In contrast, China's spending in Africa is dominated by investment, infrastructure, and trade.[23] As touched on previously, although large "aid" packages are featured prominently in recent FOCAC statements by Chinese leaders, most of this funding is commercial in nature and tied to promoting Chinese exports and services. Investment in human resources, health, and education have become more of a priority for Chinese policymakers—particularly as a public diplomacy tool to burnish China's image—but still make up just a small share of China's overall engagement in Africa.

In essence, then, the United States focuses its assistance efforts on human development to a much greater degree than China, which emphasizes economic growth and commercial activity. Because they are addressing such different development challenges and pursuing such different development goals, it is difficult to assert that Washington and Beijing are competing with each other in the economic development arena.

Business and Commercial Investment

Some U.S. officials and Africa-watchers have expressed concern that Chinese economic practices in Africa will make American companies less competitive.[24] Chinese loans are often lower-cost, more flexible, and less transparent than economic aid offered by Western financial institutions, giving Chinese enterprises an inside track (or, indeed, a guaranteed track) on projects financed through such mechanisms. Moreover, many Chinese commercial entities are subsidized or supported in some way by the state,

---

[22] U.S. Department of State, *Congressional Budget Justification: Foreign Operations, Annex: Regional Perspectives, Fiscal Year 2013,* Washington, D.C., no date, pp. 6–10.

[23] While the Chinese government does not provide financial breakdowns using similar categories or even similar levels of detail as the United States, a general analysis of press reports, aid data, and scholarly articles makes clear that the lion's share of China's spending consists of economic and commercial projects.

[24] GAO, 2013, pp. 49–51.

enabling them to offer lower-cost deals[25] or undertake projects that are less commercially viable in order to advance a government interest.[26]

Furthermore, the Chinese government very proactively promotes Chinese business and investment in Africa, according to Stephen Hayes, the chief executive officer of the Corporate Council for Africa, an American business group dedicated to promoting U.S.-African business ties. Hayes testified to a Senate committee in November 2011 that one of "the highest priorities of Chinese embassies is to support its business development in Africa."[27] China is believed to have 150 commercial attachés in Africa,[28] and "to encourage Chinese companies," writes Polish academic Łukasz Fijałkowski, "Beijing has established ten centres for investment and trade promotion in sub-Saharan Africa, which provide business consultation services, special funds and simplified approval procedures for Chinese enterprises seeking to invest in Africa."[29] The Chinese Ministry of Commerce has also partnered with the United Nations Development Programme to create the China-Africa Business Council, which organizes trade missions and helps Chinese companies establish joint ventures, train personnel and perform due diligence research.[30]

Despite China's potential commercial advantages, U.S. and Chinese firms generally do not compete in Africa, as they often do not operate in the same sectors in the same countries (with the exception of the hydrocarbons sector).[31] For the most part, U.S. firms are more active in technology, while Chinese firms are more involved in construction and infrastructure.[32] Though some of the largest American companies have a presence in Africa,[33] and though many economic commentators believe that Africa's relatively strong predicted economic growth will make it the next great economic opportunity, relatively few American companies are heavily engaged in sub-Saharan Africa. "The African market is not on the radar screen of the American busi-

---

25 Testimony of Stephen Hayes in U.S. Senate, Committee on Foreign Relations, Subcommittee on African Affairs, 2011, p. 27.

26 Remarks by Senator Christopher A. Coons in U.S. Senate, Committee on Foreign Relations, Subcommittee on African Affairs, 2011, p. 2.

27 Testimony of Stephen Hayes in U.S. Senate, Committee on Foreign Relations, Subcommittee on African Affairs, 2011, p. 28.

28 Witney Schneidman, "Transforming the U.S.-Africa Commercial Relationship," in *Top Five Reasons Why Africa Should Be a Priority for the United States*, Washington, D.C.: Brookings Institution, April 2013, p. 12.

29 Lukasz Fijalkowski," China's 'Soft Power' in Africa?" *Journal of Contemporary African Studies*, Vol. 29, No. 2, April 2011, p. 227.

30 Fijalkowski, 2011, p. 227.

31 GAO, 2013, p. 54.

32 GAO, 2013, p. 67.

33 Lydia Polgreen, "U.S., Too, Wants to Bolster Investment in a Continent's Economic Promise," *New York Times*, August 8, 2012.

ness community," writes Witney Schneidman of the Brookings Institution. "In fact, the U.S. is effectively ceding the African marketplace to companies from China, India, Brazil, Russia, Turkey, the European Union and elsewhere."[34] American firms' limited presence in Africa could, of course, grow if economic growth on the continent continues, as Africa's burgeoning middle class[35] gains more disposable income, as U.S. policy initiatives promote increased investment by American companies, and if more African countries experience greater political stability and promote respect for the rule of law.

Many obstacles hinder investment in Africa. They include political instability, corruption, inadequate or unreliable power supplies, poor transportation infrastructure, and the relatively small size of local markets, which is exacerbated by limited regional integration.[36] But why are Chinese entities willing and able to invest despite these myriad impediments while many American firms are deterred by them?

First, state subsidies enable Chinese companies to take greater political and economic risks than U.S. firms might assume. As the GAO reported in February 2013, American companies—many of which are accountable to shareholders—

> are less willing than Chinese firms to risk investments in sectors other than oil and gas because U.S. firms are concerned about risks associated with conducting business in the region, such as corruption and a lack of economic and political stability. . . . In contrast to U.S. firms, Chinese state-owned enterprises and private firms with substantial government support are more willing to be flexible in commercial dealings—for example, collaborating with local businesses—and to take on business risk.[37]

Interestingly, Yu Yongding, a Chinese academic, stated at a 2006 meeting of Chinese, American, and African nongovernment experts that China also "has graded the African investment climate as difficult," and that improvements to the business environment—in such areas as rule of law, corruption, and local workforce skills—could encourage even greater private Chinese investment.[38]

---

34 Schneidman, 2013, p. 12.

35 Mthuli Ncube and Abebe Shimeles, "The Making of the Middle Class in Africa," African Development Bank, October 2012. See also Acha Leke, Susan Lund, Charles Roxburgh, and Arend van Wamelen, "What's Driving Africa's Growth," *McKinsey Quarterly*, June 2010, pp. 4–6.

36 See Deloitte, *Deloitte on Africa: Mitigating Business Risk in Africa Through Regional Integration*, 2012. See also Vijaya Ramachandran, Alan Gelb, and Manju Kedia Shah, "Chapter 2: The Business Environment in Sub-Saharan Africa," in *Africa's Private Sector: What's Wrong with the Business Environment and What to Do About It*, Washington, DC: Center for Global Development, 2009. Also see Ernst & Young, *Mind the Gap: Africa's Infrastructure Development*, EYGM Limited, February 2013.

37 GAO, 2013, p. 58.

38 The Brenthurst Foundation, the Chinese Academy of Social Sciences, the Council on Foreign Relations, and the Leon H. Sullivan Foundation, *Africa-China-U.S. Trilateral Dialogue: Summary Report*, 2007, pp. 12–13.

Second, investment opportunities in Africa are more difficult to finance and often offer more limited returns relative to investments in other regions. The small size of African markets, former Assistant Secretary of State for Africa Chester Crocker stated in 2006, "makes it difficult to get the attention of boards of directors of American companies."[39] Furthermore, American commercial banks are generally not interested in financing projects in Africa, according to the Corporate Council for Africa's Stephen Hayes.[40] Indeed, the World Bank reported in early 2013 that access to financing is one of the leading obstacles hindering investment in Africa by businesses from any country.[41] Chinese enterprises supported by state-backed financing or benefiting from government-to-government agreements calling for the employment of Chinese firms are not limited by the availability of commercial financing.

Third, it is difficult to justify investments in countries in which the critical infrastructure needed to support business operations does not exist or is insufficient or unreliable. A factory cannot produce goods if the power supply is unreliable, and it cannot get its goods to market efficiently if the roads are poor and the railroad network limited. American companies tend to specialize in a general industrial sector, meaning that an American mining company interested in launching operations in a remote area of the Democratic Republic of Congo is going to have to find another company willing to extend rail links and a third company to upgrade the electrical grid. In contrast, large Chinese state-owned enterprises—if they are not already integrated entities that have capabilities in multiple arenas—can often harness the influence of the state to provide (or fund) all of the supporting capabilities needed to facilitate the core investment. In *China Safari*, journalists Serge Michel and Michel Beuret recount comments by the Guinean Minister of Mines, who lamented that the Chinese "are the only ones who offer us 'package' deals or turnkey contracts: a mine, a hydroelectric dam, a railroad, and a refinery—all financed by the China Exim Bank, which is paid in alumina. . . . When we ask Alcoa for the same thing, they say that their business is aluminum, not hydroelectric dams."[42]

Fourth, although former Deputy Assistant Secretary of State for African Affairs Witney Schneidman exaggerates a bit in writing that "the U.S. government provides

---

[39] Quoted in the Brenthurst Foundation, the Chinese Academy of Social Sciences, the Council on Foreign Relations, and the Leon H. Sullivan Foundation, 2007, p. 12.

[40] Testimony of Stephen Hayes in U.S. Senate, Committee on Foreign Relations, Subcommittee on African Affairs, 2011, p. 28.

[41] Miguel Heilbron, "Biggest Obstacles for Companies in Africa: Access to Power Tops Access to Finance in Many African Countries," Venture Capital for Africa.biz, February 4, 2013. Citing data from World Bank Group/International Finance Corporation, *IFC Jobs Study: Assessing Private Sector Contributions to Job Creation and Poverty Reduction*, January 2013.

[42] Michel and Beuret, 2009, p. 9.

virtually no support for American businesses seeking to trade or invest in Africa,"[43] the assistance that the U.S. government does provide is relatively small. While the U.S. Ex-Im Bank loaned a record $1.5 billion in Africa in 2012, this figure represented only 4 percent of its total $35.8 billion in export financing.[44] The Overseas Private Investment Corporation (OPIC) has dedicated just 3 percent of its total funding since 1974 ($6.3 billion out of $200 billion) to support investments in Africa.[45] The U.S. Trade and Development Agency (TDA) has provided just $90 million to facilitate American investments in Africa since 1981, an average of less than $3 million per year.[46] Overall, the Corporate Council for Africa's Stephen Hayes told the Senate Foreign Relations Committee, U.S. government trade and investment promotion institutions provide far less financing "than the Chinese counterparts provide for their private sector companies seeking to do business in Africa."[47] The U.S. government could facilitate greater American investment in Africa if OPIC, TDA, and Ex-Im Bank were to dedicate more funds to the region.

Similarly, the U.S. Commerce Department maintains few commercial offices in Africa.[48] As of early 2013, the U.S. Foreign Commercial Service (FCS), a component of the Commerce Department that promotes and facilitates U.S. business overseas, had only four dedicated offices in sub-Saharan Africa (in Ghana, Kenya, Nigeria, and South Africa),[49] with approximately 20 full-time commercial attachés, about half of whom are local nationals. (The number of offices and staff roughly doubles if Egypt and the Maghreb countries are included.)[50] In most African countries, a State Department economic officer, rather than an FCS staff member, serves as the U.S. embassy's commercial officer. Furthermore, though the Commerce Department has liaisons at the World Bank, the Asian Development Bank, the European Bank for Reconstruc-

---

43 Schneidman, 2013, p. 12.

44 Export-Import Bank of the United States, *Exports Grow Jobs*, 2012 Annual Report, pp. 4, 20.

45 Jones and Williams, 2012, p. 29.

46 Jones and Williams, 2012, p. 31.

47 Testimony of Stephen Hayes in U.S. Senate, Committee on Foreign Relations, Subcommittee on African Affairs, 2011, p. 28.

48 Testimony of Stephen Hayes in U.S. Senate, Committee on Foreign Relations, Subcommittee on African Affairs, 2011, p. 28.

49 See Foreign Commercial Service office listings at U.S. Department of Commerce, export.gov website, no date. See also Schneidman, 2013, p. 12.

50 See U.S. Department of Commerce, export.gov, website, no date—specifically country pages for Ghana, Kenya, Nigeria, and South Africa. The Department of Commerce's fiscal year 2014 budget request included an additional $40 million to place a total of 21 American Foreign Commercial Service Officers and 146 locally hired employees to promote American business in support of both the *U.S. Strategy Toward Sub-Saharan Africa* and the Administration's "rebalance" to Asia, so some portion of these additional resources will be devoted to Africa. See Rebecca M. Blank, Deputy Secretary of Commerce, *The Department of Commerce Budget in Brief: Fiscal Year 2014*, Washington, D.C.: U.S. Department of Commerce, no date, p. 57.

tion and Development, and the Inter-American Bank, it does not have such an office at the African Development Bank.[51] The Commerce Department would likely be more effective in promoting U.S. business in Africa if it increased the number of commercial attaché offices on the continent and engaged the AfDB more proactively.

President Obama's Economic Initiatives

In mid-2013, the United States decided to begin tackling the obstacles to U.S. investment in the region. Heralding "the beginning of a new level of economic engagement with Africa," President Obama used speeches in South Africa and Tanzania to announce that the United States would devote significant effort and resources to promote private-sector investment in Africa, primarily by offering government financing, loan guarantees, and insurance that would mitigate the risks that prevent American and Western companies from investing themselves.

Noting that "electricity is fundamental to opportunity,"[52] on June 30, 2013, President Obama announced the launch of the Power Africa Initiative, through which the U.S. government will commit more than $7 billion over five years—along with $9 billion in private sector commitments—to add 10,000 megawatts of electricity generation in six countries (Ethiopia, Ghana, Kenya, Liberia, Nigeria, and Tanzania). The lion's share of this funding will consist of $5 billion in loans from the Ex-Im Bank, $1.5 billion in financing and insurance guarantees from OPIC, and $1 billion in investments from the Millennium Challenge Corporation (MCC).[53] Though U.S. companies had been involved in infrastructure projects to a modest degree, these commitments mark the entry of the United States into the African infrastructure sector at economically significant levels. While the new U.S. ventures will undoubtedly make a contribution (if only a modest one) to Africa's extensive infrastructure requirements, whether and to what extent they foster direct competition between U.S. and Chinese companies remains to be seen.

The following day, the president announced an initiative to promote U.S. trade with Africa, as well as increase intra-regional trade within Africa. Working initially with the five member states of the East African Community (EAC), the Trade Africa Initiative plans to double intra-EAC trade, increase EAC exports to the United States by 40 percent, and reduce barriers that delay the movement of cargo throughout the region.[54] The initiative will also enhance the Commerce Department's "Doing Business in Africa" campaign, which works to support investments by American businesses,

---

51 See Department of Commerce website.

52 The White House, "Remarks by President Obama at the University of Cape Town," June 30, 2013.

53 The White House, "Fact Sheet: Power Africa," June 30, 2013.

54 The White House, "Fact Sheet: Trade Africa," July 1, 2013. See also The White House, "Remarks by President Obama at Business Leaders Forum," Dar es Salaam, Tanzania, July 1, 2013.

and launch U.S. Trade and Investment Centers to facilitate links between investors and exporters from both the United States and East Africa.[55]

Stating, "I want to make sure we're doing everything we can to encourage the new growth we're seeing across Africa, and more trade between our countries," President Obama also announced that the Secretaries of Commerce, Energy, and Treasury would bring American investors and corporations to Africa within a year to discuss business opportunities and to "forg[e] new partnerships in agriculture and energy and infrastructure."[56]

Competition and Suspicion

Given Washington's and Beijing's widely divergent policy objectives in Africa, it is not surprising that neither the U.S. nor the Chinese government sees the other as a competitor in Africa. In the United States, this perception has been held by both Democratic and Republican presidents. During a 2008 press conference in Accra with Ghanaian President John Kufuor, President George W. Bush stated, "I don't view Africa as zero-sum for China and the United States. I mean, I think we can pursue agendas . . . without creating a great sense of competition. I mean, inherent in your question is that I view China as a fierce competitor on the continent of Africa—no, I don't."[57] President Obama was equally clear in a statement to the press during his trip to three African countries in June and July 2013:

> I think it's a good thing that China and India and Turkey and some of these other countries—Brazil—are paying a lot of attention to Africa. This is not a zero-sum game. This is not the Cold War. You've got one global market, and if countries that are now entering into middle-income status see Africa as a big opportunity for them, that can potentially help Africa. . . . [W]e shouldn't view the participation of a country like China or Brazil in Africa as a bad thing.[58]

U.S. officials similarly do not believe China is driven by a desire to outmaneuver the United States in Africa. Senator Russ Feingold, a respected Africa expert who chaired the Senate Foreign Relations Committee's Subcommittee on African Affairs, asserted in 2008 that "China's commercial and diplomatic activities in Africa are

---

[55] The White House, "Fact Sheet: Trade Africa," 2013. See also Rebecca Blank, Deputy Secretary of Commerce, "Remarks at Launch of 'Doing Business in Africa' Campaign, Johannesburg, South Africa," November 28, 2012.

[56] The White House, "Fact Sheet: Trade Africa," 2013.

[57] The White House, "President Bush Participates in Press Availability with President Kufuor of Ghana," Accra, Ghana, February 20, 2008.

[58] The White House, "Press Gaggle by President Obama Aboard Air Force One," June 28, 2013.

not aimed at diminishing U.S. influence on the continent."[59] After visiting China in November 2011, Assistant Secretary of State for African Affairs Johnnie Carson told reporters, "We in Washington do not see China as an adversary in Africa, but as a country trying to expand its trade and investment across the continent just as we and others are also doing."[60]

Todd Moss, who served as a Deputy Assistant Secretary of State for African Affairs, claimed in 2012 that Chinese and U.S. economic activities are actually complementary. "I think in private there is very little U.S. concern about what China is doing in Africa," he told the *New York Times*. "The U.S. is not going to build highways and bridges and airports, and that is something Africa needs, so we should be grateful that the Chinese are doing this."[61]

While Chinese perceptions of U.S. influence in Africa tend to vary across government, academia, and civilian communities, many in China hold suspicions of U.S. policies in Africa. Some of these suspicions are derived from Western media reports, which some in China perceive as representing the unofficial views of the U.S. government. Tian Xuejun, the Chinese Ambassador to South Africa, vocalized these sentiments when he said, "Some Western politicians and media also tend to make irresponsible remarks on China-Africa relations, attempting to mess up our cooperation."[62] Secretary of State Hillary Clinton's veiled criticism of China's Africa policies during her 2012 11-day tour of Africa, when she said that the U.S. "seeks a model of sustainable partnership in Africa that adds value, rather than extracts it," set off a wave of anti-American sentiment within Chinese media circles and increased suspicion that the United States was out to sully China's image in Africa.[63] As a Xinhua editorial noted, "Whether Clinton was ignorant of the facts on the ground or chose to disregard them, her implication that China has been extracting Africa's wealth for itself is utterly wide of the truth." The editorial claimed that Clinton's "cheap shots" had a "hidden agenda to discredit China's engagement with Africa."[64]

China harbors suspicions toward U.S. security policy on the continent as well. An article in the *China Youth Daily*, the daily newspaper of the PRC Communist Youth League, written by Yan Wenhu, who is affiliated with the Chinese Academy of Military Sciences, cast doubt on the intentions behind AFRICOM's increase in deploy-

---

[59] Remarks by Senator Russell Feingold in U.S. Senate, Committee on Foreign Relations, Subcommittee on African Affairs, "China in Africa: Implications for U.S. Interests," Senate Hearing 110-649, June 4, 2008, p. 12.

[60] Johnnie Carson, "Briefing on Assistant Secretary Carson's Recent Travel to Asia," November 22, 2011.

[61] Polgreen, 2012.

[62] "Remarks by H.E. Ambassador Tian Xuejun at the South African Institute of International Affairs (SAIIA)," 2012.

[63] David Smith, "Hillary Clinton Launches African Tour with Veiled Attack on China," *The Guardian*, August 1, 2012.

[64] "U.S. Plot to Sow Discord Between China, Africa Is Doomed to Fail" Xinhua, August 8, 2012.

ment of 3,500 troops to 35 African countries in 2013.[65] Yan claims that the United States is attempting to use its military force to "contain" China's ever-expanding economic penetration into the African market since the "China model" may undermine the influence of the American democratic values in Africa.[66]

Some Chinese officials, however, have rejected the idea of a global U.S.-China competition. Writing about mistrust in overall U.S.-China relations stemming from the U.S. "pivot" toward Asia, He Yafei, the deputy director of the Chinese State Council's Overseas Chinese Affairs Office and former vice minister at the Chinese Ministry of Foreign Affairs, wrote in *Foreign Policy* that the "view of a rivalry among great powers for spheres of influence and the inevitability of a confrontation between existing and aspiring powers" is "outdated."[67]

Many leading nongovernment experts concur. Roughly three dozen prominent academics, businesspeople, and former government officials from the United States, China, and Africa met in 2006 and 2007 in a series of trilateral "Track 2" (non-official) discussions. One of the principal areas of agreement in this so-called Trilateral Dialogue was that "there is no strategic conflict between the U.S. and China in Africa, and there is no zero-sum dynamic between the two countries."[68] Even regarding the alleged scramble for Africa's resources, two of the American delegates to the Trilateral Dialogue wrote, "the likelihood of strategic competition for natural resources in Africa between the U.S. and China was remote, regardless of commercial competition for such resources, given the nature of supply and demand for such commodities on the world market."[69]

Outside commentators do nevertheless assert that American and Chinese interests in Africa are at odds and that the two powers are fighting to establish clear, exclusive spheres of influence in the region. Council on Foreign Relations China scholar Elizabeth Economy has asserted that China's willingness to provide aid and investment to autocratic governments "poses a clear challenge to America's stated commitment to promoting good governance in the region."[70] According to Robert Rotberg, Beijing sees Africa as an arena for U.S.-Chinese competition, fearing that Washington will apply

---

65 Yu, 2013.

66 "U.S. Military Adds Troops to Africa for Anti-Terrorism and Resources," [美军增兵非洲 为反恐也为资源], *China Youth Daily* [中国青年报], January 25, 2013.

67 He Yafei, "The Trust Deficit," *Foreign Policy*, May 13, 2013.

68 The Brenthurst Foundation, the Chinese Academy of Social Sciences, the Council on Foreign Relations, and the Leon H. Sullivan Foundation, 2007, p. 6.

69 Princeton N. Lyman and Witney W. Schneidman, "Africa-China-U.S. Trilateral Dialogue: Overview," in The Brenthurst Foundation, the Chinese Academy of Social Sciences, the Council on Foreign Relations, and the Leon H. Sullivan Foundation, *Africa-China-U.S. Trilateral Dialogue: Summary Report*, 2007, p. 4.

70 Testimony of Elizabeth Economy in U.S. Senate, Committee on Foreign Relations, Subcommittee on African Affairs, 2008, p. 27.

its policy of containing Chinese influence in Asia to Africa as well.[71] Stephanie Rupp of Lehman College claims that "it is clear that China, Europe, and the United States are engaged in a triangular competition for influence in Africa" similar to the colonial-era "scramble for Africa" between Great Britain, France, Portugal, and Germany.[72] This mentality, China scholars Andrew Scobell and Andrew Nathan write, lead some in China to "expect Western powers to resist Chinese competition for resources and higher-value-added markets."[73]

Some Western analysts do express concern that China has the capacity to "threaten" U.S. and global energy security by "locking up" oil resources in Africa. The logic goes that as Chinese energy companies increasingly strike exclusive oil deals with African governments, they will take this oil off the world market and ship it directly back to China. If true, such deals would increasingly allow China to disrupt global energy markets and exacerbate the energy insecurity of other countries dependent on resource imports from Africa. Similar arguments are made about Chinese mining companies "locking up" other critical natural resources, such as rare earth minerals.

As University of Sydney professor John Lee observes, however, this narrative—at least in relation to the oil sector—is largely false. First, he notes that Chinese national oil companies "have actually sold a significant proportion of their offshore equity oil on local and international commodity markets," which contradicts the notion that China exports all of its oil back to the mainland.[74] More importantly, Lee emphasizes the fact that the capacity for China to disrupt world energy markets and threaten global energy security is actually quite limited:

> In 2010, Beijing's offshore equity oil production was around 1.37 million barrels per day (bpd), which meets around 28 per cent of its daily importing needs. Production by the next ten largest oil producers (not including China) is around 62.37 million bpd. The global oil export trade is around 64 million bpd. By these estimates, offshore equity controlled by Chinese NOCs [national oil companies] makes up just over 2 percent of all oil exports each year. Even by 2020, the most optimistic estimates place Chinese offshore oil equity production at 2 million bpd. Estimates put the global supply of oil at a plateau of around 70 million bpd, with such production levels stable until 2035. Although these estimates cannot fully

---

71 Rotberg, 2008, p. 2.

72 Rupp, 2008, p. 67.

73 Andrew J. Nathan and Andrew Scobell, "How China Sees America," *Foreign Affairs*, September/October 2012.

74 John Lee, "The 'Tragedy' of China's Energy Policy," *The Diplomat*, October 4, 2012. Whether or not China exports all the natural resources it obtains via resource-backed loan contracts with African countries, as opposed to selling a portion on the international commodity market, is up for debate. For example, one report seems to imply that all of the oil extracted from Africa is sent back to China. See Warwick Davies-Webb, "The Emerging Asian Energy Challenge in Africa," *Petroleum Africa*, No. 26, May 2007, p. 28.

> account for all factors (such as when peak oil is reached at certain oil fields, unrest in oil producing countries, etc.) the point remains that Beijing's capacity to disrupt global supply or pricing is far less significant than is widely assumed.[75]

Furthermore, RAND Corporation energy expert James Bartis points out that because oil is a global commodity, Chinese investment that brings more oil online contributes to decreases in global prices and is therefore *beneficial* to the United States. Bartis further notes that Chinese oil companies do not "lock up" petroleum resources any more than Western companies do; when Chinese firms secure exclusive access to an overseas oil field, they are engaging in exactly the same practice as oil companies from around the world.[76] The fact that Chinese energy companies occasionally secure their access through bilateral negotiations or as payment for Chinese-built infrastructure rather than through a competitive bidding process might enable them to secure a higher profit margin, but it has little impact on the West's access to energy.

Given Washington's and Beijing's divergent interests in Africa, the zero-sum narrative of their engagement on the continent appears to be rooted in a broader perception of the United States and China as competitors. Noting that the United States and European countries have criticized China for selling arms to African autocrats despite the fact that Russia, Ukraine, and Belarus have supplied such pariah states to a far greater extent, researchers Paul Midford and Indra de Soysa hypothesize that China attracts such criticism because of "broader trade frictions and hegemonic rivalry."[77]

Whether the United States and China are competitors in Africa or whether there are enough opportunities on the continent for both to pursue profitably, it is likely that the presence of multiple investors will be beneficial for Africans. "I want everybody playing in Africa," President Obama stated during a press conference in South Africa in late June 2013. "The more, the merrier. I think that's good. . . . It gives Africans leverage" to ensure that such economic interactions are "good for Africa."[78]

Indeed, competition from American investors may drive Chinese entities to offer better financial deals, improve working conditions, provide social services to communities which host Chinese enterprises, or generally act in a more socially responsible way. The more American companies enter African markets and create local jobs, provide opportunities for training and advancement, and foster more humane working conditions, the more Chinese firms will be compelled to follow suit. As a result, increased American investment in Africa will improve Africans' economic growth and

[75] Lee, 2012.

[76] Telephone interview with James Bartis, May 14, 2013.

[77] Midford and De Soysa, 2012, p. 854.

[78] The White House, "Remarks by President Obama and President Zuma of South Africa at Joint Press Conference," Pretoria, South Africa, June 29, 2013.

living standards indirectly by incentivizing Chinese businesses to negotiate more equitable deals and to be better corporate citizens.

African Perceptions of U.S. Versus Chinese Engagement

Regardless of whether the United States and China are competing for influence in Africa, the two countries' divergent objectives and engagement mechanisms mean that Africans perceive them very differently.

While U.S. messages of private investment and good governance have had little concrete impact on the lives of ordinary Africans, it appears that China's strategy of large-scale infrastructure construction and investment in extractive industries is winning friends in Africa. As Brookings Institution researcher Yun Sun writes, "the U.S. is being increasingly edged out of the continent politically and economically" even though the Chinese engagement provides Africa only "short-term benefit . . . and has long-term negative consequences."[79]

Short-term benefits are, nevertheless, popular, and many Africans thus perceive Chinese engagement as more valuable than U.S. engagement. Chinese aid is more visible than U.S. and Western aid;[80] in addition to the construction of high-profile facilities such as parliament buildings, conference centers, and football stadiums, Chinese funds often enable large-scale construction and infrastructure initiatives that have the potential to benefit the public through job creation and improved services (transportation, electricity, etc.). Though some Western aid leads to similar projects, the long and onerous oversight processes for such large investments means that fewer of them are undertaken.

U.S. and Western foreign aid, in contrast, more often enhance the local government's ability to provide community-level services such as health and education and thereby bring credit to the government (or, by at least filling gaps in services that the government does provide, mitigate hostility to it). Indeed, the most notable U.S. economic initiative in Africa during the George W. Bush administration (2001–2009) was the President's Emergency Plan for AIDS Relief (PEPFAR). Soon after President Bush proposed the initiative in his 2003 State of the Union Address, Congress authorized $15 billion to be spent over five years in 14 countries, 12 of them in sub-Saharan Africa, to build partner-nation capacity to combat HIV/AIDS and treat and care for

---

[79] Yun Sun, "China in Africa: Implications for U.S. Competition and Diplomacy," in *Top Five Reasons Why Africa Should Be a Priority for the United States*, Washington, D.C.: Brookings Institution, April 2013, pp. 6–7.

[80] Remarks by Senator Christopher A. Coons in U.S. Senate, Committee on Foreign Relations, Subcommittee on African Affairs, 2011, p. 3.

victims of the disease.[81] Over the course of ten years (fiscal years 2004–2013), however, the program has provided more than $52 billion in funding to combat and treat HIV/AIDS, tuberculosis, and malaria[82] in 33 countries, two-thirds of them in sub-Saharan Africa.[83]

As AFRICOM Commander Carter Ham pointed out, such investments in human development are "not as visible as a football stadium."[84] Nevertheless, majorities in six African countries surveyed by the Pew Research Project in 2013 reported that U.S. economic aid has a mostly positive impact on their countries.[85]

More important than mere visibility, however, is the ways in which aid projects are selected. Western governments and aid organizations are often criticized for emphasizing donors' interests and policy prescriptions rather than African governments' own policy priorities or local residents' self-identified needs.[86] China, in contrast, contributes or invests in sectors—such as infrastructure and potentially job-creating extractive industries—that African governments want to develop and from which African publics hope to see concrete benefit.[87] David Shinn writes that the Chinese "have, indeed, gone heavily into infrastructure, but they have done that because that is precisely what the Africans have requested."[88]

Despite the fact that more than 75 percent of Africans polled by the Pew Global Attitudes Project viewed the United States favorably, and despite very high levels of support for American ways of doing business,[89] "across sub-Saharan Africa, China's influence is seen as growing faster than America's, and China is almost universally viewed as having a more beneficial impact on African countries than does the United States."[90] These views softened somewhat by 2013, when one-third to one-half of Afri-

---

[81] Myra Sessions, "Overview of the President's Emergency Plan for AIDS Relief (PEPFAR)," Center for Global Development, no date. See also U.S. Department of State, Office of the United States Global AIDS Coordinator, "Building Capacity: Partnerships for Sustainability," in *The Power of Partnerships: The President's Emergency Plan for AIDS Relief,* Third Annual Report to Congress, 2007, pp. 107–127.

[82] Henry J. Kaiser Family Foundation, "The U.S. President's Emergency Plan for AIDS Relief (PEPFAR)," March 25, 2013.

[83] GAO, *President's Emergency Plan for AIDS Relief: Per-Patient Costs Have Declined Substantially, but Better Cost Data Would Help Efforts to Expand Treatment*, GAO-13-345, Washington, D.C., March 2013, pp. 1–2, 5.

[84] Ham, 2012.

[85] Pew Global Attitudes Project, 2013, p. 17.

[86] Dambisa Moyo, "Beijing, A Boon for Africa," *New York Times*, June 27, 2012.

[87] Testimony of Deborah Brautigam in U.S. Senate, Committee on Foreign Relations, Subcommittee on African Affairs, 2011, pp. 18–19.

[88] Testimony of David H. Shinn in U.S. Senate, Committee on Foreign Relations, Subcommittee on African Affairs, 2011, p. 31.

[89] Pew Global Attitudes Project, 2007, pp. 5, 13, 26.

[90] Pew Global Attitudes Project, 2007, p. 45.

cans surveyed believed that China had already replaced or would soon replace the United States as the world's leading superpower.[91] More Africans nevertheless saw the United States as having a more significant influence on their countries than China, though majorities saw both Chinese and U.S. influence as positive.[92]

The United States has a substantial "soft power" advantage over China among Africans. Pew reported in 2013 that solid majorities in six Sub-Saharan African countries polled admire the United States for its science and technology, popular culture, ideas about democracy, and ways of doing business.[93] China, in contrast, is admired for its science and technology and its business acumen, though far fewer viewed Chinese ideas, customs, and pop culture favorably.[94]

The United States prioritizes security-related issues in its engagement with African nations, though U.S. military assistance is not particularly valued by African citizens; many African countries' security services are unpopular (if not feared or resented), and ordinary citizens derive few concrete or visible benefits from U.S. military cooperation. The reputation of either the United States or China could be damaged if its military assistance is perceived as propping up an illegitimate regime, but Washington risks its reputation more than Beijing does in this regard given its more extensive military engagement.

U.S. and Chinese Public Diplomacy Activities

With Beijing's new emphasis on people-to-people exchanges, media outreach, and more socially responsible community engagement by large commercial enterprises, China is taking robust steps to improve its image in Africa and make its political and economic activities more palatable to Africans, which will facilitate the maintenance—or even expansion—of relations with their governments. The United States, in contrast, is scaling back its budgets for global public diplomacy and educational exchanges, and its efforts in Africa remain relatively small-scale. Although Washington and Beijing are each using such initiatives to create segments of African societies that are sympathetic to, and familiar with, their values and policy priorities, it is clear that China is placing a far higher priority on public diplomacy in Africa than the United States.

The scale of U.S. outreach efforts in Africa is relatively stagnant. The State Department's FY2014 budget request noted that Africa is one of two priority regions for public diplomacy in FY2014. However, although the public diplomacy budget request for the Africa Bureau increased about 7 percent from FY2012 (from $48.5 million to $52.2 million), half of the increase was to adjust the salaries of local public diplomacy

---

91 Pew Global Attitudes Project, 2013, p. 5.

92 Pew Global Attitudes Project, 2013, p. 40.

93 Pew Global Attitudes Project, 2013, p. 16.

94 Pew Global Attitudes Project, 2013, pp. 27–28.

employees for inflation.[95] The department reduced its request for worldwide educational and cultural exchange programs by $36 million (about 6 percent) from FY2012, though it plans to shift an unspecified amount of resources to support programs in Africa and Asia.[96]

In contrast, China is significantly increasing its global public diplomacy activities, both around the world and in Africa. *The Guardian* reported in December 2011 that Beijing is spending an estimated $6 billion to expand official media activities alone, including by launching television news channels in English, Russian, and Arabic and increasing this size of CCTV's overseas staff by a factor of 10 between 2012 and 2016.[97] In Africa, China has launched a multi-pronged public diplomacy effort to promote Chinese culture, enhance people-to-people engagement, and highlight China's contributions to Africa's development—a campaign intended "to change the narrative of China's involvement in Africa from one of exploitation to one of opportunity . . . challeng[e] negative perceptions and make investment possibilities seem more attractive," as CNN reported in September 2012.[98] As discussed, Beijing has greatly expanded its media outreach, primarily by opening a broadcasting studio for CCTV in Nairobi, creating an African edition of the English-language newspaper *China Daily*,[99] and expanding the number of African bureaus for the official Xinhua news service.[100] It has expanded the number of Confucius Institutes in Africa to promote Chinese language and culture.[101] Chinese officials announced at the 2012 FOCAC meeting that China would expand training, education, and cultural exchange initiatives with African partners. Beijing's multifaceted, proactive, and well-resourced efforts to convey its messages in Africa are likely to significantly enhance its image on the continent.

Despite ambitious public diplomacy efforts on the Chinese side, however, the United States still enjoys clear comparative advantages in the soft power realm in Africa.[102] Africans positively identify with U.S. ideals of individualism, freedom, democracy, and the rule of law. American sports and Hollywood movies are still very popular among most Africans.[103] Thus, even without the public diplomacy resources to

---

95 U.S. Department of State, *Congressional Budget Justification, Volume 1: Department of State Operations, Fiscal Year 2014*, Washington, D.C., no date, pp. 182, 191–192.

96 U.S. Department of State, no date, pp. 182, 191–192.

97 Tania Branigan, "Chinese State TV Unveils Global Expansion Plan," *The Guardian*, December 8, 2011.

98 McKenzie, 2012.

99 "China Daily Newspaper Launches Africa Edition," 2012.

100 Wu, 2012.

101 Jintao, 2012.

102 See Pew Global Attitudes Project, 2013, pp. 16–18, 27–30, 39–41.

103 Rohit Kachroo, "My Head Says That China Is Number One, My Heart Always Says America'," NBC News.com, June 27, 2012.

augment an official public diplomacy "message," Africans still generally identify with broad aspects of U.S. culture, society, and forms of governance that place the United States at a soft power advantage vis-à-vis China.

Opportunities for U.S.-Chinese Collaboration in Africa

So if the United States and China are not strategic competitors in Africa, do opportunities exist for the two to collaborate? Perhaps, but because the two countries have such different objectives in Africa, any such cooperation is likely to be small-scale and on the margins of what both of them see as their core interests.

Officially, the United States demands little of China in Africa except that it act responsibly. Assistant Secretary of State Johnnie Carson told reporters in November 2011,

> What we do say when we look at China is to act as a responsible player as it goes about undertaking its economic activities on the continent. We hope that as they invest, as we invest, and others invest in the continent that they will employ African labor. That they will follow local labor standards. That they will pay decent wages. That they will train their personnel. That they will impart technology and that the trade that they have will be beneficial as it should for both parties to the process. But we have no objection to China as we have no objection to Germany, France or Japan engaging in trade and investment in Africa. We ask that everybody live up to their responsibilities in doing so and do it in a manner which is beneficial to not only the country but the citizens of the country as well.[104]

Washington and Beijing already have a senior-level forum for discussing Africa: the U.S.-China Subdialogue on Africa, which was launched in November 2005.[105] In a collection of firsthand accounts of U.S. Africa policy by 15 Assistant Secretaries of State for African Affairs, Jendayi Frazer, who held the position from 2005 to 2009, explained U.S. hopes for the Sub-Dialogue:

> AF [the State Department's Bureau of African Affairs] operated on the basis that we could work with China to further Africa's development and stability just as we do with other countries like France that have interests that span the continent but

[104] Carson, 2011.

[105] Bates Gill, J. Stephen Morrison, and Chin-Hao Huang, "China-Africa Relations: An Early, Uncertain Debate in the United States," in Chris Alden, Daniel Large, and Ricardo Soares de Oliveira, eds., *China Returns to Africa: A Rising Power and a Continent Embrace,* New York, Columbia University Press, 2008, 177. Also see Bates Gill, *Meeting the Challenges and Opportunities of China's Rise: Expanding and Improving Interaction Between the American and Chinese Policy Communities*, Washington, D.C.: Center for Strategic and International Studies, 2006, p. 13. The Subdialogue also met in March 2007 and October 2008.

> are not always congruent with US interests. This approach was partly driven by the need for enhanced donor coordination to avoid duplication of efforts and optimize all existing sources of assistance in order to achieve our mutual objectives. It remains important to encourage China to support the work of international financial institutions in encouraging good economic management and to not overload African countries with new unsustainable debts owed to China. Our challenge was finding ways the US and China could work together in Africa to advance the wider goals of peace, stability, [and] economic development while also encouraging China to support good governance, rule of law, and access to free and transparent markets in Africa.[106]

These expectations are extremely ambitious. Beijing clearly has little interest in reducing the extent of African debt to China or in promoting free and transparent markets; indeed, Chinese economic policy toward Africa has been predicated on investments—many of which are approved by host nations through less-than-transparent means—that increase African indebtedness to China.

Not surprisingly, therefore, the Subdialogue has generated few concrete cooperative initiatives. After the most recent meeting (the fifth) in November 2011, the State Department reported that U.S. and Chinese representatives "discussed how the United States and China can work together in promoting a number of trilateral development initiatives in a number of African countries"; the announcement quoted Assistant Secretary of State for African Affairs Johnnie Carson as saying, "We are eager to see if we can work with China to leverage our comparative advantages to help Africa overcome some of its economic challenges, particularly in the area of agriculture, health and clean water."[107] Although the Subdialogue meeting offered "an opportunity to exchange views with the vice foreign minister, Zhai Jun, about how China views the current situation on the continent,"[108] no joint programs were announced.

Collaboration on Economic Development Initiatives

Washington and Beijing may be able identify opportunities to collaborate in the sphere of human development, as both provide assistance to African countries in areas such as health, education, and agriculture. However, while both the United States and China pursue similar development priorities in Africa, they have tended to pursue parallel—rather than collaborative—efforts.

---

[106] Jendayi E. Frazer, "Africa Policy: A Record of Success," in Claudia E. Anyaso, ed., *Fifty Years of U S African Policy: Reflections of Assistant Secretaries of African Affairs and U.S. Embassy Officials*, Washington, D.C.: Association for Diplomatic Studies and Training, 2011, p. 252.

[107] Merle David Kellerhals, Jr., "U.S. Diplomat Discusses Africa with Asian Counterparts," U.S. Embassy, IIPdigital.com, November 22, 2011.

[108] Kellerhals, 2011.

Principal Deputy Assistant Secretary of State for Africa Affairs Donald Yamamoto told a congressional committee in March 2012, for example, that "in order to serve the people on the African continent more effectively, China and the United States should work together, as we can achieve more with our collective resources. We are actively looking for areas of development cooperation with the Chinese. . . . It is important for the United States and China to cooperate in areas of mutual interest for the benefit of Africa as a whole."[109]

As David Shinn noted in a May 2011 conference in Beijing, however, while "collaboration by the United States and China in an effort to improve life for Africans would seem to be an obvious winning combination . . . experience has shown that it is not easy. . . . The dialogue has been underway for about six years and has produced little."[110] Shinn cites nascent efforts to work jointly on security reform in the Democratic Republic of Congo, irrigation in Ethiopia, malaria eradication in Liberia, and road construction in Tanzania but notes that such efforts either came to naught or remained limited because of "lack of interest by key American and Chinese personnel in the field," staff turnover, and a decision by the American Millennium Challenge Corporation (MCC) to award contracts only to non-state-owned companies.[111] If U.S.-Chinese cooperation were truly a priority for either country, field staff would have ensured that such initiatives were implemented, and the MCC would have found a way to include Chinese state-owned enterprises in African initiatives.

The few economic development challenges that Washington and Beijing have agreed to tackle jointly appear to be token efforts, at best. For example, although Principal Deputy Assistant Secretary of State Yamamoto told a congressional committee that "the United States and China have identified the Liberian health sector as an area for joint collaboration to support global poverty reduction and development,"[112] it is abundantly clear that the Liberian health sector is an extremely low priority for both countries. Although Secretary of State Hillary Clinton and Liberian President Ellen Johnson-Sirleaf agreed in January 2013 to establish a "Partnership Dialogue" to expand bilateral cooperation, Secretary Clinton explained that the three areas of focus for this initiative would be agriculture and food security, energy and power infrastructure, and

---

[109] Quoted in U.S. House of Representatives, Committee on Foreign Affairs, Subcommitee on Africa, Global Health, and Human Rights, "Assessing China's Role and Influence in Africa," March 29, 2012.

[110] David H. Shinn, "United States-China Collaboration on Health and Agriculture in Africa," Paper Presented at a Joint Conference Hosted by The Center for Strategic and International Studies and the China Institute of International Studies, Beijing, May 24, 2011, pp. 1, 7.

[111] Shinn, 2011, pp. 1–2. Also, Shinn, correspondence with authors, September 2, 2013.

[112] Testimony of Donald Yamamoto, Principal Deputy Assistant Secretary of State for Africa Affairs, in U.S. House of Representatives, Committee on Foreign Affairs, Subcommitee on Africa, Global Health, and Human Rights, 2012, p. 2.

human development with an emphasis on education and employment.[113] During the first meeting of the Partnership Dialogue in Washington in May 2013, working groups met to discuss only the first two focus areas.[114] Health care was not on the agenda.

U.S. foreign assistance spending levels also indicate that Liberia itself—not to mention its health sector—is a relatively low priority. The Partnership Dialogue notwithstanding, the U.S. aid request for Liberia in fiscal year 2013 ranked 13th out of 47 Sub-Saharan countries for which State and the U.S. Agency for International Development (USAID) sought bilateral assistance funds,[115] and overall aid to Liberia decreased by 25 percent between fiscal years 2009 and 2013. The State Department and USAID allocated a combined $40.7 million to the Liberian health sector in FY2013—a decrease of 21 percent ($10.6 million) from the previous year and the lowest amount allocated to health since FY2009.[116]

For Beijing's part, Chinese health-related assistance to Liberia included funds for two medical projects provided under a $17 million Economic and Technical Cooperation Agreement that also included money for broadcasting, agriculture, vocational training, and a sports initiative; one of the two initiatives, a Chinese medical team assigned to a Liberian hospital, had been funded at $1 million per year in 2006–2008.[117] Beijing's commitments to Liberia's health sector are negligible compared with the $5 billion in bilateral trade in 2011[118] and with the $2.6 billion Chinese investment in Liberia's Bong iron ore mine,[119] which the Chinese ambassador in Monrovia stated in 2012 is China's largest single investment in all of Africa.[120] If the Liberian

---

[113] Hillary Rodham Clinton, "Remarks at the U.S.-Liberia Partnership Dialogue Signing Ceremony," Washington, D.C., January 15, 2013.

[114] Wendy Sherman, Under Secretary of State for Political Affairs, *U.S.-Liberia Partnership Dialogue Closing Remarks*, Washington, D.C., May 7, 2013. See also Embassy of the Republic of Liberia to the United States, "13/05/2013: Inaugural Session of U.S.-Liberia Partnership Dialogue Held in United States," press release, May 13, 2013.

[115] U.S. Department of State, *Congressional Budget Justification, Volume 2: Foreign Operations, Fiscal Year 2013*, no date, pp. 507–508.

[116] See Liberia data at U.S. Agency for International Development, foreignassistance.gov website, no date.

[117] "Liberia, China Sign U.S.$17 Million Pact," *The New Dawn* (Monrovia), April 19, 2013. See also African Center for Economic Transformation, *Looking East: China-Africa Engagements—Liberia Case Study,* December 2009, p. 20.

[118] Alaskai Moore, "Chinese Business Association of Liberia Launched, As China's Trade with Liberia Passes US$5 Billion in 2011," *Daily Observer* (Liberia), April 24, 2012. Also, Solomon Watkins, "China, US Relations with Liberia: Which Is Best? As China Reports $5 Billion Trade in 2011," *African Standard* (Liberia), April 21, 2012.

[119] "Can China Union Restore Smiles to Bong Mines?" *The Independent* (Liberia), January 21, 2013.

[120] "Liberia Lauded for Upholding One-China Policy," *Heritage* (Liberia), August 1, 2012. See also "Tainting the China Brand: Beijing Must Emphasize Quality Over Quantity," *Front Page Africa* (Liberia), August 20, 2012.

health sector is truly the most fruitful arena for U.S.-Chinese collaboration in Africa, it appears that few strategically important opportunities for joint efforts exist.

Collaboration on Promoting Regional Integration

Both the United States and China have a stake in promoting African regional integration, which would create larger markets and reduce transaction costs not only for U.S. and Chinese firms but for local, regional, and global trade as a whole. The U.S. government's U.S.-East African Community Trade and Investment Initiative is one effort to reduce the barriers to trade and investment flows in Africa, whose goals include "trade facilitation, customs modernization, and standards harmonization," among others.[121] However, to date such U.S. government-led initiatives remain aspirational at best and typically are underfunded.

As mentioned previously in this report, the Chinese government is also focused on African integration as an increasingly important policy objective, with "transnational and trans-regional infrastructural development" featured as one of Hu Jintao's Five Point Proposal at the 2012 FOCAC.[122] China seems to be matching word with action in this regard, albeit employing state-backed Chinese infrastructure firms as proxies. For example, Kenya's "historic milestone" railway project—currently being built by the China Road and Bridge Corporation (CRBC), a Chinese state-owned enterprise—is financed by the Chinese government and aims to link the port city of Mombasa to Nairobi, Kenya.[123] The $13.8 billion project hopes to eventually extend to neighboring Uganda, Rwanda, and South Sudan. The project is one of the biggest intra-regional railway networks ever to be built in Africa, and its completion has the potential to greatly decrease barriers to trade for Chinese enterprises and global commerce. Similar to other areas of possible collaboration between the U.S. and China in Africa, however, agreement on mutual interest of enhancing regional integration in Africa has yet to lead to concerted efforts among the governments of each country to cooperate.

Collaboration on Shared Security Challenges

Some of the few collaborative Sino-American initiatives in Africa have addressed shared security concerns. American and Chinese special envoys for Sudan and South Sudan have consulted on ways to resolve the continued conflict between Khartoum and Juba.[124] Because China shares the United States' concerns about threats to commercial shipping off the Horn of Africa, China has contributed constructively to inter-

---

[121] The White House, *U.S. Strategy Toward Sub-Saharan Africa*, June 2012, pp. 3.

[122] "President Hu Proposes New Measures to Boost China-Africa Ties," Chinese government official website (gov.cn), July 19, 2012.

[123] "Kenya Launches Mega $13.8bn Railway Project" Al Jazeera, November 28, 2013.

[124] Jane Perlez, "South Sudan to Get Aid from China; No Oil Deal," *New York Times*, April 25, 2012.

national efforts to counter piracy off the coast of Somalia; U.S. Defense Secretary Chuck Hagel and Chinese Defense Minister Chang Wanquan agreed in August 2013 to conduct joint counter-piracy exercises off the Somali coast.[125] (Africa-related cooperation is clearly subordinate to other issues in the bilateral relationship, however; China canceled previous such exercises in late 2011 after the United States announced new arms sales to Taiwan.[126])

There are, however, limits on opportunities for U.S.-Chinese cooperation in the security arena. AFRICOM Commander Carter Ham suggested that the United States and China could collaborate by each "apply[ing] their strengths to the benefit to a particular African military," noting as an example that Tanzania asked China to build its National Defense College and the United States to develop the curriculum.[127] It seems unlikely, however, that China would willingly enter into a joint effort in which its companies build an African military facility so that the U.S. military can then shape that country's strategic outlook in its own image.

Given the shared U.S.-Chinese interest in ensuring freedom of navigation from pirates and criminals, Washington could encourage China to collaborate on efforts to improve security in the Gulf of Guinea—another region in which piracy has threatened commercial shipping—or help African nations enhance the capabilities of their coast guards and naval forces.[128] Successful collaboration in this area would advance mutual U.S., Chinese, and African interests in a far more strategically important area than would coordinated assistance to the Liberian health sector.

The expansion of Chinese engagement in peacekeeping may provide an avenue for the United States to engage with China more closely. The United States has a long history of participation in peacekeeping abroad, and China appears keen to increase its already robust peacekeeping operation presence in Africa and elsewhere. Washington should work with other Western countries to explore concrete ways in which China could play a more active part in planning and coordinating at the UN Department of Peacekeeping Operations, perhaps by working with China to facilitate peacekeeping seminars, training courses, and other capacity-building programs. In the long run, collaboration on peacekeeping and other related forms of military-to-military exchange would contribute to building greater openness and transparency within the PLA.

---

[125] Paul Eckert, "U.S., China to Expand Military Exchanges Amid Rows Over Cyber Security, Territory," Reuters, August 19, 2013.

[126] Andrew Erickson and Austin Strange, "'Selfish Superpower' No Longer? China's Anti-Piracy Activities and 21st-Century Global Maritime Governance," *Harvard Asia Quarterly*, Vol. 14, Nos. 1–2, Spring/Summer 2012, p. 100.

[127] Ham, 2012.

[128] Jennifer Cooke, "Introduction," in *U.S and Chinese Engagement in Africa: Prospects for Improving U.S.-China-Africa Cooperation*, Center for Strategic and International Studies, July 2008, p. 7.

Recommendations for Promoting Better Chinese Behavior in Africa

Ultimately, however, U.S. relations with China are dominated by so many critical challenges—such as Iranian sanctions, North Korea, and avoiding conflict in the South China Sea—that neither country is likely to spend much diplomatic capital to advance its interests in Africa. Indeed, when Presidents Obama and Xi met in California in June 2013, Africa was not even on their agenda. U.S. officials are more likely to promote responsible Chinese engagement by encouraging Africans to demand better behavior from China. But as long as African governments see benefit in accepting Chinese aid and investment, such arguments are likely to fall on deaf ears.

China is more likely to change course in Africa if African publics—through their governments, labor unions, and civil society—demand it themselves. China has modified its Africa policy—pledging to create more local jobs, transfer more technology, and improve working conditions—because African public opinion had become increasingly hostile to its foreign and economic policies. The best way for Washington to promote a change in Chinese policy toward the continent, therefore, is not to pressure Beijing directly, but rather to do even more to promote democracy, accountability, and transparency in the region. Continued U.S. assistance focused on promoting good governance and eliminating corruption is thus likely to be one of the most effective tools Washington has to encourage China to be a more responsible actor in Africa.[129] Such efforts could be undertaken through State Department and USAID programs that foster democracy, transparency, and a strong civil society. However, the U.S. Department of Defense can also do a great deal to promote good governance, civilian control of the military, transparent procurement/contracting mechanisms, and other aspects of accountable government through its professional military education initiatives, such as the International Military Education and Training (IMET) program and the department's Africa Center for Strategic Studies.

To promote such messages without lecturing, the United States would benefit by cultivating good relations with a wider range of African countries, much as China does through FOCAC and through high-level visits. Generally speaking, most African governments will welcome opportunities to engage the world's sole superpower on just about any topic. However, as Ian Taylor writes, when African officials visit Washington, "unless they are from South Africa, Egypt, or one of the few other states deemed strategically important, they are barely afforded a few minutes and even then they are more likely to be admonished for their chronic failures in governance than they are to be toasted as dear friends or, more important, credible statesmen." China's efforts to

---

[129] See Larry Hanauer and Lyle Morris, "Agreeing to Disagree About Africa," *U.S. News & World Report*, June 5, 2013.

"massag[e] the egos of Africa's leaders" pays off, Taylor asserts, by winning allies who are willing to offer political support when called upon.[130]

Furthermore, if the United States wants to encourage China to refrain from selling military materiel to autocratic regimes, it could begin by being more discriminating itself. However, it is not so easy in practice to determine which governments are sufficiently pure to merit military assistance in a continent where only 11 of 54 countries are ranked "free" by Freedom House[131]—and where even some of those face difficulties reining in official corruption and abuses of power.[132] The United States is unlikely to end its security relationship with Kenya, one of its closest partners on the continent, because its newly elected president has been indicted by the International Criminal Court for fomenting ethnic violence after the country's 2007 elections. A further challenge is that if Washington decides to withhold weapons and military equipment from a repressive government, China or other arms exporters are likely to fill the gap—leading to an authoritarian regime that is just as heavily armed but also less open to U.S. influence.

Similarly, U.S. efforts to promote greater private investment can force Chinese businesses to change their behavior. Competition from American industry will force Chinese enterprises to offer better deals to African governments and private partners, as well as drive Chinese firms to be more socially responsible and generate greater benefits for the communities in which they operate. Again, the more American companies enter African markets and create local jobs, provide opportunities for training and advancement, and foster more humane working conditions, the more Chinese firms will be compelled to follow suit. The Power Africa and Trade Africa initiatives that President Obama announced in June 2013—in addition to bringing billions of dollars in private capital to Africa—will likely enable African nations to secure better infrastructure deals and investment terms from Beijing.[133]

Recommendations for Further Study

Western analysts and policymakers face enormous challenges in understanding China's engagement in Africa. One of the most difficult obstacles is the lack of clear, transparent data on Chinese aid and investment projects, as has been discussed. Researchers

---

130 Taylor, 2009, p. 24.

131 Freedom House, 2013, pp. 14–18.

132 In South Africa, the national prosecutor's office estimated in late 2011 that around $3.8 billion—one-fifth to one-quarter of the government's procurement budget—is lost to waste and corruption. See "Corruption in South Africa: A Can of Worms," *The Economist*, October 29, 2011.

133 See Larry Hanauer and Lyle Morris, "To Help Africa, Do Business There," *U.S. News & World Report*, June 27, 2013.

at AidData, a partnership of the College of William and Mary and Brigham Young University, have made a valiant effort to compile information on Chinese economic engagement, but the vehement debate over whether their methodology yields reliable data demonstrates that enormous gaps in understanding remain.[134]

Even more troubling than opaque statistics, however, is that U.S. and Western policymakers lack a strategic understanding into how China sees Africa.[135] China is not a monolithic actor,[136] and its policies are not static, as demonstrated by Beijing's recent adaptations to African popular sentiment. Yet the U.S. government has little insight into how Chinese policymakers and government agencies—such as those listed in Chapter Three—develop, prioritize, implement, and adjust China's policy toward Africa. A study of these agencies' interests, objectives, internal interactions, and outreach to African partners would generate a far more nuanced understanding of the making of Chinese foreign policy.

In a related area, little research has been conducted on how China uses soft power tools, such as the expanding network of Confucius Institutes and foreign-language media outlets, as well as the types of people-to-people exchanges and scholarships that President Xi announced during his March 2013 trip to the continent. An examination of how China formulates its outreach strategy and allocates soft power resources would also add significantly to an understanding of Chinese policymaking—not just regarding Africa, but worldwide.

Furthermore, while the United States wants China to become a "responsible stakeholder" in Africa and encourages it to take steps (such as making its assistance more transparent) that advance Western priorities, Washington has given little thought to how it might shape Chinese policies toward Africa by appealing to Beijing's interests.[137] Haranguing Beijing about good governance is likely to have little impact given the centrality of non-interference to China's foreign policy; similarly, pressuring China to improve worker safety is unlikely to lead to improvements unless African governments themselves enforce labor standards that are already in place. However, promoting a dialogue on corporate social responsibility that emphasizes the positive impact on both community welfare and profits—something that many American companies

---

[134] See, for example, Deborah Brautigam, "Rubbery Numbers on Chinese Aid," *China in Africa: The Real Story* blog, April 30, 2013.

[135] Chin-Hao Huang, "China's Renewed Partnership with Africa: Implications for the United States," in Robert I. Rotberg, ed., *China Into Africa: Trade, Aid, and Influence*, Washington, D.C.: Brookings Institution Press, 2008, p. 304.

[136] Cooke, 2008, p. 7.

[137] Huang, 2008, p. 305.

have long recognized[138]—could successfully advance U.S. development priorities by acknowledging and furthering Beijing's interests.

---

[138] See, for example, Michael Barnett, "The New CSR: This Time It's Profitable," *Marketing Week*, April 14, 2011. See also Chong Wei Nurn and Gilbert Tan, "Obtaining Intangible and Tangible Benefits from Corporate Social Responsibility," *International Review of Business Research Papers*, Vol. 6, No. 4, September 2010, pp. 360–371.

Bibliography

"1,072 Chinese Gold Miners Return from Ghana," *People's Daily Online*, June 14, 2013. As of December 5, 2013:
http://english.peopledaily.com.cn/90777/8284052.html

Abdelaziz, Khalid, "Four Abducted Chinese Workers Released in Sudan's Darfur," Reuters, January 16, 2013. As of August 11, 2013:
http://www.reuters.com/article/2013/01/16/us-sudan-china-idUSBRE90F0JK20130116

"About FOCAC," ChinAfrica.cn, web page, no date. As of July 30, 2013:
http://www.chinafrica.cn/english/txt/2012-07/12/content_467915.htm

Abramson, Mark, "U.S. Plans Land-Based UAV Patrols to Combat Piracy," *Stars and Stripes*, August 29, 2009. As of November 13, 2013:
http://www.stripes.com/news/u-s-plans-land-based-uav-patrols-to-combat-piracy-1.94339

Adebayo, Ismail, "Nigeria: China to Build Four Airport Terminals in the Country," *The Daily Trust* (Nigeria), September 23, 2012. As of August 15, 2013:
http://allafrica.com/stories/201209230243.html

"Africa and China: More Than Minerals," *The Economist*, March 23, 2013. As of July 30, 2013:
http://www.economist.com/news/middle-east-and-africa/21574012-chinese-trade-africa-keeps-growing-fears-neocolonialism-are-overdone-more

"Africa: Fourth International Roundtable on China-Africa Health Cooperation 6–7 May 2013, Gaborone, Botswana," press release, May 16, 2013. As of July 26, 2013:
http://allafrica.com/stories/201305161396.html

"Africa Should Cut Reliance on Commodity Exports—Ministers," *IMF Survey Magazine*, April 16. 2011. As of April 11, 2013:
http://www.imf.org/external/pubs/ft/survey/so/2011/car041611a.htm

African Center for Economic Transformation, *Looking East: China-Africa Engagements—Liberia Case Study*, December 2009. As of May 13, 2013:
http://acetforafrica.org/wp-content/uploads/2010/08/Looking-East-Liberia-China-case-study-August-20101.pdf

———, *Looking East: China-Africa Engagements—Ghana Country Case Study*, December 2009. As of October 15, 2013:
http://acetforafrica.org/wp-content/uploads/2010/08/Looking-East-Ghana-China-Case-Study-2010.pdf

"African Culture Promoted in China," Xinhua, May 25, 2012. As of June 12, 2013:
http://www.focac.org/eng/zfgx/rwjl/t936170.htm

African Development Bank Group, "Chinese Trade and Investment Activities in Africa," Policy Brief, Vol. 1, No. 4, July 29, 2010. As of October 15, 2013:
http://www.afdb.org/fileadmin/uploads/afdb/Documents/Publications/Chinese%20Trade%20%20Investment%20Activities%20in%20Africa%2020Aug.pdf

African Development Bank and African Union, *Oil and Gas in Africa: Joint Study by the African Development Bank and the African Union,* Oxford, UK: Oxford University Press, 2009, p. xxvvi. As of August 22, 2013:
http://www.afdb.org/fileadmin/uploads/afdb/Documents/Publications/Full%20Document%20-%20Oil%20and%20Gas%20in%20Africa.pdf

Akkermans, Joost, "China Plans 45 Billion Yuan Media Expansion, Morning Post Says," Bloomberg.com, January 12, 2009. As of May 1, 2013:
http://www.bloomberg.com/apps/news?pid=newsarchive&sid=aQ2W6WFUvMqM

Alden, Chris, *China in Africa*, London: Zed Books, 2007.

———, *China's Growing Role in African Peace and Security*, London: Saferworld, January 2011, p. 51. As of August 15, 2013:
http://www.saferworld.org.uk/downloads/pubdocs/Chinas%20Growing%20Role%20in%20African%20Peace%20and%20Security.pdf

Alden, Chris, Daniel Large, and Ricardo Soares de Oliveira, eds., *China Returns to Africa: A Rising Power and a Continent Embrace*, New York: Columbia University Press, 2008.

Ampiah, Kweku, and Sanusha Naidu, "Introduction: Africa and China in the Post–Cold War Era," in Sanusha Naidu and Kweku Ampiah, eds., *Crouching Tiger, Hidden Dragon? Africa and China*, Scottsville, South Africa: University of KwaZulu-Natal Press, 2008, p. 11.

Anthony, Ross, "Should China Keep Its 'Africa Dreams' to Itself?" *The Diplomat*, April 3, 2013. As of July 29, 2013:
http://thediplomat.com/china-power/should-china-keep-its-africa-dreams-to-itself/

———, "Obama 'Playing Catch-Up' as Africa Looks to China," CNN.com, June 26, 2013. As of July 29, 2013:
http://www.cnn.com/2013/06/26/opinion/obama-catch-africa-china-anthony

"Assistant Foreign Minister Zhai Jun Accepts an Exclusive Interview by Foreign Media Concerning the Beijing Summit of the Forum on China-Africa Cooperation," Forum on China-Africa Cooperation (FOCAC) Summit, Beijing, October 26, 2006.

Ayenagbo, Kossi, Tommie Njobvu, James V. Sossou, and Biossey K. Tozoun, "China's Peacekeeping Operations in Africa: From Unwilling Participation to Responsible Contribution," *African Journal of Political Science and International Relations,* Vol. 6, No. 2, February 2012, pp. 22–32.

Badkar, Mamta, "Check Out the Massive Chinese-Built Ghost Town in the Middle of Angola," *Business Insider*, July 3, 2012. As of April 19, 2013:
http://www.businessinsider.com/chinese-built-ghost-town-kilamba-angola-2012-7

Bakano, Otto, "Multiple Barriers Hamper Trade Within Africa," Agence France Presse, January 26, 2012. As of April 11, 2013:
http://www.trademarksa.org/news/multiple-barriers-hamper-trade-within-africa

Bariyo, Nicholas, "Chinese-Owned Miner in Zambia Fires 1,000 Striking Workers," *Wall Street Journal*, October 21, 2011. As of April 23, 2013:
http://online.wsj.com/article/SB10001424052970204618704576642392413811456.html

Barnett, Michael, "The New CSR: This Time It's Profitable," *Marketing Week*, April 14, 2011. As of May 13, 2013:
http://www.marketingweek.co.uk/the-new-csr-this-time-its-profitable/3025435.article

Baynton-Glen, Sarah, *Beyond Trade—China-Africa Investment Trends*, Standard Chartered Global Research, February 22, 2012.

"Beijing Review Launches China's First Africa-Oriented Print Media Company in South Africa," Xinhua, May 8, 2012. As of December 5, 2013:
http://www.focac.org/eng/zfgx/rwjl/t929900.htm

Biggeri, Mario, and Marco Sanfilippo, "Understanding China's Move into Africa: An Empirical Analysis," *Journal of Chinese Economic and Business Studies*, Vol. 7, No. 1, 2009, pp. 31–54.

Blank, Rebecca M., Deputy Secretary of Commerce, *The Department of Commerce Budget in Brief: Fiscal Year 2014*, Washington, D.C.: U.S. Department of Commerce, no date. As of December 5, 2013:
http://osec.doc.gov/bmi/Budget/FY14BIB/ENTIREBIB.pdf

———, "Remarks at Launch of 'Doing Business in Africa' Campaign, Johannesburg, South Africa," November 28, 2012. As of May 7, 2013:
http://www.commerce.gov/news/acting-secretary-speeches/2012/11/28/remarks-launch-doing-business-africa-campaign-johannesburg

Bowman, Andrew, "Africa's Chinese Diaspora: Under Pressure," *Financial Times*, August 8, 2012. As of April 19, 2013:
http://blogs.ft.com/beyond-brics/2012/08/08/africas-chinese-diaspora-under-pressure/#axzz2Qw7ZYOyB

Branigan, Tania, "Chinese State TV Unveils Global Expansion Plan," *The Guardian*, December 8, 2011. As of August 15, 2013:
http://www.guardian.co.uk/world/2011/dec/08/china-state-television-global-expansion

Brautigam, Deborah, *The Dragon's Gift: The Real Story of China in Africa*, Oxford, UK: Oxford University Press, 2009.

———, "China in Africa: Think Again," *European Financial Review*, August 16, 2010. As of April 12, 2013:
http://www.europeanfinancialreview.com/?p=1336

———, "Aid 'With Chinese Characteristics': Chinese Foreign Aid and Development Finance Meet the OECD-DAC Aid Regime," *Journal of International Development*, Vol. 23, 2011a, p. 760.

———, "Chinese Development Aid to Africa: What, Where, Why and How Much?" in Jane Golley and Ligang Song, eds., *Rising China: Global Challenges and Opportunities*, Canberra: Australia National University Press, 2011b, pp. 203–211. As of October 15, 2013:
http://epress.anu.edu.au/wp-content/uploads/2011/08/whole3.pdf

———, "Rubbery Numbers on Chinese Aid," *China in Africa: The Real Story* blog, April 30, 2013. As of August 15, 2013:
http://www.chinaafricarealstory.com/2013/04/rubbery-numbers-on-chinese-aid.html

The Brenthurst Foundation, the Chinese Academy of Social Sciences, the Council on Foreign Relations, and the Leon H. Sullivan Foundation, *Africa-China-U.S. Trilateral Dialogue: Summary Report*, 2007. As of May 14, 2013:
http://i.cfr.org/content/publications/attachments/Trilateral_Report.pdf

Callimachi, Rukmini, "China Courts Africa With Aid, Projects," Associated Press, January 4, 2007. As of August 15, 2013:
http://www.washingtonpost.com/wpdyn/content/article/2007/01/04/AR2007010401031.html

"Can China Union Restore Smiles to Bong Mines?" *The Independent* (Liberia), January 21, 2013. As of August 15, 2013:
http://theindependentliberia.com/index.php/politics/113-can-china-union-bring-back-smiles-to-bong-miners

Carson, Johnnie, "Briefing on Assistant Secretary Carson's Recent Travel to Asia," November 22, 2011. As of May 9, 2013:
http://southafrica.usembassy.gov/mediahub_111123a.html

———, "Remarks to Panel Discussion on 'Consolidating Democratic Gains, Promoting African Prosperity,'" U.S. Institute of Peace, Washington, D.C., March 29, 2013. As of May 7, 2013:
http://www.state.gov/p/af/rls/rm/2013/206811.htm

Chalmers, Malcolm, and Owen Greene, "The UN Register of Conventional Arms: A Progress Report," *Disarmament Diplomacy*, No. 35, March 1999.

"Checkbook Diplomacy? China Pledges $20 Billion in Credit to Africa," nbcnews.com, July 19, 2012. As of July 30, 2013:
http://worldnews.nbcnews.com/_news/2012/07/19/12828957-checkbook-diplomacy-china-pledges-20-billion-in-credit-to-africa?lite

Chen, Deming, Chinese Minister of Commerce, "China and Africa Poised to Embrace a Brighter Future for Economic Cooperation and Trade," speech to Fifth Ministerial Conference of Forum on China-Africa Cooperation, July 18, 2012. As of July 19, 2013:
http://www.focac.org/eng/dwjbzjjhys/zyjh/t952591.htm

———, "China and Africa Poised to Embrace a Brighter Future for Economic Cooperation and Trade," Embassy of The People's Republic of China in the Republic of Malawi, web page, July 19, 2012. As of August 15, 2013:
http://mw.china-embassy.org/eng/sghdhzxxx/t953449.htm

Chêne, Marie, "U4 Expert Answer: Overview of Corruption and Anti-Corruption in Angola," Anti-Corruption Resource Center Expert Answer No. 257, February 25, 2010. As of April 22, 2013:
http://www.u4.no/publications/overview-of-corruption-and-anti-corruption-in-angola/

"China and Africa Join Hands in Media Cooperation," CCTV News in English, August 23, 2012. As of May 20, 2013:
http://english.cntv.cn/program/newsupdate/20120823/105929.shtml

"China Attaches Importance to Africa's Concerns, Interests: FM," Forum on China-Africa Cooperation (FOCAC), January 6, 2012. As of June 1, 2013:
http://www.focac.org/eng/zfgx/dfzc/t893413.htm

"China Beefs Up Training of African Diplomats," China Radio International, November 25, 2013. As of January 21, 2014:
http://english.cri.cn/6909/2013/11/25/2982s800429.htm

"China Daily Newspaper Launches Africa Edition," BBC News.com, December 14, 2012. As of August 15, 2013:
http://www.bbc.co.uk/news/world-asia-china-20722952

"China Industrial Relocation Boosts 'Made in Africa' Products," Xinhua, July 20, 2012. As of July 17, 2013:
http://www.focac.org/eng/ltda/dwjbzjjhys/t954298.htm

"China Signs $260m Airport Deal with Mauritius," *China Daily*, February 17, 2009. As of August 15, 2013:
http://www.chinadaily.com.cn/bizchina/2009-02/17/content7487685.htm

"China to Begin Constructing Burundi's Presidential Palace in Early 2011," Xinhua, November 12, 2010. As of December 5, 2013:
http://english.cri.cn/6909/2010/11/12/2021s604625.htm

"China to Build $1.2 Billion Airport in Sudan," Associated Press, February 15, 2011. As of August 15, 2013:
http://gulfnews.com/news/region/sudan/china-to-build-1-2-billion-airport-in-sudan-1.762493

"China to Help Build South Sudan Airport," *Ventures Africa*, August 21, 2012. As of August 15, 2013:
http://www.ventures-africa.com/2012/08/china-to-help-build-south-sudan-airport/

"China to Send Peacekeeping Forces to Mali," Xinhua, July 12, 2013. As of December 5 2013:
http://www.china.org.cn/china/2013-07/12/content_29419357.htm

"China Will Be Africa's All-Weather Friend and Partner: Chinese President," *People's Daily Online*, May 30, 2013. As of December 5, 2013:
http://english.peopledaily.com.cn/90883/8188942.html

"China's African Policy," Chinese government paper, January 2006. As of July 30, 2013:
http://english.peopledaily.com.cn/200601/12/eng20060112_234894.html

"China's Development Model Good Example for African Nations: CCM Vice-Chairman of Tanzania," Xinhua, June 21, 2012. As of December 5, 2013:
http://english.sina.com/china/2012/0619/478579.html

"China's 'Stadium Diplomacy' in Africa and Its Top Beneficiaries," *Ventures Africa* (Nigeria), March 29, 2013. As of April 20, 2013:
http://www.ventures-africa.com/2013/03/
chinas-stadium-diplomacy-in-africa-and-its-top-beneficiaries/

"China-Africa Business Council," website, no date. As of May 1, 2013:
http://www.cabc.org.cn/enindex/index.jhtml

"China-Africa Cooperation Contributes to African Growth: FM Spokeswoman," *People's Daily Online*, April 19, 2013. As of December 5, 2013:
http://english.peopledaily.com.cn/90883/8214932.html

The China-African Development Fund (CADFund) as a Sovereign Wealth Fund for Africa's Development? Policy Briefing, The Centre for Chinese Studies, Stellenbosch University, July 2013.

China-Africa Development Fund homepage, "Introduction," no date. As of October 11, 2013:
http://www.cadfund.com/en/NewsInfo.aspx?NId=48

"China-Africa Economic and Trade Cooperation (2013)," *People's Daily Online*, August 29, 2013. As of December 5, 2013:
http://english.peopledaily.com.cn/102774/8382258.html

"China-Africa: Much More Than Resources," *Emerging Markets Monitor*, Vol. 17, No. 32, November 21, 2011.

"China-Africa Relations Based on Equality, Mutual Benefit and Common Development," *China People's Daily*, February 26, 2010. As of July 30, 2013:
http://english.peopledaily.com.cn/90001/90780/6903736.html

"The Chinese Are Everywhere," *The Economist*, August 5, 2010. As of August 13, 2013:
http://www.economist.com/node/16750131

"Chinese Envoy Briefs UN on China-Africa Relations," Xinhua, September 11, 2007. As of December 5, 2013:
http://www.un.org/africa/osaa/press/China-Africa%20Relations.pdf

"Chinese Firms Told to Invest More in Africa," Chinese government official website (gov.cn), May 29, 2010. As of July 1, 2013:
http://english.gov.cn/2010-05/29/content_1616248.htm

"Chinese Firms Urged to Invest in Africa," Associated Press, March 18, 2013. As of May 19, 2013:
http://www.fin24.com/Economy/Chinese-firms-urged-to-invest-in-Africa-20130318

Chinese Foreign Ministry, "Relations with South Africa," June 14, 2006. As of November 5, 2013:
http://www.china.org.cn/english/features/wenjiabaoafrica/171412.htm

"The Chinese in Africa: Trying to Pull Together," *The Economist*, April 20, 2011. As of April 19, 2013:
http://www.economist.com/node/18586448

"Chinese Investment in Africa Examined; Stalemate in Middle East Peace Discussed," transcript, *CNN's Amanpour*, March 28, 2013. As of August 13, 2013:
http://transcripts.cnn.com/TRANSCRIPTS/1303/28/ampr.01.html

"Chinese Labour Practices Haunt Zim Factory Workers," *Mail & Guardian* (South Africa), January 6, 2012. As of February 12, 2013:
http://mg.co.za/article/2012-01-06-chinese-labour-practices-haunt-zim-factory-workers

"Chinese Leaders on Sino-African Relations," China.org.cn, December 10, 2003. As of December 10, 2013:
http://www.china.org.cn/english/features/China-Africa/82054.htm

"Chinese Leader Boosts Sudan Ties," BBC News, February 2, 2007. As of August 15, 2013:
http://news.bbc.co.uk/2/hi/6323017.stm

Chinese Ministry of Commerce website, "Foreign Investment," no date. As of October 17, 2013:
http://english.mofcom.gov.cn/article/statistic/foreigninvestment/

Chivara, Inyasha, "Construction of Chinese-Built Zim Defense College Under Scrutiny," *Mail & Guardian* (South Africa), February 8, 2013. As of February 12, 2013:
http://mg.co.za/article/2013-02-08-construction-of-chinese-built-zim-defence-college-under-scrutiny

CITIC Construction Co., Ltd., "Angola Social Housing: Project Overview," web page, March 17, 2009. As of December 5, 2013:
http://www.cici.citic.com/iwcm/null/
LGY6LGM6MmM5NDgyOTYyMDEzNmIwMzAxMjAxMzdlYzA1YTAwMDEscDosYTosbTo=/
show.vsml

Clinton, Hillary Rodham, "Remarks at the U.S.-Liberia Partnership Dialogue Signing Ceremony," Washington, D.C., January 15, 2013. As of May 24, 2013:
http://www.state.gov/secretary/rm/2013/01/202201.htm

Cloete, Rod, Felix Faulhaber, and Markus Zils, "Infrastructure: A Long Road Ahead," in *McKinsey Quarterly—Africa's Path to Growth: Sector by Sector*, McKinsey & Company, 2010, p. 8. As of August 22, 2013:
http://www.mckinsey.com/insights/economic_studies/africas_path_to_growth_sector_by_sector

"Contact a Trade Specialist Near You," foreign commercial service office listings, web page, April 3, 2009. As of August 22, 2013:
http://export.gov/eac/index.asp

Conway-Smith, Erin, "Zambian Election Results Check Chinese Influence in Africa," *GlobalPost*, September 25, 2011. As of April 15, 2013:
http://www.globalpost.com/dispatch/news/regions/africa/110924/zambian-election-results-check-chinese-influence-africa

Cooke, Jennifer, "Introduction," in *U.S and Chinese Engagement in Africa: Prospects for Improving U.S.-China-Africa Cooperation*, Center for Strategic and International Studies, July 2008, p. 7.

"Corruption in South Africa: A Can of Worms," *The Economist*, October 29, 2011. As of October 17, 2013:
http://www.economist.com/node/21533410

Cropley, Ed, "Zambia Opposition Slates China, Malaysia Investors," Reuters, January 20, 2010. As of April 16, 2013:
http://www.reuters.com/article/2010/01/20/ozatp-zambia-opposition-idAFJOE60J0ER20100120

Dagne, Ted, *Africa: U.S. Foreign Assistance Issues*, Washington, D.C.: Congressional Research Service, Report RL33591, September 15, 2011, pp. 7, 9. As of April 13, 2013:
http://www.fas.org/sgp/crs/row/RL33591.pdf

Davies, Martyn, "How China Is Influencing Africa's Development," background paper for *Perspectives on Global Development 2010: Shifting Wealth*, OECD Development Center, April 2010, p. 19. As of July 23, 2012:
http://www.oecd.org/dataoecd/34/39/45068325.pdf

Davies-Webb, Warwick, "The Emerging Asian Energy Challenge in Africa," *Petroleum Africa*, No. 26, May 2007, p. 28.

"Declaration of the First Meeting of the China-Africa Think Tank Forum," Forum on China-Africa Cooperation (FOCAC), November 23, 2011. As of April 23, 2013:
http://www.focac.org/eng/xsjl/zflhyjjljh/t880276.htm

De Pina, Constanca, "China Assists Cape Verde with Military Equipment," *A Semana Online*, May 14, 2013.

Deloitte, *Deloitte on Africa: Mitigating Business Risk in Africa Through Regional Integration*, 2012. As of May 7, 2013:
http://www.deloitte.com/assets/Dcom-SouthAfrica/Local%20Assets/Documents/Regional_Intergration.pdf

Dietz, Ton, Kjell Havnevik, Mayke Kaag, and Terje Oestigaard, eds., *African Engagements: Africa Negotiating an Emerging Multipolar World*, Leiden and Boston: Brill Publishers, 2011.

Dollar, David, "Supply Meets Demand: Chinese Infrastructure Financing in Africa," World Bank blog, July 10, 2008. As of May 17, 2013:
http://blogs.worldbank.org/eastasiapacific/supply-meets-demand-chinese-infrastructure-financing-in-africa

Du Venage, Gavin, "China, Africa Show Lessons Learnt with $20 bn Pledge," *Asia Times Online*, August 9, 2012. As of July 12, 2013:
http://www.atimes.com/atimes/China_Business/NH09Cb01.html

Duddy, Jo-Mare, "China Blocks Nam on Internet," *The Namibian*, July 30, 2009. As of April 22, 2013:
http://www.namibian.com.na/index.php?id=28&txttnews[ttnews]=57927&nocache=1

"East Africa Branch Co. of CJI," China Jiangsu International Economic and Technical Cooperation Group, Ltd., web page, no date. As of August 15, 2013:
http://www.zjgj.com/en/view.asp?id=116&class=81

"Easy Riches Draw Chinese to Ghana," *News 24* (South Africa), June 12, 2013. As of July 2, 2013:
http://www.news24.com/Africa/News/Easy-riches-draw-Chinese-to-Ghana-20130612

Eckert, Paul, "U.S., China to Expand Military Exchanges Amid Rows Over Cyber Security, Territory," Reuters, August 19, 2013. As of October 15, 2013:
http://www.reuters.com/article/2013/08/19/us-usa-china-military-idUSBRE97I0WM20130819

Eisenman, Joshua, "China's Post–Cold War Strategy in Africa: Examining Beijing's Methods and Objectives," in Joshua Eisenman, Eric Heginbotham, and Derek Mitchell, eds., *China and the Developing World*, New York: M. E. Sharpe, 2008.

Elegant, Simon, "Could Corruption Probe Be Linked to Son Hurt Hu?" *Time*, July 22, 2009. As of April 22, 2013:
http://www.time.com/time/world/article/0,8599,1912117,00.html

Embassy of the People's Republic of China in the Republic of Zambia, "Brief Introduction to Zambia-China Economic and Trade Cooperation Zone," May 16, 2011. As of July 30, 2013:
http://zm2.mofcom.gov.cn/aarticle/practicalenglish/201105/20110507552746.html

Embassy of the Republic of Liberia to the United States, "13/05/2013: Inaugural Session of U.S.-Liberia Partnership Dialogue Held in United States," press release, May 13, 2013. As of May 24, 2013:
http://www.liberianembassyus.org/index.php?mact=News,cntnt01,detail,0&cntnt01articleid=94&cntnt01origid=15&cntnt01detailtemplate=newsdetail&cntnt01returnid=69

England, Andrew, "Sata Gives Chinese Investors Guarded Welcome," *Financial Times*, September 26, 2011. As of April 16, 2013:
http://www.ft.com/intl/cms/s/0/a44aaffa-e850-11e0-ab03-00144feab49a.html#axzz2QeMhO67J

Erickson, Andrew S., and Austin M. Strange, *No Substitute for Experience: Chinese Antipiracy Operations in the Gulf of Aden,* China Maritime Study No. 10, Newport, R.I.: U.S. Naval War College, 2013. As of November 7, 2013:
http://www.usnwc.edu/Research---Gaming/China-Maritime-Studies-Institute/Publications/documents/CMS10_Web_2.aspx

———, "'Selfish Superpower'" No Longer? China's Anti-Piracy Activities and 21st-Century Global Maritime Governance," *Harvard Asia Quarterly*, Vol. 14, Nos. 1–2 ,Spring/Summer 2012. As of October 15, 2013:
http://www.andrewerickson.com/wp-content/uploads/2012/07/Erickson-Strange_Selfish-Superpower-No-Longer_PRC-Anti-Piracy_HAQ_2012-1-2.pdf

Ernst & Young, *Building Bridges: Ernst & Young's 2012 Attractiveness Survey—Africa, 2012*, EYGM Limited, 2012. As of February 25, 2013:
http://www.ey.com/Publication/vwLUAssets/EY_2012_Africa_attractiveness_survey/$FILE/attractiveness_2012_africa_v17.pdf

———, *Mind the Gap: Africa's Infrastructure Development*, EYGM Limited, February 2013. As of May 7, 2013:
http://www.ey.com/Publication/vwLUAssets/Mind_the_gap:_Africas_infrastructure_development/$FILE/130219_SGF_TL_Infrastructure_email_version.pdf

Export-Import Bank of the United States, *Exports Grow Jobs*, 2012 Annual Report, 2012, p. 4. As of May 9, 2013:
http://www.exim.gov/about/library/reports/annualreports/2012/files/exim_2012annualreport.pdf

Eze, Chinedu, "Nigeria: Chinese Firm to Build Four Airport Terminals in Nigeria, *This Day* (Nigeria), March 12, 2013. As of August 15, 2013:
http://allafrica.com/stories/201303120201.html

"Fan Changlong Meets with Tanzanian Guests," *PLA Daily*, April 18, 2013. As of August 15, 2013:
http://english.peopledaily.com.cn/90786/8212261.html

Fan, Victoria, "Sizing Up China's Role in Global Health Aid to Africa," Center for Global Development blog, March 29, 2013. As of July 26, 2013:
http://www.cgdev.org/blog/sizing-chinas-role-global-health-aid-africa

Farole, Thomas, *Special Economic Zones in Africa: Comparing Performance and Learning from Global Experience*, Washington, D.C.: The World Bank, 2011.

"Fifth Meeting of China-South Africa Defense Committee Held in South Africa," *PLA Daily*, July 23, 2012. As of October 11, 2013:
http://english.peopledaily.com.cn/90786/7883528.html

Fijalkowski, Lukasz, "China's 'Soft Power' in Africa?" *Journal of Contemporary African Studies*, Vol. 29, No. 2, April 2011, pp. 223–232.

Fine, David, Arend van Wamelen, Susan Lund, Armando Cabral, Mourad Taoufiki, Norbert Dörr, Acha Leke, Charles Roxburgh, Jörg Schubert, and Paul Cook, *Africa at Work: Job Creation and Inclusive Growth*, McKinsey Global Institute, August 2012, pp. 14–20, 27–31. As of May 17, 2013:
http://www.mckinsey.com/insights/africa/africa_at_work

"The First Forum on China-Africa Local Government Cooperation Closes in Beijing; Dai Bingguo Attends and Addresses the Closing Ceremony," PRC Ministry of Foreign Affairs, August 28, 2012. As of June 2, 2013:
http://www.fmprc.gov.cn/eng/wjb/zzjg/fzs/xwlb/t965016.shtml

"FOCAC Beijing Declaration Calls for More Just and Reasonable International Order," *China Daily*, July 20, 2012. As of December 5, 2013:
http://www.chinadaily.com.cn/xinhua/2012-07-20/content_6499276.html

"Forum on China-Africa Cooperation Sharm El Sheikh Action Plan (2010–2012)," Forum on China-Africa Cooperation, November 12, 2009.

Ford, Peter, "Why Chinese Workers Are Getting Kidnapped Abroad," *Christian Science Monitor*, February 1, 2012. As of May 18, 2013:
http://www.csmonitor.com/World/Asia-Pacific/2012/0201/
Why-Chinese-workers-are-getting-kidnapped-abroad

Forum on China-Africa Cooperation, "FOCAC ABC," website, April 9, 2013. As of October 16, 2013:
http://www.focac.org/eng/ltda/ltjj/t933522.htm

Foster, Vivien, and Cecilia Briceño-Garmendia, *Africa's Infrastructure: A Time for Transformation*, Washington, D.C.: World Bank Africa Infrastructure Country Diagnostic, 2010. As of March 25, 2013:
http://www.infrastructureafrica.org/system/files/Africa%27s%20Infrastructure%20A%20Time%20for%20Transformation%20FULL%20TEXT.pdf

Foster, Vivien, William Butterfield, Chuan Chen, and Nataliya Pushak, *Building Bridges: China's Growing Role as Infrastructure Financier for Sub-Saharan Africa*, Washington, D.C.: World Bank, 2008.

Fransman, Marius, South African Deputy Minister of International Relations and Cooperation, "Keynote Address to the Ambassadorial Forum on China—South Africa Diplomatic Relations at 15 Years," Pretoria, South Africa, September 19, 2013. As of October 11, 2013: http://www.dfa.gov.za/docs/speeches/2013/frans0919.html

Fraser, Alastair, and John Lungu, *For Whom the Windfalls? Winners and Losers in the Privatisation of Zambia's Copper Mines*, Lusaka: Civil Society Trade Network of Zambia and the Catholic Centre for Justice, Development and Peace, no date (2006 or after), pp. 48–51. As of April 23, 2013: http://www.sarpn.org/documents/d0002403/Zambia_copper-mines_Lungu_Fraser.pdf

Frazer, Jendayi E., "Africa Policy: A Record of Success," in Claudia E. Anyaso, ed., *Fifty Years of U S African Policy: Reflections of Assistant Secretaries of African Affairs and U.S. Embassy Officials*, Washington, D.C.: Association for Diplomatic Studies and Training, 2011, p. 252.

Freedom House, *Freedom in the World 2013*, 2013. As of December 5, 2013: http://freedomhouse.org/sites/default/files/FIW%202013%20Booklet_0.pdf

French, Howard W., "The Next Empire," *The Atlantic*, May 2010. As of April 19, 2013: http://www.theatlantic.com/magazine/archive/2010/05/the-next-empire/308018/

———, "In Africa, an Election Reveals Skepticism of Chinese Involvement," *The Atlantic*, September 29, 2011. As of April 15, 2013: http://www.theatlantic.com/international/archive/2011/09/in-africa-an-election-reveals-skepticism-of-chinese-involvement/245832/

Friedberg, Aaron, *A Contest for Supremacy: China, America, and the Struggle for Mastery in Asia*, W. W. Norton & Company, 1st edition, 2012.

Gadzala, Aleksandra, and Marek Hanusch, *African Perspectives on China-Africa: Gauging Popular Perceptions and Their Economic and Political Determinants*, Afrobarometer Working Paper No. 117, January 2010. As of July 20, 2012: http://www.afrobarometer.org/files/documents/working_papers/AfropaperNo117.pdf

Gamache, Lauren, Alexander Hammer, and Lin Jones, *China's Trade and Investment Relationship with Africa*, United States International Trade Commission Executive Briefings on Trade, April 2013.

GAO—*See* U.S. Government Accountability Office.

Gao, Wenzhi, Economic and Commercial Counselor, Embassy of China in Ghana, "Work by Mutual Efforts to Promote Trade and Economic Collaboration between Ghana and China," remarks to Standard Chartered Bank professional forum, Accra, Ghana, October 1, 2013. As of October 15, 2013: http://english.mofcom.gov.cn/article/newsrelease/counselorsoffice/westernasiaandafricareport/201310/20131000332843.shtml

Gerardy, Justine, "Africa Must Raise Quality of Trade with China: WEF," Agence France Presse, May 6, 2011. As of July 23, 2012: http://www.google.com/hostednews/afp/article/ALeqM5iBA6tXoT4LJLGL65rpW0GMxLbnkg?docId=CNG.c0bb0d28621ce10d14542a3563c84669.1b1

Gill, Bates, *Meeting the Challenges and Opportunities of China's Rise: Expanding and Improving Interaction Between the American and Chinese Policy Communities*, Washington, D.C.: Center for Strategic and International Studies, 2006, p. 13.

Gill, Bates, J. Stephen Morrison, and Chin-Hao Huang, "China-Africa Relations: An Early, Uncertain Debate in the United States," in Chris Alden, Daniel Large, and Ricardo Soares de Oliveira, eds., *China Returns to Africa: A Rising Power and a Continent Embrace*, New York: Columbia University Press, 2008, pp. 167–180.

Gill, Bates and Huang, Chin-hao, *China's Expanding Role in Peacekeeping: Prospects and Policy Implications*, SIPRI Policy Paper No. 25, November 2009. As of November 6, 2013:
http://books.sipri.org/files/PP/SIPRIPP25.pdf

Global Witness, *China and Congo: Friends in Need*, March 2011. As of May 16, 2013:
http://www.globalwitness.org/sites/default/files/library/friends_in_need_en_lr_1.pdf

Government of China, "China's National Defense in 2010," web page, no date. As of December 5, 2013:
http://english.gov.cn/official/2011-03/31/content_1835499_11.htm

Grimmett, Richard F., *Conventional Arms Transfers to Developing Nations, 2002–2009*, Congressional Research Service, Report R41403, September 10, 2010, pp. 52–58.

Grobler, John, "Nuctec 'Corruption' Spreads to Namibia," *Mail & Guardian* (South Africa), July 18, 2009. As of April 19, 2013:
http://mg.co.za/article/2009-07-18-nuctec-corruption-spreads-to-namibia

"Guinea Bissau Takes Delivery from China of Refurbished National Stadium," Macauhub.com, March 7, 2013. As of August 22, 2013:
http://www.macauhub.com.mo/en/2013/03/07/guinea-bissau-takes-delivery-from-china-of-refurbished-national-stadium/

"Guinea-Bissau: Possibilities and Pitfalls Following President's Death," IRIN, UN Office for the Coordination of Humanitarian Affairs, January 20, 2012. As of August 15, 2013:
http://www.irinnews.org/report/94693/guinea-bissau-possibilities-and-pitfalls-following-president-s-death

Haglund, Dan, "Blessing or Curse: The Rise of Mineral Dependence Among Low- and Middle-Income Countries," Oxford, UK: Oxford Policy Management, December 2011. As of July 29, 2013:
http://www.eisourcebook.org/submissions/1325523556OPMBlessingorcursereport2011.pdf

Hai, Tao, "Is the Navy Establishing the First Batch of Overseas Strategic Support Points?" [海军建首批海外战略支撑点?] *Guoji Xianqu Daobao* (in Chinese), January 10, 2013. As of August 15, 2013:
http://ihl.cankaoxiaoxi.com/2013/0110/148665.shtml

Ham, Carter, "Transcript: General Ham at the Chatham House, London," November 21, 2012. As of May 9, 2013:
http://www.africom.mil/Newsroom/Transcript/10110/transcript-general-ham-at-the-chatham-house-londo

Han, Wei, and Shen Hu, "Zambian President Embraces Chinese Investment," Caixin Online, October 30, 2011. As of April 15, 2013:
http://english.caixin.com/2011-10-30/100318969.html

Hanauer, Larry, and Lyle Morris, "Agreeing to Disagree About Africa," *U.S. News & World Report*, June 5, 2013. As of July 19, 2013:
http://www.usnews.com/opinion/blogs/world-report/2013/06/05/us-and-china-dont-need-to-compete-in-africa

———, "To Help Africa, Do Business There," *U.S. News & World Report*, June 27, 2013. As of July 19, 2013:
http://www.usnews.com/opinion/blogs/world-report/2013/06/27/obama-can-counter-china-by-bringing-africa-business

Harman, Danna, "How China's Support of Sudan Shields a Regime Called 'Genocidal,'" *Christian Science Monitor*, June 26, 2007. As of July 30, 2013:
http://www.csmonitor.com/2007/0626/p01s08-woaf.html

He, Wenping, "China's Perspective on Contemporary China-Africa Relations," in Chris Alden, Daniel Large, and Ricardo Soares de Oliveira, eds., *China Returns to Africa: A Rising Power and a Continent Embrace*, New York: Columbia University Press, 2008, p. 157.

He, Yafei, "The Trust Deficit," *Foreign Policy*, May 13, 2013. As of May 14, 2013:
http://www.foreignpolicy.com/articles/2013/05/13/how_china_sees_the_us_pivot_to_asia

Heilbron, Miguel, "Biggest Obstacles for Companies in Africa: Access to Power Tops Access to Finance in Many African Countries," Venture Capital for Africa.biz, February 4, 2013. As of May 7, 2013:
http://vc4africa.biz/blog/2013/02/04/biggest-obstacles-for-companies-in-africa-access-to-power-tops-access-to-finance-in-many-countries/

Heng, He, "Ghana Gold Mines Suggest Larger Crisis for China," *Epoch Times*, June 12, 2013. As of August 15, 2013:
http://www.ghanaweb.com/GhanaHomePage/NewsArchive/artikel.php?ID=276946

Henry J. Kaiser Family Foundation, "The U.S. President's Emergency Plan for AIDS Relief (PEPFAR)," March 25, 2013. As of July 30, 2013:
http://kff.org/global-health-policy/fact-sheet/the-u-s-presidents-emergency-plan-for/

Hille, Kathrin, "China Commits Combat Troops to Mali," *Financial Times*, June 27, 2013.

Hilsum, Lindsey, "The Chinese Are Coming," *The New Statesman* (UK), July 4, 2005. As of April 16, 2013:
http://www.newstatesman.com/node/150988

———, "Africa's Chinese Love Affair," *Channel 4* (UK), November 3, 2006. As of April 16, 2013:
http://www.channel4.com/news/articles/politics/international_politics/africas+chinese+love+affair/171520.html

Hitchens, Peter, "How China Has Created a New Slave Empire in Africa," *Daily Mail* (UK), September 28, 2008. As of April 19, 2013:
http://www.dailymail.co.uk/news/article-1063198/PETER-HITCHENS-How-China-created-new-slave-empire-Africa.html

Holslag, Jonathan, "China's New Security Strategy for Africa," *Parameters*, Summer 2009, p. 32. As of May 7, 2013:
http://www.carlisle.army.mil/usawc/parameters/Articles/09summer/holslag.pdf

———, "China and the Coups: Coping with Political Instability in Africa," *African Affairs,* Vol. 110, No. 44, June 24, 2011, pp. 367–386.

Hook, Leslie, "Zuma Warns on Africa's Trade Ties to China," *Washington Post*, July 19, 2012. As of June 11, 2013:
http://articles.washingtonpost.com/2012-07-19/world/35489561_1_african-president-jacob-zuma-trade-ties-african-nations

Horta, Loro, *Guinea-Bissau: China Sees a Risk Worth Taking*, Washington, D.C.: Center for Strategic and International Studies, no date. As of August 15, 2013:
http://csis.org/print/13863

———, *Defense and Military Education: A Dimension of Chinese Power*, Power and Interest News Report, September 29, 2006. As of August 22, 2013:
http://www.gees.org/documentos/Documen-01492.pdf

Howe, Marc, "South African Report Highlights Chinese Labor Abuses in the Sub-Sahara," mining.com, November 9, 2012. As of July 2, 2013:
http://www.mining.com/south-african-report-highlights-chinese-labor-abuses-in-zimbabwe-and-zambia-80476/

Hu, Jintao, president of the People's Republic of China, "Open Up New Prospects for a New Type of China-Africa Strategic Partnership," speech at the opening ceremony of the Fifth Ministerial Conference of the Forum on China-Africa Cooperation, Beijing, July 19, 2012. As of August 15, 2013:
http://www.focac.org/eng/ltda/dwjbzjjhys/zyjh/t953172.htm

"Hu Jintao Proposes Measures in Five Priority Areas to Boost China-Africa Ties," Xinhua, July 19, 2012. As of December 5, 2013:
http://news.xinhuanet.com/english/china/2012-07/19/c_131725353.htm

Hu, Yihan, "China Has No Colonial Designs on Africa," *China Daily*, December 9, 2011. As of May 29, 2013:
http://www.chinadaily.com.cn/cndy/2011-12/09/content_14236672.htm

Huang, Chin-Hao, "China's Renewed Partnership with Africa: Implications for the United States" in Robert I. Rotberg, ed., *China Into Africa: Trade, Aid, and Influence*, Washington, D.C.: Brookings Institution Press, 2008, pp. 296–312.

Human Rights First, "China's Arms Sales to Sudan," no date. As of April 25, 2013:
http://www.humanrightsfirst.org/wp-content/uploads/pdf/080311-cah-arms-sales-fact-sheet.pdf

Human Rights Watch, *Transparency and Accountability in Angola: An Update*, April 2010. As of April 22, 2013:
http://www.hrw.org/sites/default/files/reports/angola0410webwcover1.pdf

———, *"You'll Be Fired If You Refuse": Labor Abuses in Zambia's Chinese State-Owned Copper Mines*, November 4, 2011. As of August 22, 2013:
http://www.hrw.org/reports/2011/11/03/you-ll-be-fired-if-you-refuse-0

———, "Zambia: Safety Gaps Threaten Copper Miners: Government, Chinese State-Owned Subsidiaries Make Uneven Progress," news release, February 20, 2013. As of April 1, 2013:
http://www.hrw.org/news/2013/02/20/zambia-safety-gaps-threaten-copper-miners

IMF Direction of Trade Statistics (DOTS), website, no date. As of January 7, 2014:
http://elibrary-data.imf.org/finddatareports.aspx?d=33061&e=170921

Information Office of the State Council, People's Republic of China, "China's Foreign Aid," April 2011. As of August 22, 2013:
http://english.gov.cn/official/2011-04/21/content_1849913.htm

"Initiative for the China-Africa Think Tanks 10+10 Partnership Plan," Beijing, China, October 2103. As of January 21, 2014:
http://www.saiia.org.za/doc_download/379-think-tank-10-10-partnership-plan

International Energy Agency, *World Energy Outlook 2011*, November 9, 2011. As of August 22, 2013:
http://www.iea.org/publications/freepublications/publication/WEO2011_WEB.pdf

Jacks, Mzwandile, "CADFund to Invest $2.4 Billion in Africa Projects," July 1, 2013. As of December 5, 2013:
http://www.ventures-africa.com/2013/07/cadfund-to-invest-4-2-billion-in-african-projects/

Jacques, Martin, *When China Rules the World: The End of the Western World and the Birth of a New Global Order*, second edition, New York: Penguin Books, 2012.

Jeuck, Lukas, *Arms Transfers to Zimbabwe: Implications for an Arms Trade Treaty*, SIPRI Background Paper, Stockholm International Peace Research Institute, March 2011, pp. 1–2, 7. As of April 13, 2013:
http://books.sipri.org/files/misc/SIPRIBP1103.pdf

Jia, Qinglin, "Towards a Better Future with Stronger China-Africa Solidarity and Cooperation," speech to 18th Summit of the African Union, Addis Ababa, Ethiopia, January 29, 2012. As of August 15, 2013:
http://www.focac.org/eng/zt/jqlAfrica2012/t899821.htm

Jones, Vivian C., and Brock R. Williams, *U.S. Trade and Investment Relations with Sub-Saharan Africa and the African Growth and Opportunity Act*, Washington, D.C.: Congressional Research Service report, RL31772, November 14, 2012. As of May 7, 2013:
http://www.fas.org/sgp/crs/row/RL31772.pdf

Kachroo, Rohit, "'My Head Says That China Is Number One, My Heart Always Says America,'" NBC News.com, June 27, 2012. As of August 15, 2013:
http://worldnews.nbcnews.com/_news/2012/06/27/12422593-my-head-says-that-china-is-number-one-my-heart-always-says-america

Kandu, Frank, "China to Build New Malawi Stadium," BBC Sport.com, October 31, 2012. As of April 22, 2013:
http://www.bbc.co.uk/sport/0/football/20153471

Kellerhals, Merle David, Jr., "U.S. Diplomat Discusses Africa with Asian Counterparts," U.S. Embassy, IIPdigital.com, November 22, 2011. As of December 5, 2013:
http://iipdigital.usembassy.gov/st/english/article/2011/11/20111122153617elrem0.1062281.html#axzz2So5DeFep

"Kenya Launches Mega $13.8bn Railway Project" Al Jazeera, November 28, 2013. As of January 22, 2014:
http://www.aljazeera.com/news/africa/2013/11/kenya-launches-mega-138bn-railway-project-201311281442720658.html.

"Kidnapped Chinese Workers Freed in Sudan," Al Jazeera.com, February 7, 2012. As of May 24, 2013:
http://www.aljazeera.com/news/africa/2012/02/20122718057383606.html

Kotch, Nicholas, "News Analysis: Khama Wants Fewer Chinese Firms to Receive State Contracts," *Business Day Live* (South Africa), February 20, 2013. As of April 19, 2013:
http://www.bdlive.co.za/world/africa/2013/02/20/news-analysis-khama-wants-fewer-chinese-firms-to-receive-state-contracts

Kotch, Nick, "Zambia Seizes Chinese Mine Over Safety," *Business Day Live* (South Africa), February 21, 2013. As of April 16, 2013:
http://www.bdlive.co.za/business/mining/2013/02/21/zambia-seizes-chinese-mine-over-safety

Kuyela, Teddy, "Sata Back from China," *Zambia Daily Mail*, April 13, 2013. As of April 15, 2013:
http://www.daily-mail.co.zm/?p=4060

Kwenda, Stanley, "Zimbabwe: Chinese Become Unwelcome Guests," *China in Africa*, August 15, 2012. As of September 10, 2012:
http://www.sinoafrica.org/en/print/2085

LaFraniere, Sharon, "Uneasy Engagement: China Helps the Powerful in Namibia," *New York Times*, November 19, 2009. As of April 22, 2013:
http://www.nytimes.com/2009/11/20/world/asia/20namibia.html?pagewanted=all

LaFraniere, Sharon, and John Grobler, "China Spreads Aid in Africa, with a Catch," *New York Times*, September 21, 2009. As of April 22, 2013:
http://www.nytimes.com/2009/09/22/world/africa/22namibia.html?pagewanted=all

Laing, Aislinn, "Zambia's President Rupiah Banda Congratulates Rival Michael Sata, Bows Out in Tears," *The Telegraph*, September 23, 2011. As of April 16, 2013:
http://www.telegraph.co.uk/news/worldnews/africaandindianocean/zambia/8784129/Zambias-president-Rupiah-Banda-congratulates-rival-Michael-Sata-bows-out-in-tears.html

Le Belzic, Sébastien, *China's Exim Bank: Africa's Largest Financier Looks for an Even Bigger Role*, The Africa Report.com, October 25, 2012. As of July 30, 2013:
http://www.theafricareport.com/North-Africa/chinas-exim-bank-africas-largest-financier-looks-for-an-even-bigger-role.html

Lee, Ching Kwan, "Raw Encounters: Chinese Managers, African Workers and the Politics of Casualization in Africa's Chinese Enclaves," *The China Quarterly*, Vol. 199, 2009.

Lee, John, "The 'Tragedy' of China's Energy Policy," *The Diplomat*, October 4, 2012. As of August 15, 2013:
http://thediplomat.com/china-power/the-tragedy-of-chinas-energy-policy

Leggett, Karby, "Staking a Claim: China Flexes Economic Muscle Throughout Burgeoning Africa," *Wall Street Journal*, March 29, 2005. As of April 22, 2013:
http://online.wsj.com/article/0,,SB111205419351091336,00.html

Leke, Acha, Susan Lund, Charles Roxburgh, and Arend van Wamelen, "What's Driving Africa's Growth," *McKinsey Quarterly*, June 2010. As of October 11, 2013:
http://www.mckinsey.com/insights/economic_studies/whats_driving_africas_growth

Levin, Dan, "Ghana's Crackdown on Chinese Gold Miners Hits One Rural Area Hard," *New York Times*, June 29, 2013. As of August 15, 2013:
http://www.nytimes.com/2013/06/30/world/asia/ghanas-crackdown-on-chinese-gold-miners-hits-one-rural-area-hard.html?pagewanted=all

Li, Anshan, *Chinese Medical Cooperation in Africa*, Discussion Paper 52, Uppsala, Sweden: Nordiska Afrikainstitutet, 2011, p. 9.

Li, Jiao, "Africa: Chinese 'Container Hospitals' Ready to Deploy in Africa," allAfrica.com, June 13, 2013. As of July 26, 2013:
http://allafrica.com/stories/201306131687.html

Liu, Dong, "Chinese Miners Lured by Ghana's Gold Rush Hit Rock Bottom After Crackdown," *Global Times*, June 13, 2013. As of July 2, 2013:
http://www.globaltimes.cn/content/788641.shtml

Liu, Guangyuan, H.E. Ambassador, "Deepen China-Africa Media Cooperation and Enrich the China-Africa Community of Shared Destinies," speech at the seminar on China-Africa Media Cooperation on 18th November 2013, Chinese Embassy in Kenya, November 19, 2013. As of January 22, 2014:
http://www.fmprc.gov.cn/eng/wjb/zwjg/zwbd/t1100583.shtml

"Liberia Lauded for Upholding One-China Policy," *Heritage* (Liberia), August 1, 2012. As of May 13, 2013:
http://www.news.heritageliberia.net/index.php/inside-heritage/business-finance/334-liberia-lauded-for-upholding-one-china-policy

"Liberia, China Sign U.S. $17 Million Pact," *The New Dawn* (Monrovia), April 19, 2013. As of May 13, 2013:
http://allafrica.com/stories/201304190964.html

Loa, Lok-Sin, and Jenny W. Hsu, "China Plans to Take Over Projects in Malawi: Report," *Taipei Times*, January 24, 2008. As of October 16, 2013:
http://www.taipeitimes.com/News/taiwan/archives/2008/01/24/2003398585

Lo, Wing, *China-Africa Trade—Setting the Scene for the Future*, Standard Chartered Global Research Special Report, April 1, 2011. As of October 15, 2013:
https://research.standardchartered.com/configuration/ROW%20Documents/China-Africa%20trade%20%E2%80%93%20Setting%20the%20scene%20for%20the%20future_01_04_11_17_31.pdf

Lopes, Carlos, "Large Scale Commodity-Based Industrialization in Africa Is Imperative, Possible and Beneficial," United Nations Economic Commission for Africa, *Africa Cheetah Run* blog, March 1, 2013. As of April 11, 2013:
http://www.uneca.org/es-blog/large-scale-commodity-based-industrialization-africa-imperative-possible-and-beneficial

Lu, Shaye, *Seizing Opportunities and Overcoming Difficulties to Promote the Development of China-Africa Relations*, China Institute of International Studies, April 19, 2013. As of June 15, 2013:
http://www.ciis.org.cn/english/2013-04/19/content_5888785.htm

Lum, Thomas, Hannah Fischer, Julissa Gomez-Granger, and Anne Leland, *China's Foreign Aid Activities in Africa, Latin America, and Southeast Asia*, Washington, D.C.: Congressional Research Service, Report R40361, February 25, 2009.

Lyman, Princeton N., and Witney W. Schneidman, "Africa-China-U.S. Trilateral Dialogue: Overview," in The Brenthurst Foundation, the Chinese Academy of Social Sciences, the Council on Foreign Relations, and the Leon H. Sullivan Foundation, *Africa-China-U.S. Trilateral Dialogue: Summary Report*, 2007. As of May 14, 2013:
http://i.cfr.org/content/publications/attachments/Trilateral_Report.pdf

Lynch, Colum, "China's Arms Exports Flooding Sub-Saharan Africa," *Washington Post*, August 25, 2012. As of July 30, 2013:
http://www.washingtonpost.com/world/national-security/chinas-arms-exports-flooding-sub-saharan-africa/2012/08/25/16267b68-e7f1-11e1-936a-b801f1abab19_story.html

Marques de Morais, Rafael, "The Ill-Gotten Gains Behind Angola's Kilamba Housing Development," *Pambazuka News*, No. 552, October 12, 2011. As of April 19, 2013:
http://pambazuka.org/en/category/features/77070

———, "Growing Wealth, Shrinking Democracy," *New York Times*, August 29, 2012. As of August 31, 2012:
http://www.nytimes.com/2012/08/30/opinion/in-angola-growing-wealth-but-shrinking-democracy.html

Marton, Peter, and Tamas Matura, "The 'Voracious Dragon,' the 'Scramble' and the 'Honey Pot': Conceptions of Conflict over Africa's Natural Resources," *Journal of Contemporary African Studies*, Vol. 29, No. 2, April 2011, pp. 155–167.

"Mbeki Warns on China-Africa Ties," BBC News.com, December 14, 2007. As of August 28, 2012:
http://news.bbc.co.uk/2/hi/business/6178897.stm

McDonald, Mark, "China Confirms Naval Role in Gulf of Aden," *New York Times*, December 18, 2008. As of November 7, 2013:
http://www.nytimes.com/2008/12/19/world/asia/19patrols.html?_r=0

McKenzie, David, "Chinese Media Make Inroads into Africa," CNN, September 25, 2012. As of August 15, 2013:
http://edition.cnn.com/2012/09/05/business/china-africa-cctv-media

McLaughlin, Kathleen E., "Counterfeit Medicine from Asia Threatens Lives in Africa," *The Guardian*, December 23, 2012. As of July 26, 2013:
http://www.guardian.co.uk/world/2012/dec/23/africa-counterfeit-medicines-trade

———, "Malaria Is Not Going Away Because We Are Getting Fake Treatment," *The Guardian*, December 23, 2012. As of July 26, 2013:
http://www.guardian.co.uk/world/2012/dec/23/malaria-fake-medicines-africa-china

McNamee, Terence, *Africa in Their Words: A Study of Chinese Traders in South Africa, Lesotho, Botswana, Zambia and Angola*, Brenthurst Foundation Discussion Paper 2012/03, April 2012, p. 20. As of December 5, 2013:
http://www.thebrenthurstfoundation.org/files/brenthurst_commisioned_reports/Brenthurst-paper-201203-Africa-in-their-Words-A-Study-of-Chinese-Traders.pdf

Menges, Werner, "Finance Scanners Trial in the Starting Blocks," *The Namibian*, April 16, 2013. As of April 22, 2013:
http://www.namibian.com.na/news/full-story/archive/2013/april/article/finance-scanners-trial-in-the-starting-blocks/

———, "Lameck and Co. Turn Charges Against ACC," *The Namibian*, April 19, 2013. As of April 22, 2013:
http://www.namibian.com.na/news/full-story/archive/2013/april/article/lameck-and-co-turn-charges-against-acc/

Meyer, Nathan William, "China's Dangerous Game: Resource Investment and the Future of Africa," Foreign Policy Association blogs, October 12, 2012. As of April 19, 2013:
http://foreignpolicyblogs.com/2012/10/12/chinas-dangerous-game-resource-investment-and-the-future-of-africa/

Michel, Serge, and Michel Beuret, *China Safari: On the Trail of Beijing's Expansion in Africa*, New York: Nation Books, 2009.

Midford Paul, and Indra De Soysa, "Enter the Dragon! An Empirical Analysis of Chinese Versus US Arms Transfers to Autocrats and Violators of Human Rights, 1989–2006," *International Studies Quarterly*, Vol. 56, 2012. As of October 16, 2013:
http://stockholm.sgir.eu/uploads/Midford%20de%20Soysa%20AUG%2022%202010_final.pdf

Ministry of Commerce of the People's Republic of China, "Department of Aid to Foreign Countries," web page, no date. As of July 30, 2013:
http://english.mofcom.gov.cn/departments/yws2/

———, "Department of Western Asian and African Affairs," web page, no date. As of July 30, 2013:
http://english.mofcom.gov.cn/departments/xyf2/

———, "Department of Outward Investment and Economic Cooperation," web page, no date. As of July 30, 2013:
http://english.mofcom.gov.cn/departments/hzs2/

———, "China and Malawi," web page, August 22, 2011. As of August 15, 2013:
http://www.fmprc.gov.cn/eng/wjb/zzjg/fzs/gjlb/Malawi/t780178.htm

Ministry of Foreign Affairs of the People's Republic of China, "Xi Jinping Delivers a Speech at the Parliament of the Republic of Congo Calling for Writing New Chapters in Friendship between Chinese and African People," web page, March 30, 2013. As of August 13, 2013:
http://www.fmprc.gov.cn/eng/zxxx/t1027264.shtml

———, "Department of African Affairs," website, no date. As of October 16, 2013:
http://www.fmprc.gov.cn/eng/wjb/zzjg/fzs/

———, "Department of West Asian and North African Affairs," website, no date. As of October 16, 2013:
http://www.fmprc.gov.cn/eng/wjb/zzjg/xybfs/

Mirle, Mitali, *The Question of Small Arms and Light Weapons (SALWs) in Africa*, General Assembly 1—Disarmament and International Security, Dubai International Academy Model United Nations, Fourth Annual Session, March 4, 2012. As of August 13, 2013:
http://www.diamun.org/pdf/2012/research_reports/GA1_1.pdf

Moore, Alaskai, "Chinese Business Association of Liberia Launched, As China's Trade with Liberia Passes US$5 Billion in 2011," *Daily Observer* (Liberia), April 24, 2012. As of May 13, 2013:
http://www.liberianobserver.com/index.php/business/item/1105-chinese-business-association-of-liberia-launched-as-china's-trade-with-liberia-passes-us$5-billion-in-2011

"More Than 1,000 Chinese Gold Miners Return from Ghana," UPI.com, June 14, 2013. As of August 15, 2013:
http://www.upi.com/Top_News/World-News/2013/06/14/More-than-1000-Chinese-gold-miners-return-from-Ghana/UPI-66541371185710/

Moyo, Dambisa, "Beijing, A Boon for Africa," *New York Times*, June 27, 2012. As of August 15, 2013:
http://www.nytimes.com/2012/06/28/opinion/beijing-a-boon-for-africa.html

Moyo, Last, "From Sudan to Zimbabwe, China Is Part of the Problem," newzimbabwe.com, November 12, 2009. As of August 15, 2013:
http://www.newzimbabwe.com/pages/opinion335.18494.html

Muekalia, Domingos Jardo, "Africa and China's Strategic Partnership, *African Security Review*, Vol. 13, No. 1, 2004, pp. 5–11.

Namusa, Kaiko, "Chinese to Engage in West Rice Production," *Times of Zambia*, April 15, 2013. As of April 15, 2013:
http://www.times.co.zm/?p=5197

Nathan, Andrew J., and Andrew Scobell, "How China Sees America," *Foreign Affairs*, September/October 2012a.

———, *China's Search for Security*, second edition, New York: Columbia University Press, 2012b.

National Institute of Parasitic Diseases; Chinese Center for Disease Control and Prevention (China CDC), Shanghai; and World Health Organization China Representative Office, Beijing, *China-Africa Collaborative Project on Malaria Control and Elimination*, May 2013. As of July 26, 2013:
http://www.igh.pku.edu.cn/PDF/China-Africa%20Health%20Cooperation%20Study%204_China-Africa%20Collaborative%20Project%20on%20Malaria%20Control%20and%20Elimination%20(English).pdf

Ncube, Mthuli, and Abebe Shimeles, "The Making of the Middle Class in Africa," African Development Bank, October 2012. As of October 11, 2013:
http://www.afdb.org/fileadmin/uploads/afdb/Documents/Knowledge/AEC%202012%20-%20%20The%20Making%20of%20the%20Middle%20Class%20in%20Africa.pdf

"New Palace for Togo's New Leader," BBC News.com, April 25, 2006. As of August 15, 2013:
http://news.bbc.co.uk/2/hi/africa/4941502.stm

"News Analysis: African Scholars Call on China to Participate in Continent's Security," Xinhua, August 9, 2012. As of December 5, 2013:
http://www.focac.org/eng/xsjl/xzzs/t959643.htm

Ng'wanakilala, Fumbuka, and George Obulutsa, "China's Xi Tells Africa He Seeks Relationship of Equals," Reuters, March 25, 2013. As of July 29, 2013:
http://www.reuters.com/article/2013/03/25/us-china-africa-idUSBRE92O0D220130325

Ngozo, Claire, "Malawi's New Law Targeting Chinese Traders in Rural Areas Draws Criticism," *The Guardian* (UK), August 9, 2012. As of April 24, 2013:
http://www.guardian.co.uk/global-development/2012/aug/09/new-law-targets-chinese-traders-malawi

"Nigeria 'Frees Chinese Traders,'" BBC News.com, May 25, 2012. As of April 24, 2013:
http://www.bbc.co.uk/news/world-africa-18205032

"Nigeria Accuses Chinese Traders of 'Scavenging' in Kano," BBC News.com, May 22, 2012. As of April 24, 2013:
http://www.bbc.co.uk/news/world-africa-18169983

Njal, Jorge, "The 'Chinese Connection' in Mozambique's Hosting the 2011 Maputo All-Africa Games," *African-East Asian Affairs: The China Monitor*, No. 72, June 2012, p. 14. As of August 13, 2013:
http://www.ccs.org.za/wp-content/uploads/2012/06/China_Monitor_JUNE_2012_FINAL.pdf

Nossiter, Adam, and Bree Feng, "Ghana Arrests Chinese in Gold Mines," *New York Times*, June 6, 2013. As of July 2, 2013:
http://www.nytimes.com/2013/06/07/world/africa/ghana-arrests-chinese-in-gold-mining-regions.html

Nossiter, Adam, and Yiting Sun, "Chasing a Golden Dream, Chinese Miners Are on the Run in Ghana," *New York Times*, June 10, 2013. As of July 2, 2013:
http://www.nytimes.com/2013/06/11/world/africa/ghana-cracks-down-on-chinese-gold-miners.html?pagewanted=all/

Nuland, Victoria, State Department Daily Press Briefing, October 28, 2011. As of November 13, 2013:
http://www.state.gov/r/pa/prs/dpb/2011/10/176352.htm#ETHIOPIA.

Nurn, Chong Wei, and Gilbert Tan, "Obtaining Intangible and Tangible Benefits from Corporate Social Responsibility," *International Review of Business Research Papers*, Vol. 6, No. 4, September 2010, pp. 360–371. As of May 13, 2013:
http://www.bizresearchpapers.com/29.%20Gilbert%20Tan-FINAL.pdf

Obayuwana, Oghogho, "China Wants to Partner Nigeria on Gulf of Guinea," *The Guardian* (Nigeria), August 2, 2012. As of July 30, 2013:
http://www.ngrguardiannews.com/index.php?option=com_content&view=article&id=94354:china-wants-to-partner-nigeria-on-gulf-of-guinea-&catid=1:national&Itemid=559

Obulutsa, George, and Fumbuka Ng'wanakilala, "Africa's Trade Ties with China in Spotlight as Xi Visits," *Business Day Live*, March 24, 2013. As of April 16, 2013:
http://www.bdlive.co.za/africa/africanbusiness/2013/03/24/africas-trade-ties-with-china-in-spotlight-as-xi-visits

OECD—*See* Organisation for Economic Co-operation and Development.

"Of Emperors and Kings," *The Economist*, November 12, 2011. As of July 30, 2013:
http://www.economist.com/node/21538159

Ogodo, Ochieng, "China-Africa Joint Medical Research to Deepen," SciDev.Net, July 5, 2013. As of July 26, 2013:
http://www.scidev.net/global/health/news/china-africa-joint-medical-research-to-deepen-.html

Okere, Roseline, "Leveraging on Potential of Nigeria's Free Trade Zones for Economic Transformation," *The Guardian* (Nigeria), August 8, 2012. As of July 30, 2013:
http://www.ngrguardiannews.com/index.php?option=com_content&view=article&id=94808:leveraging-on-potential-of-nigerias-free-trade-zones-for-economic-transformation&catid=89:industry-watch&Itemid=594

Organisation for Economic Co-operation and Development, "Glossary of Statistical Terms, Official Development Assistance (ODA)," web page, August 28, 2003. As of August 22, 2013:
http://stats.oecd.org/glossary/detail.asp?ID=6043

———, "Is it ODA? Fact Sheet," November, 2008. As of August 22, 2013:
http://www.oecd.org/dataoecd/21/21/34086975.pdf

———, *Mapping Support for Africa's Infrastructure Investment*, 2012, pp. 12–13. As of August 15, 2013:
http://www.oecd.org/daf/inv/investmentpolicy/MappingReportWeb.pdf

Palitza, Kristin, "Why Zambia's Elections Will Be All About China," *Time*, September 19, 2011. As of April 15, 2013:
http://www.time.com/time/world/article/0,8599,2093381,00.html

Pang, Zhongying, "From Non-Interference to Constructive Intervention? Defining the Good Intervention," in *African Security and External Interference: Exploring the Role of a Newcomer, China*, London School of Economics, Department of International Relations and Africa Talks Public Debate, January 29, 2013.

Parenti, Jennifer, "China-Africa Relations in the 21st Century," *Joint Forces Quarterly*, No. 52, 1st Quarter, 2009.

Park, Yoon Jung, "Chinese Migration in Africa," Occasional Paper No. 24, China in Africa Project, South African Institute of International Affairs (SAIIA), January 2009, p. 3.

Parrish, Karen, "U.S. Supports Pushback Against Lord's Resistance Army," American Forces Press Service, April 25, 2012. As of April 29, 2013:
http://www.defense.gov/News/NewsArticle.aspx?ID=116080

People's Republic of China Ministry of Foreign Affairs, "Implementation of the Follow-Up Actions of the Fourth Ministerial Conference of the Forum on China-Africa Cooperation," July 18, 2012. As of June 9, 2013:
http://www.focac.org/eng/dwjbzjjhys/hxxd/t952532.htm

Perlez, Jane, "South Sudan to Get Aid from China; No Oil Deal," *New York Times*, April 25, 2012. As of October 15, 2013:
http://www.nytimes.com/2012/04/26/world/asia/china-to-aid-south-sudan-but-pipeline-efforts-stall.html?_r=0

Pew Global Attitudes Project, *Global Unease with Major World Powers: 47-Nation Pew Global Attitudes Survey*, public opinion survey, Washington, D.C.: Pew Research Center, June 27, 2007. As of July 19, 2012:
http://www.pewglobal.org/2007/06/27/global-unease-with-major-world-powers/

———, *America's Global Image Remains More Positive Than China's*, Washington, D.C.: Pew Research Center, July 18, 2013. As of July 18, 2013:
http://www.pewglobal.org/files/2013/07/Pew-Research-Global-Attitudes-Project-Balance-of-Power-Report-FINAL-July-18-2013.pdf

Polgreen, Lydia, "U.S., Too, Wants to Bolster Investment in a Continent's Economic Promise," *New York Times*, August 8, 2012. As of May 7, 2013:
http://www.nytimes.com/2012/08/09/world/africa/us-seeks-to-step-up-africa-investment.html?pagewanted=all

"Police in Ghana Detain Illegal Chinese Miners Killing One in the Process," *African Globe*, October 16, 2012. As of August 15, 2013:
http://www.africanglobe.net/africa/police-ghana-detain-illegal-chinese-miners-killing-process/

"President Hu Meets Five African Presidents in Beijing," Xinhua, November 3, 2006. As of December 5, 2013:
http://www.gov.cn/misc/2006-11/03/content_431680.htm

"President Hu Proposes New Measures to Boost China-Africa Ties," Chinese government official website (gov.cn), July 19, 2012. As of May 14, 2013:
http://english.gov.cn/2012-07/19/content_2187416.htm

Provost, Claire, and Rich Harris, "China Commits Billions in Aid to Africa as Part of Charm Offensive—Interactive," *The Guardian*, April 29, 2013. As of August 22, 2013:
http://www.guardian.co.uk/global-development/interactive/2013/apr/29/china-commits-billions-aid-africa-interactive

Qi Li, "The 'Secrets' Behind the Success of China-Africa Relations," *China Daily*, July 20, 2012. As of October 11, 2013:
http://www.chinadaily.com.cn/opinion/2012-07/20/content_15603361.htm

Quartey, Lawrence, "China to Construct Ghana's Second International Airport," *The Africa Report*, October 15, 2012. As of August 15, 2013:
http://www.theafricareport.com/West-Africa/china-to-construct-ghanas-second-international-airport.html

"The Queensway Syndicate and the Africa Trade," *The Economist*, August 13, 2011. As of April 22, 2013:
http://www.economist.com/node/21525847

Raghavan, Sudarsan, "With Oil at Stake, South Sudan's Crisis Matters to Its Customers," *Washington Post*, January 20, 2014.

Ramachandran, Vijaya, Alan Gelb, and Manju Kedia Shah, "Chapter 2: The Business Environment in Sub-Saharan Africa," in *Africa's Private Sector: What's Wrong with the Business Environment and What to Do About It*, Washington, D.C.: Center for Global Development, 2009. As of May 7, 2013:
http://www.cgdev.org/sites/default/files/9781933286280-Ramachandran-Gelb-Shah-africa-private-sector.pdf

Rebol, Max, "Public Perceptions and Reactions: Gauging African Views of China in Africa," *Alternatives: Turkish Journal of International Relations*, Vol. 9, No. 4, Winter 2010, pp. 149–186. As of July 20, 2012:
http://www.alternativesjournal.net/new/download_pdf.php?id=10&f=10_rev1.pdf

Redvers, Louise, "Angola's Chinese-Built Ghost Town," BBC News.com, July 2, 2012. As of April 19, 2013:
http://www.bbc.co.uk/news/world-africa-18646243

"Re-Launch of 'ChinAfrica' Magazine to Strengthen China-Africa Friendly Exchanges," Xinhua, October 31, 2009. As of November 7, 2013:
http://english.people.com.cn/90001/90776/90883/6799591.html

"Remarks by H.E. Ambassador Tian Xuejun at the South African Institute of International Affairs (SAIIA)," Forum on China-Africa Cooperation, July 4, 2012. As of May 17, 2013: http://www.focac.org/eng/dwjbzjjhys/t951978.htm

Rijia, Ding, "Mining for Growth," *China Daily*, March 8, 2013. As of April 19, 2013: http://africa.chinadaily.com.cn/weekly/2013-03/08/content16291583.htm

Robison, Peter, and Ekow Dontoh, "Losing Faith in Gold from Ghana to Vancouver Proves Rout," Bloomberg, August 14, 2013. As of October 11, 2013: http://www.bloomberg.com/news/2013-08-13/losing-faith-in-gold-from-ghana-to-vancouver-proves-rout.html

Rogers, Philippe D., "Dragon with a Heart of Darkness? Countering Chinese Influence in Africa," *Joint Forces Quarterly*, No. 47, 4th Quarter 2007, pp. 22–27.

Rotberg, Robert I., ed., *China into Africa: Trade, Aid, and Influence*, Washington, D.C.: Brookings Institution Press, 2008.

———, "China's Quest for Resources, Opportunities, and Influence in Africa," in Robert I. Rotberg, ed., *China into Africa: Trade, Aid, and Influence*, Washington, D.C.: Brookings Institution Press, 2008, pp. 1–20.

Roxburgh, Charles, Norbert Dörr, Acha Leke, Amine Tazi-Riffi, Arend van Wamelen, Susan Lund, Mutsa Chironga, Tarik Alatovik, Charles Atkins, Nadia Terfous, and Till Zeino-Mahmalat, *Lions on the Move: The Progress and Potential of African Economies*, McKinsey Global Institute, June 2010. As of August 15, 2013: http://www.mckinsey.com/insights/mgi/research/productivity_competitiveness_and_growth/lions_on_the_move

Rupp, Stephanie, "Africa and China: Engaging Postcolonial Interdependencies," in Robert I. Rotberg, ed., *China into Africa: Trade, Aid, and Influence*, Washington, D.C.: Brookings Institution Press, 2008, pp. 65–86.

Saine, Pap, and Michael Gold, "Gambia to Cut Ties with Taiwan, China Says Unaware," Reuters, November 15, 2013. As of January 21, 2014: http://www.reuters.com/article/2013/11/15/us-africa-china-taiwan-idUSBRE9AE04Z20131115

Sandrey, Ron, *The Trade and Economic Implications of the South African Restrictions Regime on Imports of Clothing from China*, TRALAC Working Paper No. 2006/16, Stellenbosch, South Africa: Trade Law Center, 2006. As of July 30, 2013: http://www.tralac.org/wpcontent/blogs.dir/12/files/2011/uploads/20061024_Sandrey_SouthAfrica-China_clothingquotas.pdf

Sanusi, Lamido, "Africa Must Get Real About Its Romance with China," *Financial Times*, March 26, 2013. As of June 14, 2013: http://www.ft.com/intl/cms/s/0/562692b0-898c-11e2-ad3f-00144feabdc0.html#axzz2biT3Nimb

Sautman, Barry, and Yan Hairong, "Friends and Interests: China's Distinctive Links with Africa," in Firoze Manji and Dorothy-Grace Guerrero, eds., *China's New Role in Africa and the South: A Search for a New Perspective*, Oxford, UK: Fahamu, 2008; also in *African Studies Review*, 2007. As of August 22, 2013: http://users.polisci.wisc.edu/schatzberg/ps362/Sautman2007.pdf

———, "African Perspectives on China–Africa Links," *China Quarterly*, Vol. 199, September 2009, pp. 728–759. As of April 17, 2013: http://journals.cambridge.org/abstract_S030574100999018X

———, "Trade, Investment, Power and the China-in-Africa Discourse," *Asia-Pacific Journal*, Vol. 9, No. 52, December 28, 2009. As of July 23, 2012:
http://www.japanfocus.org/-Barry-Sautman/3278

Schiere, Richard, Léonce Ndikumana, and Peter Walkenhorst, eds., *China and Africa: An Emerging Partnership for Development?* Tunis: African Development Bank Group, September 30, 2011, p. 96. As of November 20, 2012:
http://www.afdb.org/fileadmin/uploads/afdb/Documents/Publications/Anglaischina.pdf

Schneidman, Witney, "Transforming the U.S.-Africa Commercial Relationship," in *Top Five Reasons Why Africa Should Be a Priority for the United States*, Washington, D.C.: Brookings Institution, April 2013, p. 12. As of April 26, 2013:
http://www.brookings.edu/~/media/Research/Files/Reports/2013/04/africa%20priority%20united%20states/04_africa_priority_united_states.pdf

Sessions, Myra, "Overview of the President's Emergency Plan for AIDS Relief (PEPFAR)," Center for Global Development, no date. As of July 30, 2013:
http://www.cgdev.org/doc/HIVAIDSMonitor/OverviewPEPFAR.pdf

Shambaugh, David, *China Goes Global: The Partial Power*, New York: Oxford University Press, 2013.

Shanker, Thom, "Djibouti Outpost Behind Somalia Rescue Is Part of New Defense Strategy," *New York Times*, January 25, 2012. As of April 29, 2013:
http://www.nytimes.com/2012/01/26/world/africa/camp-lemonier-in-djibouti-played-crucial-role-in-somalia-rescue.html

Shen, Hu, and Han Wei, "China's Harsh Squeeze in Zambia's Copper Belt," Caixin Online, November 10, 2011. As of April 15, 2013:
http://english.caixin.com/2011-11-10/100324752.html

Sherman, Wendy, Under Secretary of State for Political Affairs, *U.S.-Liberia Partnership Dialogue Closing Remarks*, Washington, D.C., May 7, 2013. As of May 24, 2013:
http://www.state.gov/p/us/rm/2013/202680.htm

Shinn, David H., "China and the Conflict in Darfur," *Brown Journal of World Affairs*, Vol. 16, No. 1, Fall/Winter 2009, pp. 85–100. As of October 15, 2013:
http://web.ebscohost.com/ehost/pdfviewer/pdfviewer?sid=2144578b-4ae1-4e60-936f-ad9fe7281163%40sessionmgr13&vid=8&hid=112.

———, "The Impact of China's Growing Influence in Africa," *The European Financial Review*, April–May 2011.

———, "Military and Security Relations: China, Africa, and the Rest of the World," in Robert I. Rotberg, ed., *China into Africa: Trade, Aid, and Influence*, Washington, D.C.: Brookings Institution Press, 2008, pp. 155–196.

———, "United States-China Collaboration on Health and Agriculture in Africa," Paper Presented at a Joint Conference Hosted by the Center for Strategic and International Studies and the China Institute of International Studies, Beijing, May 24, 2011. As of October 15, 2013:
http://www.scribd.com/doc/56154100/United-States-China-Collaboration-on-Health-and-Agriculture-in-Africa

Shinn, David H., and Joshua Eisenman, *China and Africa: A Century of Engagement*, Philadelphia: University of Pennsylvania Press, 2012.

Sibanda, Newton, "We Want Own Airline," *Zambia Daily Mail*, April 11, 2013. As of April 15, 2013:
http://www.daily-mail.co.zm/?p=3850

"Sierra Leone Signs $190mn Agreement with China for Airport Construction," StarAfrica.com, December 14, 2012. As of August 15, 2013:
http://en.starafrica.com/news/sierra-leone-signs-190mn-agreement-with-china-for-airport-construction.html

Smith, David, "China's Booming Trade with Africa Helps Tone Its Diplomatic Muscle," *The Guardian*, March 22, 2012. As of October 16, 2013:
http://www.theguardian.com/world/2012/mar/22/chinas-booming-trade-africa-diplomatic

———, "Hillary Clinton Launches African Tour with Veiled Attack on China," *The Guardian*, August 1, 2012. As of November 5, 2013:
http://www.theguardian.com/world/2012/aug/01/hillary-clinton-africa-china

South African Institute of International Affairs, "SAIIA Attends China-Africa Think Tanks 10+10 Partnership," November 3, 2013. As of January 21, 2014:
http://www.saiia.org.za/news/saiia-attends-china-africa-think-tanks-10-10-partnership

"Sudan-South Sudan Oil Conflict Brings New Role for Beijing" *Future Directions*, May 29, 2013. As of October 11, 2013:
http://www.futuredirections.org.au/publications/indian-ocean/29-indian-ocean-swa/1070-sudan-south-sudan-oil-conflict-brings-new-role-for-beijing.html

"Sudan: China Urges Govt and South Sudan to Break Oil Deadlock," *All Africa*, December 11, 2011. As of October 13, 2013:
http://allafrica.com/stories/201112121129.html

Spiegel, Samuel J., and Philippe Le Billon, "China's Weapons Trade: From Ships of Shame to the Ethics of Global Resistance," *International Affairs*, Vol. 85, No. 2, 2009.

Svan, Jennifer H., "Air Force Investigating Cause of Drone Crash in Seychelles," *Stars and Stripes*, December 13, 2011. As of November 13, 2013:
http://www.stripes.com/news/air-force-investigating-cause-of-drone-crash-in-seychelles-1.163399

"Tainting the China Brand: Beijing Must Emphasize Quality over Quantity," *Front Page Africa* (Liberia), August 20, 2012. As of May 13, 2013:
http://frontpageafricaonline.com/op-ed-editorial/editorial/3953-tainting-the-china-brand-beijing-must-emphasize-quality-over-quantity.html

"Tanzania Orders Chinese Out of Dar es Salaam Market," BBC News.com, January 7, 2011. As of April 19, 2013:
http://www.bbc.co.uk/news/world-africa-12138811

Taylor, Ian, *China's New Role in Africa*, Boulder, Colo.: Lynne Rienner Publishers, 2009.

———, "China's Oil Diplomacy in Africa," *International Affairs*, Vol. 82, No. 5, September 1, 2006.

———, "Sino-African Relations and the Problem of Human Rights," *African Affairs*, Vol. 107, No. 426, 2008, p. 67.

Tian, Xuejun, Chinese ambassador to South Africa, "Friendship and Cooperation for a Better Future of China-Africa Relations," speech to the South African Institute of International Affairs (SAIIA), Johannesburg, South Africa, July 4, 2012a. As of August 15, 2013:
http://www.focac.org/eng/dwjbzjjhys/t951978.htm

———, "Remarks at the South African Institute of International Affairs," Johannesburg, South Africa, July 17, 2012b. As of July 30, 2013:
http://www.focac.org/eng/dwjbzjjhys/t951978.htm

———, "Address at the Joint Conference of Confucius Institutes in Africa," Stellenbosch, South Africa, September 13, 2012c. As of July 29, 2013:
http://allafrica.com/stories/201209141266.html

Transparency International, *Corruption Perceptions Index 2012*, December 5, 2012. As of October 9, 2013:
http://transparency.org/whatwedo/pub/corruption_perceptions_index_2012

Tull, Dennis, "The Political Consequences of China's Return to Africa," in Chris Alden, Daniel Large, and Ricardo Soares de Oliveira, eds., *China Returns to Africa: A Rising Power and a Continent Embrace*, New York: Columbia University Press, 2008, p. 118.

Ungerleider, Neil, "Bill Gates and the Chinese Government Want to Take on World Hunger," Fast Company.com, October 31, 2011. As of July 26, 2013:
http://www.fastcompany.com/1791617/bill-gates-and-chinese-government-want-take-world-hunger

United Nations, "No. 4307: India and People's Republic of China," *United Nations Treaty Series*, Vol. 299, 1958, pp. 57–81. As of January 7, 2014:
http://treaties.un.org/doc/publication/unts/volume%20299/v299.pdf

United Nations Comtrade, "United Nations Commodity Trade Statistics Database," website, no date. As of August 22, 2013:
http://comtrade.un.org/

United Nations Conference on Trade and Development, *Economic Development in Africa Report 2013—Intra-African Trade: Unlocking Private Sector Dynamism*, July 11, 2013, p. 84. As of July 19, 2013:
http://unctad.org/en/PublicationsLibrary/aldcafrica2013_en.pdf

United Nations Disarmament Yearbook, Volume 31, 2006. As of January 28, 2014:
http://www.un.org/disarmament/HomePage/ODAPublications/Yearbook/2006/HTML/Ch%20III.html

United Nations Economic Commission for Africa, *Making the Most of Africa's Commodities: Industrializing for Growth, Jobs and Economic Transformation*, United Nations: Addis Ababa, Ethiopia, 2013.

United Nations Office of the Special Advisor on Africa and the NEPAD-OECD Africa Investment Initiative, *Infrastructure in Africa*, Policy Brief No. 2, October 2010. As of May 17, 2013:
http://www.oecd.org/daf/inv/investmentfordevelopment/46148647.pdf

United Nations Security Council, S/RES/1769 (2007), July 27, 2007.

United Nations Security Council, *Report of the Security Council Committee Established Pursuant to Resolution 1591 (2005) Concerning the Sudan*, S/2006/1045, December 28, 2006, p. 2. As of April 25, 2013:
http://www.sipri.org/databases/embargoes/un_arms_embargoes/sudan/report-of-the-security-council-committee-established-pursuant-to-resolution-1591-2005-s-2006-1045-2006

———, *Resolution 1591*, March 29, 2005.

U.S. Africa Command, "Fact Sheet: Foreign Military Financing," October 2012. As of October 10, 2013:
http://www.africom.mil/Newsroom/Document/9840/fact-sheet-foreign-military-financing

———, "Fact Sheet: Exercise Flintlock," October 24, 2012.

U.S. Agency for International Development, foreignassistance.gov website, no date. As of December 5, 2013:
http://www.foreignassistance.gov/web/default.aspx

———, "Where Is the Money Going?" web page, no date. As of May 10, 2013:
http://foreignassistance.gov/OU.aspx?OUID=185&FY=2013&AgencyID=0&budTab=tab_Bud_Planned#ObjAnchor

U.S. Combined Joint Task Force—Horn of Africa, "CNIC//Camp Lemonier, Djibouti," web page, no date. As of April 29, 2013:
http://www.cnic.navy.mil/cldj/

U.S. Department of Commerce, website, no date. As of May 7, 2013:
http://export.gov/worldwide_us/index.asp

———, export.gov, website, no date. As of August 22: 2013:
http://export.gov/index.asp

U.S. Department of State, Office of the Historian, "A Guide to the United States' History of Recognition, Diplomatic, and Consular Relations, by Country, Since 1776: Equatorial Guinea," no date. As of December 5, 2013:
http://history.state.gov/countries/equatorial-guinea

———, "Travels of the President," web page, no date. As of December 5, 2013:
http://history.state.gov/departmenthistory/travels/president

———, "Travels of the Secretary," web page, no date. As of December 5, 2013:
http://history.state.gov/departmenthistory/travels/secretary

U.S. Department of State, Office of the United States Global AIDS Coordinator, "Building Capacity: Partnerships for Sustainability," in *The Power of Partnerships: The President's Emergency Plan for AIDS Relief*, Third Annual Report to Congress, 2007, pp. 107–127. As of July 30, 2013:
http://www.pepfar.gov/press/c21604.htm

U.S. Department of State, *Quadrennial Diplomacy and Development Review (QDDR)*, 2010. As of May 8, 2013:
http://www.state.gov/documents/organization/153142.pdf

———, *Congressional Budget Justification, Volume 1: Department of State Operations, Fiscal Year 2014*, Washington, D.C., no date. As of May 10, 2013:
http://www.state.gov/documents/organization/207266.pdf

———, *Congressional Budget Justification, Volume 2: Foreign Operations, Fiscal Year 2013*, no date. As of May 24, 2013:
http://www.state.gov/documents/organization/185014.pdf

———, *Congressional Budget Justification: Foreign Operations, Annex: Regional Perspectives, Fiscal Year 2013*, Washington, D.C., no date. As of May 8, 2013:
http://transition.usaid.gov/performance/cbj/185015.pdf

———, *Country Reports on Terrorism 2012*, May 2013. As of October 10, 2013:
http://www.state.gov/documents/organization/210204.pdf.

———, "Fact Sheet: African Contingency Operations Training and Assistance (ACOTA) Program," February 6, 2013. As of May 7, 2013:
http://www.state.gov/r/pa/prs/ps/2013/02/203841.htm

———, "U.S. Relations with Equatorial Guinea: Fact Sheet," web page, April 1, 2013. As of May 16, 2013:
http://www.state.gov/r/pa/ei/bgn/7221.htm

U.S. Energy Information Administration, *China Country Report*, September 2012. As of August 22, 2013:
http://www.eia.gov/countries/cab.cfm?fips=CH

U.S. Government Accountability Office, *Sub-Saharan Africa—Trends in U.S. and Chinese Economic Engagement*, GAO-13-199, Washington, D.C., February 2013.

———, *President's Emergency Plan for AIDS Relief: Per-Patient Costs Have Declined Substantially, but Better Cost Data Would Help Efforts to Expand Treatment*, GAO-13-345, Washington, D.C., March 2013, pp. 1–2, 5. As of July 30, 2013:
http://www.gao.gov/assets/660/653066.pdf

U.S. House of Representatives, Committee on Armed Services, *Report on H.R. 1960, National Defense Authorization Act for Fiscal Year 2014*, H.Rpt. 113-102, 113th Cong., 1st sess., June 7, 2013, p. 326. As of November 13, 2013:
http://www.gpo.gov/fdsys/pkg/CRPT-113hrpt102/pdf/CRPT-113hrpt102.pdf

U.S. House of Representatives, Committee on Foreign Affairs, Subcommitee on Africa, Global Health, and Human Rights, "Assessing China's Role and Influence in Africa," March 29, 2012. As of January 7, 2014:
http://archives.republicans.foreignaffairs.house.gov/112/73538.pdf

"U.S. Military Adds Troops to Africa for Anti-Terrorism and Resources," [美军增兵非洲 为反恐也为资源], *China Youth Daily* [中国青年报], January 25, 2013. As of November 5, 2013:
http://www.people.com.cn/24hour/n/2013/0125/c25408-20318598.html

"U.S. Plot to Sow Discord Between China, Africa Is Doomed to Fail," Xinhua, August 8, 2012. As of November 5, 2013:
http://news.xinhuanet.com/english/indepth/2012-08/03/c_131759593.htm

U.S. Senate, Committee on Foreign Relations, Subcommittee on African Affairs, "China in Africa: Implications for U.S. Interests," Senate Hearing 110-649, June 4, 2008. As of December 5, 2013:
http://www.gpo.gov/fdsys/pkg/CHRG-110shrg45811/html/CHRG-110shrg45811.htm

———, "China's Role in Africa: Implications for U.S. Policy," Senate Hearing 112-203, November 1, 2011. As of December 5, 2013:
http://www.gpo.gov/fdsys/pkg/CHRG-112shrg72397/pdf/CHRG-112shrg72397.pdf

U.S. Senate, Committee on Homeland Security and Governmental Affairs, Permanent Subcommittee on Investigations, *Keeping Foreign Corruption Out of the United States: Four Case Histories, Majority and Minority Staff Report,* Washington, D.C., February 4, 2010, p. 320. As of April 22, 2013:
http://www.hsgac.senate.gov/download/report-psi-staff-report-keeping-foreign-corruption-out-of-the-united-states-four-case-histories

"U.S. to Open 'Mini Embassy' in Equatorial Guinea," Voice of America.com, November 19, 2002. As of May 16, 2013:
http://www.voanews.com/content/a-13-a-2002-11-19-14-us-67410252/383403.html

van de Looy, Judith, "Africa and China: A Strategic Partnership?" ASC Working Paper 67/2006, Leiden, The Netherlands: African Studies Center, 2006. As of August 13, 2013:
https://openaccess.leidenuniv.nl/bitstream/handle/1887/12883/ASC-075287668-172-01.pdf?sequence=2

Voice of America, "US to Open 'Mini Embassy' in Equatorial Guinea," November 19, 2002.

Wade, Abdoulaye, "Time for the West to Practise What It Preaches," *Financial Times*, January 23, 2008. As of April 1, 2013:
http://www.ft.com/intl/cms/s/0/5d347f88-c897-11dc-94a6-0000779fd2ac.html#axzz2PDxW5KjA

Wagner, Joanne, "'Going Out': Is China's Skillful Use of Soft Power in Sub-Saharan Africa a Threat to U.S. Interests?" *JFQ*, No. 64, 1st Quarter 2012. As of August 15, 2013:
http://www.ndu.edu/press/lib/pdf/jfq-64/JFQ-64_99-106_Wagner.pdf

Wang, Bingfei, "Interview: China Plays Active, Responsible Role in Angola's Post-War Reconstruction," *People's Daily Online*, August 20, 2011. As of December 5, 2013: http://english.peopledaily.com.cn/90777/7574997.html

Watkins, Solomon, "China, U.S. Relations with Liberia: Which Is Best? As China Reports $5 Billion Trade in 2011," *African Standard* (Liberia), April 21, 2012. As of May 13, 2013: http://www.africanstandardnews.org/index.php?option=com_content&view=article&id=256:solomon-watkins-monrovia-liberia&catid=3:newsflash

Weisbrod, Aaron, and John Whalley, *The Contribution of Chinese FDI to Africa's Pre Crisis Growth Surge*, National Bureau of Economic Research Working Paper 17544, October 2011, p. 2. As of April 25, 2013:
http://www.nber.org/papers/w17544.pdf?new_window=1

Weitz, Richard, "Operation Somalia: China's First Expeditionary Force?" *China Security*, Vol. 5, No. 1, Winter 2009, pp. 27–42.

Wezeman, Pieter D., Siemon T. Wezeman, and Lucie Béraud-Sudreau, *Arms Flows to Sub-Saharan Africa*, SIPRI Policy Paper 30, Stockholm: Stockholm International Peace Research Institute, December 2011.

The White House, "Fact Sheet: Power Africa," June 30, 2013. As of July 2, 2013: http://www.whitehouse.gov/the-press-office/2013/06/30/fact-sheet-power-africa

———, "Fact Sheet: Trade Africa," July 1, 2013. As of July 2, 2013: http://www.whitehouse.gov/the-press-office/2013/07/01/fact-sheet-trade-africa

———, "President Bush Participates in Press Availability with President Kufuor of Ghana," Accra, Ghana, February 20, 2008. As of October 10, 2013: http://georgewbush-whitehouse.archives.gov/news/releases/2008/02/20080220-2.html

———, "Press Gaggle by President Obama Aboard Air Force One," June 28, 2013. As of July 2, 2013:
http://www.whitehouse.gov/the-press-office/2013/06/28/press-gaggle-president-obama-aboard-air-force-one

———, "Remarks by President Obama and President Zuma of South Africa at Joint Press Conference," Pretoria, South Africa, June 29, 2013. As of July 2, 2013: http://www.whitehouse.gov/the-press-office/2013/06/29/remarks-president-obama-and-president-zuma-south-africa-joint-press-conf

———, "Remarks by President Obama at Business Leaders Forum," Dar es Salaam, Tanzania, July 1, 2013. As of July 2, 2013:
http://www.whitehouse.gov/the-press-office/2013/07/01/remarks-president-obama-business-leaders-forum

———, "Remarks by President Obama at the University of Cape Town," June 30, 2013. As of July 2, 2013:
http://www.whitehouse.gov/the-press-office/2013/06/30/remarks-president-obama-university-cape-town

———, *U.S. Strategy Toward Sub-Saharan Africa*, June 2012.

Whitlock, Craig, "U.S. Drone Base in Ethiopia Is Operational," *Washington Post*, October 27, 2011. As of April 29, 2013:
http://articles.washingtonpost.com/2011-10-27/world/35276956_1_drone-flights-drone-operations-reaper-drones

———, "Drone Crashes Mount at Civilian Airports," *Washington Post*, November 30, 2012. As of November 13, 2013:
http://www.washingtonpost.com/world/national-security/drone-crashes-mount-at-civilian-airports-overseas/2012/11/30/e75a13e4-3a39-11e2-83f9-fb7ac9b29fad_story.html

———, "Drone Base in Niger Gives U.S. a Strategic Foothold in West Africa," *Washington Post*, March 21, 2013. As of November 13, 2013:
http://articles.washingtonpost.com/2013-03-21/world/37905284_1_drone-bases-unarmed-predator-drones-surveillance-drones

Whitlock, Craig, and Greg Miller, "U.S. Assembling Secret Drone Bases in Africa, Arabian Peninsula, Officials Say," *Washington Post*, September 20, 2011. As of April 29, 2013:
http://articles.washingtonpost.com/2011-09-20/world/35273162_1_undeclared-drone-wars-seychelles-president-james-michel-unmanned-aircraft

"Why Beijing Succeeds in Africa," *Washington Times*, editorial, January 7, 2007. As of April 16, 2013:
http://www.washingtontimes.com/news/2007/jan/7/20070107-095330-5402r/

Wines, Michael, "Graft Inquiry in Namibia Finds Clues in China," *New York Times*, July 21, 2009. As of April 19, 2013:
http://www.nytimes.com/2009/07/22/world/africa/22namibia.html

Wolf, Charles, Jr., Xiao Wang, and Eric Warner, *China's Foreign Aid and Government-Sponsored Investment Activities: Scale, Content, Destinations, and Implications*, Santa Monica, Calif.: RAND Corporation, RR-118, 2013. As of December 4, 2013:
http://www.rand.org/pubs/research_reports/RR118.html

World Bank, *Africa's Pulse*, Vol. 6, October 2012, pp. 15–17.

World Bank Group/International Finance Corporation, *IFC Jobs Study: Assessing Private Sector Contributions to Job Creation and Poverty Reduction*, January 2013. As of May 7, 2013:
http://www1.ifc.org/wps/wcm/connect/0fe6e2804e2c0a8f8d3bad7a9dd66321/IFC_FULL+JOB+STUDY+REPORT_JAN2013_FINAL.pdf?MOD=AJPERES

World Economic Forum, *Enabling Trade: Valuing Growth Opportunities*, 2013, p. 6. As of April 11, 2013:
http://www3.weforum.org/docs/WEFSCTEnablingTradeReport2013.pdf

Wroughton, Lesley, "IMF Finds Most of Angola's Missing $32 bln," Reuters, January 25, 2012. As of April 19, 2013:
http://www.reuters.com/article/2012/01/25/ozatp-imf-angola-idAFJOE80O00O20120125

Wu, Yu-Shan, *The Rise of China's State-Led Media Dynasty in Africa*, South African Institute of International Affairs Occasional Paper No. 117, June 2012. As of May 10, 2013:
http://www.saiia.org.za/images/stories/pubs/occasional_papers_above_100/saia_sop_%20117_wu_20120618.pdf

Wu, Yu-Shan, and Chris Alden, "BRICS' Public Diplomacy and the Nuances of Soft Power," South African Institute of International Affairs (SAIIA), January 16, 2014. As of January 21, 2014:
http://www.saiia.org.za/opinion-analysis/brics-public-diplomacy-and-the-nuances-of-soft-power

Xu, Ming, "Daily Life of Chinese Family Is TV Hit in Africa," *Global Times*, April 12, 2013. As of June 12, 2013:
http://english.peopledaily.com.cn/90782/8204299.html

Yamamoto, Donald, *Assessing China's Role and Influence in Africa*, Testimony Before the Subcommittee on Africa, Global Health, and Human Rights, Committee on Foreign Affairs, U.S. House of Representatives, Washington, D.C., March 29, 2012, p. 2. As of May 9, 2013: http://archives.republicans.foreignaffairs.house.gov/112/HHRG-112-FA16-WState-YamamotoD-20120329.pdf

Yang, Jiechi, "Advance Friendly Cooperation" *China Daily*, July 17, 2012. As of August 15, 2013: http://www.chinadaily.com.cn/opinion/2012-07/17/content_15588248.htm

Yang, Mian, and Song Fei, "Further Reminding the Chinese Enterprises and Workforces in Africa of the Risks and Necessary Safety Measures" [一步提升 非企 和 工的 意 和安全措施], *Asia & Africa Review*, Vol. 2, 2012.

Yin, Beibei, "Chinese Investment in Tanzania Bears Bitter Fruit," *The Guardian*, March 2, 2012. As of August 15, 2013:
http://www.theguardian.com/globaldevelopment/2012/mar/02/chinese-investment-tanzania-airport-eviction

———, "Reality Check Casts Doubts on Chinese Health Aid to Africa," *The Guardian*, June 10, 2013. As of July 26, 2013:
http://www.guardian.co.uk/global-development-professionals-network/2013/jun/06/reality-check-chinese-health-aid-africa

"You Can't Stay Aloof Forever: The Political Economy of Chinese Investment in Africa," *The East African* (Kenya), February 11, 2012. As of August 15, 2013:
http://www.theeastafrican.co.ke/OpEd/comment/The+political+economy+of+Chinese+investment+in+Africa/-/434750/1324594/-/ll08drz/-/index.html

Yu, Miles, "After Policy Disasters, U.S. AFRICOM to Deploy Troops to 35 Countries," *World Tribune*, January 21, 2013.

Yueh, Linda, "China's 'Going Out, Bringing In' Policy: The Geo-economics of China's Rise," presented at A New Era of Geo-economics: Assessing the Interplay of Economic and Political Risk International Institute of Strategic Studies (IISS) Seminar, March 23–25, 2012. As of August 15, 2013:
http://www.iiss.org/en/events/geo-economics%20seminars/geo economics%20seminars/archive/a-new-era-of-geo-economics-617d/chinas-going-out-bringing-in-policy-the-geo-economics-of-chinas-rise-a541

Yun, Sun, "China in Africa: Implications for U.S. Competition and Diplomacy," in *Top Five Reasons Why Africa Should Be a Priority for the United States*, Washington, D.C.: Brookings Institution, April 2013, pp. 6–7. As of April 26, 2013:
http://www.brookings.edu/~/media/Research/Files/Reports/2013/04/africa%20priority%20united%20states/04_africa_priority_united_states.pdf

"Zambian Miners Kill Chinese Manager During Pay Protest," BBC News.com, August 5, 2012. As of August 30, 2012:
http://www.bbc.co.uk/news/world-africa-19135435

Zenawi, Meles, Ethiopian Prime Minister, "Remarks at the Inauguration of the New African Union Commission Conference Center and Office Complex," Addis Ababa, Ethiopia, January 28, 2012. As of July 29, 2013:
http://au.int/en/sites/default/files/Remarkes%20by%20H.E.Ato%20Meles%20Zenawi1.pdf

Zhang, Rui, "Culture Forum Hosts African Officials in Beijing," China.org.cn, June 19, 2012. As of June 14, 2013:
http://www.china.org.cn/world/2012-06/19/content_25690053.htm

Zhang, Xiaoling, "China Makes Voice Heard Above Din," *China Daily*, January 21, 2013. As of June 2, 2013:
http://usa.chinadaily.com.cn/weekly/2013-01/18/content_16135976.htm

Zhong, Jianhua, "The Sudan-South Sudan Reconciliation: More Patience and Efforts Needed," *Global Review*, Winter 2012, Special Issue, pp. 1–2.

"Zimbabwe Overhauls Major Tourist Airport on Chinese Loan," *People's Daily Online*, April 12, 2012. As of December 5, 2013:
http://english.peopledaily.com.cn/90883/8204505.html